THE MAINE WOODS

THE MAINE WOODS

HENRY DAVID THOREAU

PERENNIAL LIBRARY

Harper & Row, Publishers, New York
Cambridge, Philadelphia, San Francisco, Washington
London, Mexico City, São Paulo, Singapore, Sydney

First PERENNIAL LIBRARY edition published 1987.

Library of Congress Cataloging-in-Publication Data
Thoreau, Henry David, 1817–1862.
    The Maine woods.
    Reprint. Originally published: Boston: Ticknor and Fields, 1864.
With new introd.
    1. Piscataquis County (Me.)—Description and travel. 2. Maine—Description and travel. 3. Thoreau, Henry David, 1817–1862—Journeys—Maine. 4. Authors, American—19th century—Journeys—Maine. I. Title. F27.P5T43 1987   917.4'1043   86-46105
ISBN 0-06-091404-1 (pbk.)

---

87 88 89 90 91 MPC 10 9 8 7 6 5 4 3 2 1

CONTENTS

DEEP IN THE WOODS
WITH HENRY THOREAU

The Maine Woods were and are a breeding ground for mysticism, as much so as the Himalayas, the Amazon, or the Plains of Serengeti. I think it must be the piercing voice of the white-throated sparrow or the cry of the loon that makes the damp and mossy coniferous woods of Maine so conducive to mysticism. Or perhaps it is the pagoda-like white pine reflected on the clear waters of an unnamed pond. Or then again it might be the ghost of Henry Thoreau seen faintly through the flickering flames of a campfire.

Twenty-five years ago, I and some companions camped at Chimney Pond before our first ascent of Mount Katahdin. It was late August, and the nighttime sky throbbed with colored threads of Northern Lights. We had difficulty closing our eyes to get some sleep. And yet seemingly only moments later, we rolled up our sleeping bags all covered with hoarfrost at 5 A.M. and, like French Jesuits of old, followed a trail through thick black spruce. The high-rising exposed granite of Baxter Peak loomed above us; if our eyes focused correctly, we thought we saw a skein of fresh snow on the summit. The spruce and aspen around us seemed so utterly still and silent!

Before long we had worked our way through Katahdin's timberline of matted dwarf spruce; sometimes we'd sink up to our knees trying to get through it, and our boots got soaked in rivulets of spring water which trickled under the dense matting. With each ten or fifteen feet gained, we could see more and more of the boreal forests of northern Maine, giving off an aroma like incense at some Buddhist temple in Kyoto or Nikko. And when our feet touched nothing but naked granite, we began to see distant Moosehead Lake and the cow-moose-shaped Mount Kineo, mythologized by the Penobscot Indians. We paused to take a few swallows of icy spring water gushing out of a crevice; the sudden chill made our teeth hurt. Though the sky was bright and sunny, a chill wind drilled through us up here four thousand feet above the relatively flat terrain around Katahdin's base.

Finally we stood on the rugged and spiny summit of Mount Katahdin, over five thousand feet tall, and peered down sheer granite cliffs into the glacial cirque of Chimney Pond. We hadn't expected to see such sweeping alpine terrain east of the Mississippi, but wild and sweeping it was! As clouds gathered and poured over Katahdin's Knife Edge Ridge to the east, the temperature dropped twenty degrees, helping preserve the tiny crests of fresh snow between the rocks. Dense clouds seemed to be born at our very feet. We elected to descend. Thoreau, a hundred years earlier, called this rocky perch an unfinished part of the globe that robbed him of his "divine faculties." In a sense, all of us standing there could have agreed with him in that the flood of sensations was too quick, too vast to be absorbed in a reasonable period of time. This one day's climb entered our spirit's core in undecipherable ways. Thoreau's book, however, offers ways in which one can at least begin to decipher the impact of the Maine woods, with its pagodas of pine, its eerie and plaintive bird calls, its mossy and damp fragrance, and its alpine heights.

Henry David Thoreau gained immeasurable metaphysical knowledge from his two-year experiment on the shores of Walden Pond (1845–47), but his three excursions into the wilderness of Maine (1846, 1853, 1857) afforded him a primal contact with the generative forces of the universe itself. In Maine he experienced an unfinished wilderness as opposed to a humanized Walden Pond and its surrounding woods. But in Maine he overcame the shock of "inhuman nature" to arrive at a new level of understanding of Nature which foreshadowed writers like John Muir, Loren Eiseley, and Edward Abbey.

Let us begin by examining some significant and crucial passages in the more famous book, *Walden* (1854). As Thoreau writes, "My purpose in going to Walden Pond was not to live cheaply nor to live dearly there, but to transact some private business with the fewest obstacles; to be hindered from accomplishing which for want of a little enterprise and business talent, appeared not so sad as foolish." While his chief business consisted of becoming a writer (for at Walden he would write an homage to his deceased brother, *A Week on the Concord and Merrimack Rivers* [1849], and portions of his *Journal*), he also conducted some rather serious metaphysical business. He writes, "I have thought that Walden Pond would be a good port and a good foundation."

Once he set up his living quarters on the shores of Walden, or "God's Drop," as he calls it, what did Thoreau discover about Nature that he would not have, had he continued living in Concord Village? By reducing his life to the simplest terms and living on a one-to-one basis with his environment, he developed the most receptive ear to the spiritual tunes of nature in nineteenth-century America.

During his first week of residence at the pond, he became engrossed by nature's inner spirit: "For the first week, whenever I looked out on the pond it impressed me like a tarn high up on the side of a mountain, its bottom far above the surface of other lakes, and, as the sun rose, I saw it throwing off its nightly clothing of mist and here and there, by degrees, its soft ripples on its smooth surface was revealed, while the mists, like ghosts were

stealthily withdrawing in every direction
into the woods, as at the breaking up of
some nocturnal conventicle." Here we can
see Thoreau's mind seeking planes of correspondence. Mists are like ghosts at a
conventicle. Walden Pond's revealed surface is like an ultimate reality which can
be discovered only after nocturnal veils
are removed. All of this requires the light
of the sun, a universal symbol of the light
of knowledge. Morning, therefore, is a
time of enlightenment, and enlightenment
is the central theme of *Walden:* "They say
that characters were engraven on the
bathing tub of king Tching-Thang to this
effect: 'Renew thyself completely each day;
do it again, and again, and forever again.'
I can understand that. Morning brings
back the heroic ages." Thoreau would
have heartily approved of the rising sun
as a national symbol.

Nature can be a wise teacher, revealer
of truths to the soul. Thoreau writes, "I
have read in a Hindoo book that 'there
was a king's son, who, being expelled in
infancy from his native city, was brought
up by a forester, and, growing up to ma-
turity in that state, imagined himself to
belong to the barbarous race with which

xiii

he lived. One of his father's ministers having discovered him, revealed to him what he was, and the misconception of his character was removed, and he knew himself to be a prince. So soul,' continues the Hindoo philosopher, 'from the circumstances in which it is placed, mistakes its own character, until the truth is revealed to it by some holy teacher, and then it knows itself to be Brahme.' " The woods of Walden, along with Oriental and Western classics as spiritual guidebooks, served as a teacher, a revealer of soul. As Thoreau illustrates, "Sometimes, in a summer morning, having taken my accustomed bath, I sat in my sunny doorway from sunrise till noon, rapt in a revery, amidst the pines and hickories and sumachs, in undisturbed solitude and stillness, while the birds sang around or flitted noiseless through the house, until by the sun falling in at my west window, or the noise of some traveller's wagon on the distant highway, I was reminded of the lapse of time. I grew in those seasons like corn in the night, and they were far better than any work of the hands would have been. They were not time subtracted from my life, but so much over and above my usual allowance. I realized what the Orientals mean by contemplation and the foresaking of works."

Nature can reveal as much of night and darkness as it can of light and wisdom. The screech owls of Walden serve as a case in point: "They are the spirits, the low spirits and melancholy forebodings of fallen souls that once in human shape night-walked the Earth and did the deeds of darkness, now expiating their sins with their wailing hymns or threnodies in the scenery of their transgressions. They give me a new sense of the variety and capacity of that nature which is our common dwelling. *Oh-o-o-o-o that I never had been bor-r-rn!* sighs one on this side of the pond, and circles with the restlessness of despair to some new perch on the gray oaks. Then— *that I never had been bor-r-r-rn!* comes faintly from far in the Lincoln woods."

Such a Thoreauvian bird is surely worthy of serving as background music for Japanese Noh and Kabuki tragedies which depict some great human loss. For, as Thoreau notes, owls make sounds "admirably suited to swamps and twilight woods which no day illustrates, suggesting a vast and undeveloped nature which men have

not recognized." Here we get a definite
hint of the metaphysical value which the
deep wilderness of Maine will have for
him as expressed in *The Maine Woods.*
Plaintive whippoorwills and trumping
bullfrogs were for Thoreau yet another
example of nocturnal ghosts at a conventicle. Frogs sound as if they are "trying to
sing a catch in their Stygian lake," bellowing *"turoonk, turoonk, turoonk!"*

But it is light, sunrise and the clearing
of mists which most delighted Thoreau. As
the crowing cock celebrates the beginning
of a new day, so Thoreau depicts himself
as a chanticleer crowing to his townsmen
to wake up and renew themselves from
their nocturnal stupor. Nature's cycle of
light and darkness served as Thoreau's
constant companion, so that his solitude in
nature was only a seeming solitude. Nature was for Thoreau, as he himself puts
it in "Baker Farm" of *Walden,* a pagoda
or a shrine with its dark and foreboding
spirits as well as its great spirits of light.

Nature at Walden gave Thoreau a dual
comprehension of the nature of man and
the universe. The wild and rank aspects of
nature were as important as the spiritual
planes of correspondence produced in the

mind through these stimuli: "The wildest scenes had become unaccountably familiar," writes Thoreau in the "Higher Laws" chapter. "I found myself, and still find, an instinct toward a higher, or, as it is named, spiritual life, as do most men, and another toward a primitive rank and savage one, and I reverence them both." For this reason he became as utterly fascinated with a battle between a red and a black ant as he did with Walden Pond's "field of water" which betrayed the spirit.

But of all natural aspects, the season of spring had the most profound metaphysical significance for Thoreau during his two years at Walden Pond. Seeing thawing clay and melting ice, Thoreau exclaims, "What is man but a mass of thawing clay? The ball of the human finger is but a drop congealed. The fingers and toes flow to their extent from the thawing mass of the body. Who knows what the human body would expand and flow out to under a more genial heaven?" And regarding the greening of earth with new buds, new life, he waxes poetic: "The grass flames up on the hillsides like a spring fire . . . as if the earth sent forth an inward heat to greet the returning sun; not yellow but green is the color of its flame,—the symbol of perpetual youth, the grass-blade, like a long green ribbon, streams from the sod into the summer, checked indeed by the frost, but anon pushing on again, lifting its spear of last year's hay with the fresh life below. It grows as steadily as the rill oozes out of the ground. It is almost identical with that, for in the growing days of June, when the rills are dry, the grass blades are their channels, and from year to year the herds drink at this perennial green stream, and the mower draws from it betimes their winter supply. So our human life dies down to its root, and still puts forth its green blade to eternity."

In one last passage from *Walden,* coming from the end of "Spring," we can see clearly a foreshadowing of the metaphysical significance of Maine. Here, Thoreau makes a special plea for all Americans, if not all citizens of our planet, to maintain a close and vital contact with the mysteries of Nature: "Our village life would stagnate if it were not for the unexplored forests and meadows which surround it. We need the tonic of wilderness,—to wade sometimes in marshes where the bittern and the meadow-hen lurk, and hear the

booming of the snipe; to smell the whisper-
ing sedge where only some wilder and solitary fowl builds her nest, and the mink
crawls with its belly close to the ground.
At the same time that we are earnest to
explore and learn all things, we require
that all things be mysterious and unex-
plorable, that land and sea be infinitely
wild, unsurveyed and unfathomed by us
because unfathomable. We can never have
enough of Nature. We must be refreshed
by the sight of inexhaustible vigor, vast
and Titanic features, the sea-coast with its
wrecks, the wilderness with its living and
its decaying trees, the thunder cloud, and
the rain which lasts three weeks and pro-
duces freshets. We need to witness our
own limits transgressed, and some life
pasturing freely where we never wander."
The adjectives "mysterious," "unexplora-
ble" and "unfathomable" are the very
qualities of the Maine Woods that trans-
gress our limits. Thoreau's recordings of
metaphysical transgressions during his
three excursions to the Maine Woods indeed do supplement and enhance his experience along the shores of Walden Pond.
His journeys into Maine were not only
physical journeys but an actual practice

of what he implores his readers to attempt: "Be . . . the Lewis and Clark and Frobisher of your own streams and oceans; explore your own higher latitudes." Maine was to be Thoreau's higher latitude both physically and metaphysically.

Thoreau's first excursion into Maine, in 1846, constitutes his first true exposure to a wilderness environment. He wished to confront a frontier as mountain men had in Yellowstone or on the great western prairies. He writes, "The wild or unsettled portion [of Maine] is far more extensive. So that some hours only of travel in this direction will carry the curious to the verge of a primitive forest, more interesting, perhaps, on all accounts, than they would reach by going a thousand miles westward." When he does arrive at the edge of the wilderness, it is described in a somewhat Hawthornean manner. As he and his companions walk along a woodsy road, Thoreau remarks, "it was but a step on either hand to the grim, untrodden wilderness, whose tangled labyrinth of living, fallen, and decaying trees only the deer and moose, the bear and wolf can easily penetrate." But the road itself going

through this wilderness had a "remarkable beauty." This remarkable beauty illustrates the first phase of Thoreau's
metaphysical education deep in the woods
of Maine. First, let us explore the nature
of Maine's beauty.

One aspect of Maine which immediately
gains Thoreau's attention is that it is
"what you might call a bran-new country." Thoreau continues with "the only
roads were of Nature's making, and the
few houses were camps. Here, then, one
could no longer accuse institutions and society, but must front the true source of
evil." Isolated human presence in the
midst of a bran-new country is the source
of evil (not, as Sherman Paul contends,
nature itself). This newness or virginity
of Nature so susceptible to the destructive
forces of loggers, settlers and hunters
becomes for Thoreau a source of tremendous metaphysical complexity. First of
all, there is a certain omnipresent vigor
and perennialness. Man, who attacks and
destroys this vigor by way of lumbering
operations and the like, is, nonetheless,
affected by it, and all the more so an unob-
structive observer such as Henry Thoreau. As he remarks, "It was as if we

sucked at the very teats of Nature's pine-
clad bosom in these parts." Maine had a
naturalizing effect characterized by stern-
ness and gentleness: "It [Maine] has left
such an impression of stern, yet gentle,
wildness on my memory as will not soon be
effaced." This naturalizing effect on a mid-
nineteenth-century man is somewhat remi-
niscent of a Rousseauan mental voyage
back in time from civilization to very
primitive times, when men were close to
rocks.

When Thoreau and his party arrived at
the slopes of Mount Katahdin, they erased
eons of time, to the very beginnings of
man on this planet. The upper slopes of
Katahdin, which Thoreau climbed on his
own, were almost overwhelming to Thoreau of Walden. They were like the Rock-
ies or the Himalayas—he had never before
seen such country. He writes, "They were
the raw materials of a planet dropped
from an unseen quarry, which the vast
chemistry of nature would anon work up,
or work down, into the smiling and verdant plains and valleys of earth. This was
an undone extremity of the globe; as in
lignite, we see coal in the process of formation." This remarkable rawness of na-

ture puts man on terms with the creative forces themselves. Thoreau stood and stared and felt humble before a vast power which he had not experienced along the shores of Walden Pond and in the woods of Concord. The following passage from his 1846 excursion fully expresses this sense of awe:

> Occasionally, when the windy columns broke in to me, I caught sight of a dark, damp crag to the right or left; the mist driving ceaselessly between it and me. It reminded me of the creations of the old epic and dramatic poets, of Atlas, Vulcan, the Cyclops, and Prometheus. Such was Caucasus and the rock where Prometheus was bound. Aeschylus had no doubt visited such scenery as this. It was vast, Titanic, and such as man never inhabits. Some part of the beholder, even some vital part, seems to escape through the loose grating of his ribs as he ascends. He is more lone than you can imagine. There is less of substantial thought and fair understanding in him than in the plains where men inhabit. His reason is dispersed and shadowy, more thin and

subtile, like the air. Vast Titanic, inhuman Nature has got him at disadvantage, caught him alone, and pilfers him of some of his divine faculty. She does not smile on him as in the plains. She seems to say sternly, Why came ye here before your time.

Thoreau continues his Promethean description with a reflection: "The tops of mountains are among the unfinished parts of the globe, whither it is a slight insult to the gods to climb and pry into their secrets, and try their effect on our humanity. Only daring and insolent men, perchance, go there. Simple races, as savages, do not climb mountains,—their tops are sacred and mysterious tracts never visited by them. Pomola is always angry with those who climb to the summit of Ktaadn."

As devastating as this raw nature is with its stern, forbidding atmosphere which robs man of his divine faculties upon first contact, Thoreau *does* manage to overcome his initial shock even during his first excursion into Maine. And it is *this* point that needs to be emphasized! It is this "shock element" that makes *The*

Maine Woods almost beyond the ken of transcendentalism. Romantic concepts no longer hold water. Metaphysical aspects of Buddhism may be more apt. As Peter Matthiessen writes in *The Snow Leopard,* "The Great Compassionate One is also perceived as Mahakala . . . [who] will liberate those who can die to their past in order to be reborn." Thoreau had experienced a kind of dying on Mount Katahdin.

While this vast untamed nature shocks man with its inhuman qualities, it fosters and engenders an equally important process in Thoreau's mind, and that is the process of metaphysical speculation. Let us continue examining some crucial passages in the first essay of *The Maine Woods* which exemplify this process:

> but here not even the surface had been scarred by man, but it was a specimen of what God saw fit to make this world. What is it to be admitted to a museum, to see a myriad of particular things, compared with being shown some star's surface, some hard matter in its home! I stand in awe of my body, this matter to which I am bound has become so

strange to me. I fear not spirits, ghosts, of which I am one,—that my body might,—but I fear bodies, I tremble to meet them. What is this Titan that has possession of me? Talk of mysteries! Think of our life in nature,— daily to be shown matter, to come in contact with it,—rocks, trees, wind on our cheeks! the *solid* earth! the *actual* world! the *common sense! Contact! Contact! Who* are we? *where* are we?

One finds no such passage in *Walden.* Here in *The Maine Woods,* Thoreau is confronted with vast, titanic nature, which at first shocks him and robs him of his divine faculties. But this shock induces a philosophical inquiry into the nature of Nature. His eyes have been opened to God's matter or "making stuff" called Nature. If these very atoms are at first shocking, they compensate by giving a new perspective to mankind, who is just as much a part of nature as are rocks and trees. The stuff of nature must be in our very bodies. As Loren Eiseley contends in *The Immense Journey,* the history and evolution of man on this planet can be traced through the various elements of his own body. The place of his origin, the sea, can be found in elemental form within the bone structure of the human being. Thoreau is led from a similar induction from solid earth and actual world to Contact! and *Who* are we? *where* are we? Such a metaphysical train of thought makes him stand in as much awe of his own body as of Mount Katahdin! What God has used in the construction of the surface of a star He has also used in the construction of a human body. One could say that in Maine, Thoreau developed, long before Einstein, a metaphysical theory of relativity. Star matter and body matter are related. Could not such speculation lead to star energies and spiritual energies of Zen?

To go to Maine is to go back in time to what Thoreau calls "the red face of man," eons ago when there was no artificial separation between man and nature. Maine is a time bubble for Thoreau, which fuses man with nature—man as he was before the comforts of civilization shielded him from the elements. For this reason, he writes, "What a place to live, what a place to die and be buried in! There certainly men would live forever, and laugh at death and the grave." Why does he say this? I believe it is because he has seen an inseparable fusion between the stuff of nature and the stuff of man. This elemental essence or matter is as eternal as the universe itself.

Another important discovery Thoreau makes on this first excursion into Maine is that exploration of the unknown wilderness of outer space induces metaphysical explanations of the wilderness of inner space, as Robert Frost illustrates in his poems "Desert Places" and "Tree at My Window." While Americans of the mid-nineteenth century had barely gone beyond the shores of America in terms of complete exploration, more significantly they had not penetrated their own inner shores of thought and spirit. Maine was just the catalyst Thoreau needed. Clearly, Maine was a positive philosophical experience for him, as he returned twice more, in 1853 and in 1857.

It is important to remember that Thoreau was still living at Walden during his first excursion into Maine. Probably as a result of the philosophical impact of Maine, he wrote in his book *Walden,* published six years after he left Walden Pond, the following words:

What does Africa,—what does the west stand for? Is not our own interior white on the chart? black though it may prove, like the coast, when discovered. Is it the source of the Nile, or the Niger, or the Mississippi, or a North-West passage around this continent, that we would find? Are these the problems which most concern mankind? Is Franklin the only man who is lost, that his wife should be so earnest to find him? Does Mr. Grinnell know where he himself is? Be rather the Mungo Park, the Lewis and Clark and Frobisher of your own streams and oceans; explore your own higher latitudes, with shiploads of preserved meats to support you, if they be necessary; and pile the empty cans sky-high for a sign. Were preserved meats invented to preserve meat merely? Nay, be a Columbus to whole new continents and worlds within you, opening new channels not of trade, but of thought. Every man is the lord of realms beside which the earthly empire of the czar is but a petty state, a hummock left by the ice.

This passage, I conjecture, is a metaphysical response to the questions he raised in 1846 in Maine: "Think of our life in nature,—daily to be shown matter, to come in contact with it . . . *Who* are we? *where* are we?" Once we have made vital contact with nature, we are the Columbus and the Frobisher of our inner continents. In this sense, Thoreau was no Emersonian or Wordsworthian Romantic to whom nature meant a balm, a soothing balm from the complexities of civilization. Quite the contrary, nature was for Thoreau a catalyst for complex introspection having elements of fear, doubt, wonder and awe. In this regard, Thoreau was closer to Einstein, in that he conceived of the physics of outer nature as being an inverse correlative of the metaphysics of inner nature. If Thoreau were alive today, reading about perpetual earth-sized hurricanes on the surface of the planet Saturn, he could not help but be led to brain-wave storms on the surface of the human mind. Emerson and Wordsworth could hardly take solace in saturnal violence. So this vast titanic unfinished nature of Mount Katahdin leads Thoreau to a contact with something he didn't quite experience, at least so forcefully, at Walden Pond.

His 1853 excursion, entitled "Chesun-cook," while replete with a sense of joy in the wild, vigorous, moosey backwoods of Maine, exemplifies further mystical exploration. "I began to be exhilarated," writes Thoreau, "by the sight of the wild fir and spruce tops, and those of other primitive evergreens, peering through the mist in the horizon." But his exhilaration transcends to higher levels of thought, one hundred years ahead of his own time, regarding the metaphysical import of American Indian cultures and of wild places. Back in 1846, Thoreau writes:

> Why read history, then, if the ages and the generations are now? He lives three thousand years deep into time, an age not yet described by poets. Can you well go further back in history than this? Ay! ay!—for there turns up but now into the mouth of Millinocket stream a still more ancient and primitive man, whose history is not brought down even to the former. In a bark vessel sewn with the roots of the spruce, with horn-beam paddles, he dips his

way along. He is but dim and misty to me, obscured by the aeons that lie between the bark canoe and the batteau. He builds no house of logs, but a wigwam of skins. He eats no hot bread and sweet cake, but musquash and moose meat and the fat of bears. He glides up the Millinocket and is lost to my sight, as a more distant and misty cloud is seen flitting by behind a nearer, and is lost in space. So he goes about his destiny, the red face of man.

Thoreau caught a glimpse of this red face of man through his guide and companion Joe Aitteon, from whom he learns some of the mystical Penobscot language, a language of the soil, and native ingenuity for living, surviving in the wilderness. Thoreau writes:

While lying there listening to the Indians, I amused myself with trying to guess at their subject by their gestures, or some proper name introduced. There can be no more startling evidence of their being a distinct and comparatively aboriginal race than to hear this unaltered Indian language, which the white man cannot speak nor understand. We may suspect change and deterioration in almost every other particular but the language which is so wholly unintelligible to us. It took me by surprise, though I had found so many arrow-heads, and convinced me that the Indian was not the invention of historians and poets. . . . These Abenakis gossiped, laughed, and jested, in the language in which Eliot's Indian Bible is written, the language which has been spoken in New England who shall say how long? These were the sounds that issued from the wigwams of this country before Columbus was born; they have not yet died away; and, with remarkably few exceptions, the language of their forefathers is still copious enough for them. I felt that I stood, or rather lay, as near to the primitive man of America, that night, as any of its discoverers ever did.

This Indian language was close to nature—so close, Thoreau conjectures in his "Indian Notebooks," that the Indian looks about him in nature to find some natural object to aid his expression. The Penobscot language brought Thoreau to the very ground, as its sounds were the sounds of nature raw and undigested by civilized man. In this sense the Penobscot language was like the summit of Mount Katahdin, vast, incomprehensible (at first) and unintelligible. But as Thoreau starts to learn Penobscot, he can see the direct natural sense of it. For example, he asked what the word Sebamook meant. "Tahmunt said, 'Ugh! I know,'—and he rose up partly on the moose-hide,—'like as here is a place, and there is a place,' pointing to different parts of the hide, 'and you take water from there and fill this, and it stays here; that is *Sebamook.*' I understood him to mean that it was a reservoir of water which did not run away, the river coming in on one side and passing out again near the same place, leaving a permanent bay." Sebamook then is a word full of forces of nature uttered in three syllables. Therein lies a good bit of metaphysical significance for Thoreau. Many pages of the essay "Chesuncook" are taken up with a discussion of Indian vocabulary predominantly relating to natural phenomena (e.g., *Penobscot,* meaning Rocky River, was "originally the name of only a section of the main channel, from the head of the tide-water to a short distance above Old-town"). Every word is steeped in nature; this is important to a philosopher whose every thought is relegated to nature.

Likewise the Indian living pattern is steeped in nature, as was Thoreau's along the shores of Walden Pond. Thoreau writes, "I narrowly watched his motions, and listened attentively to his observations, for we had employed an Indian mainly that I might have an opportunity to study his ways." Joe Aitteon's native ingenuity partook of mystical qualities in that it exemplified an ideal blend of man with nature. From the bark of a birch tree, for instance, he made a hunting horn and a torch to keep insects away at night. The white lumbermen and other back-woodsmen learned much from the Indian in this regard. Thoreau marvelled at Joe's manner of silent walking during a moose hunt: ". . . he stepped lightly and grace-fully, stealing through the bushes with the least possible noise, in a way in which no white man does,—as it were, finding a place for his foot each time." The Indian's life-style, then, affected Thoreau's appreciation for the wild and inspired him to merge with the wild as very few nineteenth-century American writers did. "For my dessert," writes Thoreau, "I helped myself to a large slice of the Chesuncook woods, and took a hearty draught of its waters with all my senses." Such writing brings to mind Ernest Hemingway's story "Big Two-Hearted River" in its yearning for and appreciation of the wild.

The woods of Maine inspired Thoreau for the most part to transcendental thought supplementing his Walden experiment. In his Chesuncook essay, Thoreau quotes John Josselyn: "There are certain transcendentia in every creature, which are the indelible character of God, and which discover God." Here we get back to God's matter or the making stuff of nature. For Thoreau, the moose of the Maine woods also has such making stuff or transcendentia: "The moose will, perhaps, one day become extinct; but how naturally then, when it exists only as a fossil relic, and unseen as that, may the poet or sculptor invent a fabulous animal with similar branching and leafy horns,—a sort of fucus or lichen in bone,—to be the inhabitant of such a forest as this!" Wild places had immense spiritual significance. James

Russell Lowell wanted the following famous passage removed from the essay if it was to be published in *The Atlantic Monthly:* "It is the living spirit of the tree, not its spirit of turpentine, with which I sympathize, and which heals my cuts. It is as immortal as I am, and perchance will go to as high a heaven, there to tower above me still." Thoreau, like John Muir, who wrote in much the same vein, was a century ahead of his time; James Russell Lowell was not ahead of his time. Man and nature are fused in spirit, from Thoreau's point of view; in this sense he was indeed similar to the Oriental philosophy of Zen, and this must explain, in part, why Thoreau is popular in Asia.

Thoreau's third excursion to Maine, in 1857, ten years after his Walden experiment and three years after the publication of *Walden,* provided him with more similar experiences with an Indian guide, Joseph Polis, who was to become a good friend and a strong link between Thoreau and Indian culture. Thoreau continued his education in Indian ways by agreeing to teach Polis all that he knew if Polis would teach him all that he knew. Thoreau drilled him with questions on the Indian

language (as with Aitteon). He learned
that there is a direct connection between
language and natural phenomena. For instance, *Apmoojenegamook* "means lake that
is crossed, because the usual course lies
across, and not along it." He observed
that the Penobscot language "was a wild
and refreshing sound, like that of the
wind among the pines, or the booming of
the surf on the shore." When Joe Polis
sang aloud in his own tongue by the
campfire at night, Thoreau remarked that
"His singing carried me back to the period of the discovery of America, to San
Salvador and the Incas, when Europeans
first encountered the simple faith of the
Indian."

And, as with Aitteon, Polis teaches Thoreau much about the Indian's natural ingenuity. Certain species of plants can be
used for medicinal purposes. The inner
bark of the aspen, for instance, was good
for sore eyes. Lily bulbs made an excellent
wild soup and black spruce roots, when
split, made good threads for repairing
leaky canoes with a tree-bark patch. Certain oils made from tree barks served as
good insect repellent. The Indian always
seems to know where he is in the woods or

on a misty lake. He has an uncanny sense of direction, as Thoreau notes: "I could only occasionally perceive his trail in the moss, and yet he did not appear to look down nor hesitate an instant, but led us out exactly to his canoe. This surprised me, for without a compass, or the sight or noise of the river to guide us, we could not have kept our course many minutes, and could have retraced our steps but a short distance, with a great deal of pains and very slowly, using a laborious circumspection. But it was evident that he could go back through the forest wherever he had been during the day." All of this proved to Thoreau that men living close to nature will have nature deeply embedded into their spirits, language and life-style.

The Indian's closeness to nature can be seen clearly in his mythological fabrications, which fascinated the visitor from Concord. The Indian poet of nature invented, in ancient times, a mythological moose out of the land: "While we were crossing this bay, where Mount Kineo rose dark before us, within two or three miles, the Indian repeated the tradition respecting this mountain's having anciently been a cow moose,—how a mighty Indian hunter, whose name I forget, succeeding in killing this queen of the moose tribe with great difficulty, while her calf was killed somewhere among the islands in Penobscot Bay, and, to his eyes, this mountain had still the form of the moose in a reclining posture, its precipitous side presenting the outline of her head." Perhaps it was no small coincidence for Thoreau that Mount Kineo, so he had read, was a good source of hornstone, used for making arrowheads and hatchets. Through the Indian's knowledge of and feeling for nature, then, Thoreau gained a deeper appreciation for intangible qualities of the wilderness. He himself became Indianized somewhat in his perceptions of Maine, far more so in 1857 than during his first excursion, in 1846. Let us now examine the manner of Thoreau's growth.

Thoreau writes in this last Maine Woods essay, "The Allegash and East Branch," that "Nature must have made a thousand revelations to them [Indians] which are still secrets to us." But Thoreau began to learn some of these secrets, and nowhere better can this be seen than in the 1857 excursion.

Through the Indian Thoreau gained a

multidimensional appreciation of the wilds which he did not have on his first trip. Referring to the "will-o'-the-wisp" light coming from phosphorescent dead wood, he explains that a white man's explanation of the phenomenon would not be of interest to him:

I let science slide, and rejoiced in that light as if it had been a fellow-creature. I saw that it was excellent, and was very glad to know that it was so cheap. A scientific *explanation,* as it is called, would have been altogether out of place there. That is for pale daylight. Science with its retorts would have put me to sleep; it was the opportunity to be ignorant that I improved. It suggested to me that there was something to be seen if one had eyes. It made a believer of me more than before. I believed that the woods were not tenantless, but choke-full of honest spirits as good as myself any day,—not an empty chamber, in which chemistry was left to work alone, but an inhabited house,— and for a few moments I enjoyed fellowship with them. Your so-called wise man goes trying to persuade himself that there is no entity there but himself and his traps, but it is a great deal easier to believe the truth. It suggested, too, that the same experience always gives birth to the same sort of belief or religion. One revelation has been made to the Indian, another to the white man. I have much to learn of the Indian, nothing of the missionary. I am not sure but all that would tempt me to teach the Indian my religion would be his promise to teach me *his.* Long enough I had heard of irrelevant things; now at length I was glad to make acquaintance with the light that dwells in rotten wood. Where is all your knowledge gone to? It evaporates completely, for it has no depth.

It is the metaphysical speculation, epistemology, which attracts Thoreau, not rote science of white civilization or the Sunday school religion of the churches of Concord. The Indian has given him an epistemological pathway through the wood. In this sense, Polis is like Virgil leading Dante toward a deeper knowledge of nature and away from the idée fixe of the white man. Thoreau must learn the language of nature through the Indian. By language of nature, I mean what the French utopian writer of the seventeenth century Cyrano de Bergerac (not to be confused with Edmond Rostand's caricature) meant. At one time, according to de Bergerac, all creatures of nature could intercommunicate through the universal music of the spheres. Thoreau discovered that this ancient level of communication still existed in the forests of Maine. Thoreau would be interested in the fact that scientists at Dartmouth are now studying ways in which trees of the same species *can* communicate with each other. He describes Joe Polis's talking to a muskrat; "and, sitting flat on the bank, he began to make a curious squeaking, wiry sound with his lips, exerting himself considerably. I was greatly surprised,—thought that I had at last got into the wilderness, and that he was a wild man indeed, to be talking to a musquash! I did not know which of the two was the strangest to me. He seemed suddenly to have quite forsaken humanity, and gone over to the musquash side."

Thoreau follows Polis's lead by talking in his own language to a spruce hawk:

"One of those sombre fir and spruce woods is not complete unless you hear from out its cavernous mossy and twiggy recesses his fine alarum,—his spruce voice, like the working of the sap through some crack in a tree,—the working of the spruce-beer. Such an impertinent fellow would occasionally try to alarm the wood about me. 'O,' said I, 'I am well acquainted with your family, I know your cousins in Concord very well. Guess the mail's irregular in these parts, and you'd like to hear from 'em.' " And commenting on the call of the wild loon, Thoreau writes, "I have heard a sound exactly like it when breathing heavily through my own nostrils, half awake at ten at night, suggesting my affinity to the loon; as if its language were but a dialect of my own, after all." He, numerous times, repeats the sound of the white-throated sparrow's *ah, te-te-te,* saying, "What a glorious time they must have in that wilderness, far from mankind and election day!" In other words, Thoreau was capable of sensing through bird notes corresponding feeling for nature in his own soul. By his third trip to Maine, these feelings are no longer hindered by preconceptions and false assumptions. He lets the wilderness become an open pathway to mystical heights.

He strongly questions American utilitarian values, which rule out any mystical relationship of man with nature. The lumbering industry serves as a case in point:

> The Anglo-American can indeed cut down, and grub up all this waving forest, and make a stump speech, and vote for Buchanan on its ruins, but he cannot converse with the spirit of the tree he fells, he cannot read the poetry and mythology which retire as he advances. He ignorantly erases mythological tablets in order to print his handbills and town-meeting warrants on them. Before he has learned his a b c in the beautiful but mystic lore of the wilderness which Spenser and Dante had just begun to read, he cuts it down, coins a *pine-tree* shilling (as if to signify the pine's value to him), puts up a deestrict school-house, and introduces Webster's spelling-book.

John Muir followed Thoreau's lead to fight for wilderness conservation so that vast areas of North America could remain wild and mystical.

By this 1857 excursion, Thoreau took delight in the wild, unfinished part of the globe. The following two passages which take joy in the wild and the stormy could not have been written in 1846 and contrast greatly with his 1846 essay, "Ktaadn": "The clouds breaking away a little, we had a glorious wild view, as we ascended, of the broad lake with its fluctuating surface and numerous forest-clad islands, extending beyond our sight both north and south, and the boundless forest undulating away from its shores on every side, as densely packed as a rye-field, and enveloping nameless mountains in succession." And on the next page of the essay, he writes: "If I wished to see a mountain or other scenery under the most favorable auspices, I would go to it in foul weather, so as to be there when it cleared up; we are then in the most suitable mood, and nature is most fresh and inspiring." Such passages hardly sound like the earlier impressions of "Vast, Titanic, inhuman Nature has got him at disadvantage, caught him alone, and pilfers him of some of his divine faculty." Thoreau, in short, had metaphysically adjusted to extremely

wild, woodsy places, more wild than
Walden Pond of ten years earlier. Critics
do Thoreau a disservice by not taking into
account his later reactions in Maine.

"The Allegash and East Branch" fore-
shadows and prefigures twentieth-century
philosophers of the land, including Robert
Frost and Frank Waters. Frost believed
that North Americans must meet the expectations of the land, not have the land
meet their expectations. In other words,
North Americans should become more
mystically attuned to their continent.
Frank Waters believed that each region of
our planet has a psychic pulse and that
humans, after a certain number of generations, become so attuned to these psychic
pulses that the land actually affects their
psyche. D. H. Lawrence claimed, along
similar lines, that he felt if he had stayed
in Taos, New Mexico, any longer than he
did, he would have been in danger of losing his "white psyche." Waters believed
that Utah canyons will eventually Utah-
canyonize their inhabitants. Likewise Thoreau could see back in 1856 that the Maine
Woods had the power to affect all its inhabitants: "No doubt, the short distance
to which you can see in the woods, and the

general twilight, would at length react on the inhabitants, and make them *salvages.*"

In another remarkable passage, Thoreau makes the following comment on the Maine Woods: "My imagination personified the slopes themselves, as if by their very length they would waylay you, and compel you to camp again on them before night. Some invisible glutton would seem to drop from the trees and gnaw at the heart of the solitary hunter who threaded those woods; and yet I was tempted to walk there." The wilderness of Maine had indeed affected Thoreau's psyche to the point of his sensing invisible forces, metaphysical forces if you will, as had the Indian long before him. The damp and mossy woods of Maine gave Henry Thoreau and us insight into the nature of Nature. The text of *The Maine Woods* which here follows gives us a chance to experience inwardly an exploration of self amid pine cones and gushing rapids.

Richard F. Fleck
Takarazuka-shi, Japan, 1982
Laramie, Wyoming, 1986

INTRODUCTORY NOTE

The Maine Woods was the second volume collected from his writings after Thoreau's death.
Of the material which composed it, the first two
divisions were already in print. *Ktaadn and
the Maine Woods* was the title of a paper printed in 1848 in *The Union Magazine,* and *Chesuncook* was published in *The Atlantic Monthly*
in 1858. The book was edited by his friend,
William Ellery Channing.

It was during his second summer at Walden
that Thoreau made his first visit to the Maine
woods. It was probably in response to a request from Horace Greeley that he wrote out the
narrative from his journal, for Mr. Greeley had
shown himself eager to help Thoreau in putting
his wares on the market. In a letter to Emerson, January 12, 1848, Thoreau writes: " I read
a part of the story of my excursion to Ktaadn
to quite a large audience of men and boys, the
other night, whom it interested. It contains
many facts and some poetry." He offered the

paper to Greeley at the end of March, and on the 17th of April Greeley responded: "I inclose you $25 for your article on Maine scenery, as promised. I know it is worth more, though I have not yet found time to read it; but I have tried once to sell it without success. It is rather long for my columns, and too fine for the million; but I consider it a cheap bargain, and shall print it myself if I do not dispose of it to better advantage. You will not, of course, consider yourself under any sort of obligation to me, for my offer was in the way of business, and I have got more than the worth of my money." But this generous, high-minded friend was thinking of Thoreau's business, not his own, for in October of the same year he writes: "I break a silence of some duration to inform you that I hope on Monday to receive payment for your glorious account of *Ktaadn and the Maine Woods*, which I bought of you at a Jew's bargain and sold to *The Union Magazine*. I am to get $75 for it, and as I don't choose to *exploiter* you at such a rate, I shall insist on inclosing you $25 more in this letter, which will still leave me $25 to pay various charges and labors I have incurred in selling your articles and getting paid for them, — the latter by far the most difficult portion of the business."

In the three journeys which he made to the

Maine woods Thoreau spent in all but little more than a month. His experience, however, deepened his interest in the Indian, and Mr. Sanborn tells us that it was his purpose to expand his studies into a separate work on the subject, and that his journals show how much material he collected for this purpose from other writers. The third paper, drawn from his journals, contains evidence of this direction of his mind, and the following letter to Mr. Blake, written just after his return from his third visit sets forth clearly the movement of his thought. It was written from Concord, August 18, 1857. "I have now returned (from Maine), and think I have had a quite profitable journey, chiefly from associating with an intelligent Indian. Having returned I flatter myself that the world appears in some respects a little larger, and not as usual smaller and shallower for having extended my range. I have made a short excursion into the new world which the Indian dwells in or is. He begins where we leave off. It is worth the while to detect new faculties in man, who is so much the more divine, and anything that fairly excites our admiration expands us. The Indian who can find his way so wonderfully in the woods possesses so much intelligence which the white man does not, — and it increases my own capacity as well as faith to observe it. I rejoice to find that intelligence flows in other channels than I knew. It redeems for me portions of what seemed brutish before. It is a great satisfaction to find that your oldest convictions are permanent. With regard to essentials I have never had occasion to change my mind. The aspect of the world varies from year to year as the landscape is differently clothed, but I find that truth is still true, and I never regret any emphasis which it may have inspired. Ktaadn is there still, but much more surely my old conviction is there, resting with more than mountain breadth and weight on the world, the source still of fertilizing streams, and affording glorious views from its summit if I can get up to it again."

THE MAINE WOODS

THE MAINE WOODS

KTAADN

On the 31st of August, 1846, I left Concord in Massachusetts for Bangor and the backwoods of Maine, by way of the railroad and steamboat, intending to accompany a relative of mine, engaged in the lumber trade in Bangor, as far as a dam on the west branch of the Penobscot, in which property he was interested. From this place, which is about one hundred miles by the river above Bangor, thirty miles from the Houlton military road, and five miles beyond the last log-hut, I proposed to make excursions to Mount Ktaadn, the second highest mountain in New England, about thirty miles distant, and to some of the lakes of the Penobscot, either alone or with such company as I might pick up there. It is unusual to find a camp so far in the woods at that season, when lumbering operations have ceased, and I was glad to avail myself of the circumstance of a gang of men being employed there at that time in repairing the injuries caused by the great freshet in the spring. The

mountain may be approached more easily and
directly on horseback and on foot from the
northeast side, by the Aroostook road, and the
Wassataquoik River; but in that case you see
much less of the wilderness, none of the glorious
river and lake scenery, and have no experience
of the batteau and the boatman's life. I was
fortunate also in the season of the year, for in
the summer myriads of black flies, mosquitoes,
and midges, or, as the Indians call them, "no-
see-ems," make traveling in the woods almost
impossible; but now their reign was nearly over.

Ktaadn, whose name is an Indian word signifying highest land, was first ascended by white
men in 1804. It was visited by Professor
J. W. Bailey of West Point in 1836; by Dr.
Charles T. Jackson, the State Geologist, in
1837; and by two young men from Boston in
1845. All these have given accounts of their
expeditions. Since I was there, two or three
other parties have made the excursion, and told
their stories. Besides these, very few, even
among backwoodsmen and hunters, have ever
climbed it, and it will be a long time before the
tide of fashionable travel sets that way. The
mountainous region of the State of Maine
stretches from near the White Mountains, northeasterly one hundred and sixty miles, to the
head of the Aroostook River, and is about sixty

miles wide. The wild or unsettled portion is far
more extensive. So that some hours only of
travel in this direction will carry the curious to
the verge of a primitive forest, more interesting,
perhaps, on all accounts, than they would reach
by going a thousand miles westward.

The next forenoon, Tuesday, September 1, I
started with my companion in a buggy from
Bangor for "up river," expecting to be overtaken the next day night at Mattawamkeag
Point, some sixty miles off, by two more Ban-
goreans, who had decided to join us in a trip to
the mountain. We had each a knapsack or bag
filled with such clothing and articles as were indispensable, and my companion carried his gun.

Within a dozen miles of Bangor we passed
through the villages of Stillwater and Oldtown,
built at the falls of the Penobscot, which fur-
nish the principal power by which the Maine
woods are converted into lumber. The mills
are built directly over and across the river.
Here is a close jam, a hard rub, at all seasons;
and then the once green tree, long since white,
I need not say as the driven snow, but as a
driven log, becomes lumber merely. Here your
inch, your two and your three inch stuff begin
to be, and Mr. Sawyer marks off those spaces
which decide the destiny of so many prostrate
forests. Through this steel riddle, more or less

coarse, is the arrowy Maine forest, from Ktaadn and Chesuncook, and the head-waters of the St. John, relentlessly sifted, till it comes out boards, clapboards, laths, and shingles such as the wind can take, still, perchance, to be slit and slit again, till men get a size that will suit. Think how stood the white-pine tree on the shore of Chesuncook, its branches soughing with the four winds, and every individual needle trembling in the sunlight, — think how it stands with it now, — sold, perchance, to the New England Friction-Match Company! There were in 1837, as I read, two hundred and fifty saw-mills on the Penobscot and its tributaries above Bangor, the greater part of them in this immediate neighborhood, and they sawed two hundred millions of feet of boards annually. To this is to be added the lumber of the Kennebec, Androscoggin, Saco, Passamaquoddy, and other streams. No wonder that we hear so often of vessels which are becalmed off our coast, being surrounded a week at a time by floating lumber from the Maine woods. The mission of men there seems to be, like so many busy demons, to drive the forest all out of the country, from every solitary beaver-swamp and mountain-side, as soon as possible.

At Oldtown, we walked into a batteau-manufactory. The making of batteaux is quite a

business here for the supply of the Penobscot
River. We examined some on the stocks.
They are light and shapely vessels, calculated
for rapid and rocky streams, and to be carried
over long portages on men's shoulders, from
twenty to thirty feet long, and only four or four
and a half wide, sharp at both ends like a canoe,
though broadest forward on the bottom, and
reaching seven or eight feet over the water, in
order that they may slip over rocks as gently as
possible. They are made very slight, only two
boards to a side, commonly secured to a few
light maple or other hard-wood knees, but inward are of the clearest and widest white-pine
stuff, of which there is a great waste on account
of their form, for the bottom is left perfectly
flat, not only. from side to side, but from end to
end. Sometimes they become "hogging" even,
after long use, and the boatmen then turn them
over and straighten them by a weight at each
end. They told us that one wore out in two
years, or. often in a single trip, on the rocks,
and sold for from fourteen to sixteen dollars.
There was something refreshing and wildly musical to my ears in the very name of the white
man's canoe, reminding me of Charlevoix and
Canadian Voyageurs. The batteau is a sort of
mongrel between the canoe and the boat, a fur-
trader's boat.

The ferry here took us past the Indian island.
As we left the shore, I observed a short, shabby,
washerwoman-looking Indian — they commonly
have the woebegone look of the girl that cried
for spilt milk, — just from "up river," — land
on the Oldtown side near a grocery, and, drawing up his canoe, take out a bundle of skins in
one hand, and an empty keg or half-barrel in
the other, and scramble up the bank with them.
This picture will do to put before the Indian's
history, that is, the history of his extinction.
In 1837 there were three hundred and sixty-two
souls left of this tribe.   The island seemed deserted to-day, yet I observed some new houses
among the weather-stained ones, as if the tribe
had still a design upon life; but generally they
have a very shabby, forlorn, and cheerless look,
being all back side and woodshed, not homesteads, even Indian homesteads, but instead of
home or abroad-steads, for their life is *domi
aut militiæ*, at home or at war, or now rather
venatus, that is, a hunting, and most of the
latter.   The church is the only trim-looking
building, but that is not Abenaki, that was
Rome's doings.   Good Canadian it may be, but
it is poor Indian.   These were once a powerful
tribe.   Politics are all the rage with them now.
I even thought that a row of wigwams, with a
dance of powwows, and a prisoner tortured at
the stake, would be more respectable than this.

We landed in Milford, and rode along on the east side of the Penobscot, having a more or less constant view of the river, and the Indian islands in it, for they retain all the islands as far up as Nicketow, at the mouth of the East Branch. They are generally well-timbered, and are said to be better soil than the neighboring shores. The river seemed shallow and rocky, and interrupted by rapids, rippling and gleaming in the sun. We paused a moment to see a fish-hawk dive for a fish down straight as an arrow, from a great height, but he missed his prey this time. It was the Houlton road on which we were now traveling, over which some troops were marched once towards Mars' Hill, though not to Mars' *field*, as it proved. It is the main, almost the only, road in these parts, as straight and well made, and kept in as good repair as almost any you will find anywhere. Everywhere we saw signs of the great freshet, — this house standing awry, and that where it was not founded, but where it was found, at any rate, the next day; and that other with a waterlogged look, as if it were still airing and drying its basement, and logs with everybody's marks upon them, and sometimes the marks of their having served as bridges, strewn along the road. We crossed the Sunkhaze, a summery Indian name, the Olemmon, Passadumkeag, and other streams, which make a greater show on the map than they now did on the road.   At Passadumkeag we found anything but what the name implies, — earnest politicians, to wit, — white ones, I mean, — on the alert to know how the election was likely to go; men who talked rapidly, with subdued voice, and a sort of factitious earnestness you could not help believing, hardly waiting for an introduction, one on each side of your buggy, endeavoring to say much in little, for they see you hold the whip impatiently, but always saying little in much.   Caucuses they have had, it seems, and caucuses they are to have again, — victory and defeat.   Somebody may be elected, somebody may not.   One man, a total stranger, who stood by our carriage in the dusk, actually frightened the horse with his asseverations, growing more solemnly positive as there was less in him to be positive about.   So Passadumkeag did not look on the map.   At sundown, leaving the river road awhile for shortness, we went by way of Enfield, where we stopped for the night.   This, like most of the localities bearing names on this road, was a place to name which, in the midst of the unnamed and unincorporated wilderness, was to make a distinction without a difference, it seemed to me.   Here, however, I noticed quite an orchard of healthy and well-grown apple-trees, in a bearing state, it being the oldest settler's house in this region, but all natural fruit and comparatively worthless for want of a grafter. And so it is generally, lower down the river. It would be a good speculation, as well as a favor conferred on the settlers, for a Massachusetts boy to go down there with a trunk full of choice scions, and his grafting apparatus, in the spring.

The next morning we drove along through a high and hilly country, in view of Cold-Stream Pond, a beautiful lake four or five miles long, and came into the Houlton road again, here called the military road, at Lincoln, forty-five miles from Bangor, where there is quite a village for this country, — the principal one above Oldtown. Learning that there were several wigwams here, on one of the Indian islands, we left our horse and wagon, and walked through the forest half a mile to the river, to procure a guide to the mountain. It was not till after considerable search that we discovered their habitations, — small huts, in a retired place, where the scenery was unusually soft and beautiful, and the shore skirted with pleasant meadows and graceful elms. We paddled ourselves across to the island side in a canoe, which we found on the shore. Near where we landed sat an Indian girl, ten or twelve years old, on a rock in the water, in the sun, washing, and humming or moaning a song meanwhile. It was an aboriginal strain. A salmon - spear, made wholly of wood, lay on the shore, such as they might have used before white men came. It had an elastic piece of wood fastened to one side of its point, which slipped over and closed upon the fish, somewhat like the contrivance for holding a bucket at the end of a well-pole. As we walked up to the nearest house, we were met by a sally of a dozen wolfish-looking dogs, which may have been lineal descendants from the ancient Indian dogs, which the first voyageurs describe as "their wolves." I suppose they were. The occupant soon appeared, with a long pole in his hand, with which he beat off the dogs, while he parleyed with us. A stalwart, but dull and greasy-looking fellow, who told us, in his sluggish way, in answer to our questions, as if it were the first serious business he had to do that day, that there *were* Indians going "up river" — he and one other — to-day, before noon. And who was the other? Louis Neptune, who lives in the next house. Well, let us go over and see Louis together. The same doggish reception, and Louis Neptune makes his appearance, — a small, wiry man, with puckered and wrinkled face, yet he seemed the chief man of the two; the same, as I remem-

bered, who had accompanied Jackson to the
mountain in '37. The same questions were put
to Louis, and the same information obtained,
while the other Indian stood by. It appeared
that they were going to start by noon, with two
canoes, to go up to Chesuncook to hunt moose,
— to be gone a month. "Well, Louis, suppose
you get to the Point (to the Five Islands, just
below Mattawamkeag) to camp, we walk on
up the West Branch to-morrow, — four of us,
— and wait for you at the dam, or this side.
You overtake us to-morrow or next day, and
take us into your canoes. We stop for you, you
stop for us. We pay you for your trouble."
"Ye!" replied Louis, "may be you carry some
provision for all, — some pork, — some bread,
— and so pay." He said, "Me sure get some
moose;" and when I asked if he thought Pomola
would let us go up, he answered that we must
plant one bottle of rum on the top; he had
planted good many; and when he looked again,
the rum was all gone. He had been up two or
three times; he had planted letter, — English,
German, French, etc. These men were slightly
clad in shirt and pantaloons, like laborers with
us in warm weather. They did not invite us
into their houses, but met us outside. So we left
the Indians, thinking ourselves lucky to have
secured such guides and companions.

There were very few houses along the road, yet they did not altogether fail, as if the law by which men are dispersed over the globe were a very stringent one, and not to be resisted with impunity or for slight reasons. There were even the germs of one or two villages just beginning to expand. The beauty of the road itself was remarkable. The various evergreens, many of which are rare with us, — delicate and beautiful specimens of the larch, arbor-vitæ, ball-spruce, and fir-balsam, from a few inches to many feet in height, — lined its sides, in some places like a long, front yard, springing up from the smooth grass-plots which uninterruptedly border it, and are made fertile by its wash; while it was but a step on either hand to the grim, untrodden wilderness, whose tangled labyrinth of living, fallen, and decaying trees only the deer and moose, the bear and wolf can easily penetrate. More perfect specimens than any front-yard plot can show grew there to grace the passage of the Houlton teams.

About noon we reached the Mattawamkeag, fifty-six miles from Bangor by the way we had come, and put up at a frequented house still on the Houlton road, where the Houlton stage stops. Here was a substantial covered bridge over the Mattawamkeag, built, I think they said, some seventeen years before. We had

dinner, — where, by the way, and even at breakfast, as well as supper, at the public-houses on
this road, the front rank is composed of various
kinds of "sweet cakes," in a continuous line
from one end of the table to the other. I think
I may safely say that there was a row of ten or
a dozen plates of this kind set before us two
here. To account for which, they say that,
when the lumberers come out of the woods, they
have a craving for cakes and pies, and such
sweet things, which there are almost unknown,
and this is the *supply* to satisfy that *demand*.
The supply is always equal to the demand, and
these hungry men think a good deal of getting
their money's worth. No doubt the balance of
victuals is restored by the time they reach Bangor, — Mattawamkeag takes off the raw edge.
Well, over this front rank, I say, you, coming
from the "sweet cake" side, with a cheap phi-
losophic indifference though it may be, have to
assault what there is behind, which I do not by
any means mean to insinuate is insufficient in
quantity or quality to supply that other demand, of men, not from the woods, but from the
towns, for venison and strong country fare.
After dinner we strolled down to the "Point,"
formed by the junction of the two rivers, which
is said to be the scene of an ancient battle between the Eastern Indians and the Mohawks,

and searched there carefully for relics, though the men at the bar-room had never heard of such things; but we found only some flakes of arrow-head stone, some points of arrow-heads, one small leaden bullet, and some colored beads, the last to be referred, perhaps, to early fur-trader days. The Mattawamkeag, though wide, was a mere river's bed, full of rocks and shallows at this time, so that you could cross it almost dry-shod in boots; and I could hardly believe my companion, when he told me that he had been fifty or sixty miles up it in a batteau, through distant and still uncut forests. A batteau could hardly find a harbor now at its mouth. Deer and caribou, or reindeer, are taken here in the winter, in sight of the house.

Before our companions arrived, we rode on up the Houlton road seven miles to Molunkus, where the Aroostook road comes into it, and where there is a spacious public house in the woods, called the "Molunkus House," kept by one Libbey, which looked as if it had its hall for dancing and for military drills. There was no other evidence of man but this huge shingle palace in this part of the world; but sometimes even this is filled with travelers. I looked off the piazza round the corner of the house up the Aroostook road, on which there was no clearing in sight. There was a man just adventuring upon it this evening in a rude, original, what you may call Aroostook wagon, — a mere seat, with a wagon swung under it, a few bags on it, and a dog asleep to watch them. He offered to carry a message for us to anybody in that country, cheerfully. I suspect that, if you should go to the end of the world, you would find somebody there going farther, as if just starting for home at sundown, and having a last word before he drove off. Here, too, *was* a small trader, whom I did not see at first, who kept a store, — but no great store, certainly, — in a small box over the way, behind the Molunkus sign-post. It looked like the balance-box of a patent hay-scales. As for his house, we could only conjecture where that was; he may have been a boarder in the Molunkus House. I saw him standing in his shop-door, — his shop was so small, that, if a traveler should make demonstrations of entering in, *he* would have to go out by the back way, and confer with his customer through a window, about his goods in the cellar, or, more probably, bespoken, and yet on the way. I should have gone in, for I felt a real impulse to trade, if I had not stopped to consider what would become of him. The day before, we had walked into a shop, over against an inn where we stopped, the puny beginning of trade, which would grow at last into a firm copartnership in the future town or city, — indeed, it was already "Somebody & Co.," I forget who. The woman came forward from the penetralia of the attached house, for "Somebody & Co." was in the burning, and she sold us percussion-caps, canalès and smooth, and knew their prices and qualities, and which the hunters preferred. Here was a little of everything in a small compass to satisfy the wants and the ambition of the woods, — a stock selected with what pains and care, and brought home in the wagon-box, or a corner of the Houlton team; but there seemed to me, as usual, a preponderance of children's toys, — dogs to bark, and cats to mew, and trumpets to blow, where natives there hardly are yet. As if a child, born into the Maine woods, among the pine-cones and cedar-berries, could not do without such a sugar-man or skipping-jack as the young Rothschild has.

I think that there was not more than one house on the road to Molunkus, or for seven miles. At that place we got over the fence into a new field, planted with potatoes, where the logs were still burning between the hills; and, pulling up the vines, found good-sized potatoes, nearly ripe, growing like weeds, and turnips mixed with them. The mode of clearing and planting is to fell the trees, and burn once

what will burn, then cut them up into suitable
lengths, roll into heaps, and burn again; then,
with a hoe, plant potatoes where you can come
at the ground between the stumps and charred
logs; for a first crop the ashes sufficing for manure, and no hoeing being necessary the first
year. In the fall, cut, roll, and burn again,
and so on, till the land is cleared; and soon it
is ready for grain, and to be laid down. Let
those talk of poverty and hard times who will
in the towns and cities; cannot the emigrant
who can pay his fare to New York or Boston
pay five dollars more to get here, — I paid
three, all told, for my passage from Boston to
Bangor, two hundred and fifty miles, — and be
as rich as he pleases, where land virtually costs
nothing, and houses only the labor of building,
and he may begin life as Adam did? If he
will still remember the distinction of poor and
rich, let him bespeak him a narrower house
forthwith.

When we returned to the Mattawamkeag, the
Houlton stage had already put up there; and a
Province man was betraying his greenness to
the Yankees by his questions. Why Province
money won't pass here at par, when States'
money is good at Fredericton, — though this,
perhaps, was sensible enough. From what I
saw then, it appears that the Province man was

now the only real Jonathan, or raw country bumpkin, left so far behind by his enterprising neighbors that he did n't know enough to put a question to them. No people can long continue provincial in character who have the propensity for politics and whittling, and rapid traveling, which the Yankees have, and who are leaving the mother country behind in the variety of their notions and inventions. The possession and exercise of practical talent merely are a sure and rapid means of intellectual culture and independence.

The last edition of Greenleaf's Map of Maine hung on the wall here, and, as we had no pocket-map, we resolved to trace a map of the lake country. So, dipping a wad of tow into the lamp, we oiled a sheet of paper on the oiled table-cloth, and, in good faith, traced what we afterwards ascertained to be a labyrinth of errors, carefully following the outlines of the imaginary lakes which the map contains. The Map of the Public Lands of Maine and Massachusetts is the only one I have seen that at all deserves the name. It was while we were engaged in this operation that our companions arrived. They had seen the Indians' fire on the Five Islands, and so we concluded that all was right.

Early the next morning we had mounted our

packs, and prepared for a tramp up the West
Branch, my companion having turned his horse
out to pasture for a week or ten days, thinking
that a bite of fresh grass, and a taste of running
water would do him as much good as backwoods
fare and new country influences his master.
Leaping over a fence, we began to follow an obscure trail up the northern bank of the Penobscot. There was now no road further, the river
being the only highway, and but half a dozen
log-huts confined to its banks, to be met with
for thirty miles. On either hand, and beyond,
was a wholly uninhabited wilderness, stretching
to Canada. Neither horse nor cow, nor vehicle
of any kind, had ever passed over this ground;
the cattle, and the few bulky articles which the
loggers use, being got up in the winter on the
ice, and down again before it breaks up. The
evergreen woods had a decidedly sweet and
bracing fragrance; the air was a sort of diet-
drink, and we walked on buoyantly in Indian
file, stretching our legs. Occasionally there
was a small opening on the bank, made for the
purpose of log-rolling, where we got a sight of
the river, — always a rocky and rippling stream.
The roar of the rapids, the note of a whistler-
duck on the river, of the jay and chickadee
around us, and of the pigeon-woodpecker in the
openings, were the sounds that we heard. This

was what you might call a bran-new country; the only roads were of Nature's making, and the few houses were camps. Here, then, one could no longer accuse institutions and society, but must front the true source of evil.

There are three classes of inhabitants who either frequent or inhabit the country which we had now entered; — first, the loggers, who, for a part of the year, the winter and spring, are far the most numerous, but in the summer, except a few explorers for timber, completely desert it; second, the few settlers I have named, the only permanent inhabitants, who live on the verge of it, and help raise supplies for the former; third, the hunters, mostly Indians, who range over it in their season.

At the end of three miles we came to the Mattaseunk stream and mill, where there was even a rude wooden railroad running down to the Penobscot, the last railroad we were to see. We crossed one tract, on the bank of the river, of more than a hundred acres of heavy timber, which had just been felled and burnt over, and was still smoking. Our trail lay through the midst of it, and was wellnigh blotted out. The trees lay at full length, four or five feet deep, and crossing each other in all directions, all black as charcoal, but perfectly sound within, still good for fuel or for timber; soon they would be cut into lengths and burnt again. Here were thousands of cords, enough to keep the poor of Boston and New York amply warm for a winter, which only cumbered the ground and were in the settler's way. And the whole of that solid and interminable forest is doomed to be gradually devoured thus by fire, like shavings, and no man be warmed by it. At Crocker's log-hut, at the mouth of Salmon River, seven miles from the Point, one of the party commenced distributing a store of small, cent picture-books among the children, to teach them to read, and also newspapers, more or less recent, among the parents, than which nothing can be more acceptable to a backwoods people. It was really an important item in our outfit, and, at times, the only currency that would circulate. I walked through Salmon River with my shoes on, it being low water, but not without wetting my feet. A few miles farther we came to "Marm Howard's," at the end of an extensive clearing, where there were two or three log-huts in sight at once, one on the opposite side of the river, and a few graves, even surrounded by a wooden paling, where already the rude forefathers of *a* hamlet lie, and a thousand years hence, perchance, some poet will write his "Elegy in a Country Churchyard." The "Village Hampdens," the "mute, inglori-

ous Miltons," and Cromwells, "guiltless of"
their "country's blood," were yet unborn.

> " Perchance in this *wild* spot *there will be* laid
>   Some heart once pregnant with celestial fire ;
> Hands that the rod of empire might have swayed,
>   Or waked to ecstasy the living lyre."

The next house was Fisk's, ten miles from the
Point at the mouth of the East Branch, opposite
to the island Nicketow, or the Forks, the last of
the Indian islands.   I am particular to give the
names of the settlers and the distances, since
every log-hut in these woods is a public house,
and such information is of no little consequence
to those who may have occasion to travel this
way.   Our course here crossed the Penobscot,
and followed the southern bank.   One of the
party, who entered the house in search of some
one to set us over, reported a very neat dwelling, with plenty of books, and a new wife, just
imported from Boston, wholly new to the woods.
We found the East Branch a large and rapid
stream at its mouth, and much deeper than it
appeared.   Having with some difficulty discovered the trail again, we kept up the south side
of the West Branch, or main river, passing by
some rapids called Rock-Ebeeme, the roar of
which we heard through the woods, and, shortly
after, in the thickest of the wood, some empty
loggers' camps, still new, which were occupied

the previous winter. Though we saw a few
more afterwards, I will make one account serve
for all. These were such houses as the lumberers of Maine spend the winter in, in the wilderness. There were the camps and the hovels for
the cattle, hardly distinguishable, except that
the latter had no chimney. These camps were
about twenty feet long by fifteen wide, built of
logs, — hemlock, cedar, spruce or yellow birch,
— one kind alone, or all together, with the bark
on; two or three large ones first, one directly
above another, and notched together at the
ends, to the height of three or four feet, then of
smaller logs resting upon transverse ones at the
ends, each of the last successively shorter than
the other, to form the roof. The chimney was
an oblong square hole in the middle, three or
four feet in diameter, with a fence of logs as
high as the ridge. The interstices were filled
with moss, and the roof was shingled with long
and handsome splints of cedar, or spruce, or
pine, rifted with a sledge and cleaver. The
fire-place, the most important place of all, was
in shape and size like the chimney, and directly
under it, defined by a log fence or fender on
the ground, and a heap of ashes, a foot or two
deep within, with solid benches of split logs
running round it. Here the fire usually melts
the snow, and dries the rain before it can de-

scend to quench it. The faded beds of arbor-
vitæ leaves extended under the eaves on either
hand. There was the place for the water-pail,
pork-barrel, and wash-basin, and generally a
dingy pack of cards left on a log. Usually a
good deal of whittling was expended on the
latch, which was made of wood, in the form of
an iron one. These houses are made comfortable by the huge fires, which can be afforded
night and day. Usually the scenery about them
is drear and savage enough; and the loggers'
camp is as completely in the woods as a fungus
at the foot of a pine in a swamp; no outlook but
to the sky overhead; no more clearing than is
made by cutting down the trees of which it is
built, and those which are necessary for fuel.
If only it be well sheltered and convenient to
his work, and near a spring, he wastes no
thought on the prospect. They are very proper
forest houses, the stems of the trees collected together and piled up around a man to keep out
wind and rain, — made of living green logs,
hanging with moss and lichen, and with the
curls and fringes of the yellow-birch bark, and
dripping with resin, fresh and moist, and redo-
lent of swampy odors, with that sort of vigor
and perennialness even about them that toad-
stools suggest.[1] The logger's fare consists of

[1] Springer, in his *Forest Life* (1851), says that they first

tea, molasses, flour, pork (sometimes beef), and beans. A great proportion of the beans raised in Massachusetts find their market here. On expeditions it is only hard bread and pork, often raw, slice upon slice, with tea or water, as the case may be.

The primitive wood is always and everywhere damp and mossy, so that I traveled constantly with the impression that I was in a swamp; and only when it was remarked that this or that tract, judging from the quality of the timber on it, would make a profitable clearing, was I reminded, that if the sun were let in it would make a dry field, like the few I had seen, at once. The best shod for the most part travel with wet feet. If the ground was so wet and spongy at this, the dryest part of a dry season, what must it be in' the spring? The woods hereabouts abounded in beech and yellow birch, of which last there were some very large specimens; also spruce, cedar, fir, and hemlock; but

remove the leaves and turf from the spot where they intend to build a camp, for fear of fire; also, that "the spruce-tree is generally selected for camp-building, it being light, straight, and quite free from sap;" that "the roof is finally covered with the boughs of the fir, spruce, and hemlock, so that when the snow falls upon the whole, the warmth of the camp is preserved in the coldest weather;" and that they make the log seat before the fire, called the "Deacon's Seat," of a spruce or fir split in halves, with three or four stout limbs left on one side for legs, which are not likely to get loose.

we saw only the stumps of the white-pine here, some of them of great size, these having been already culled out, being the only tree much sought after, even as low down as this. Only a little spruce and hemlock beside had been logged here. The Eastern wood which is sold for fuel in Massachusetts all comes from below Bangor. It was the pine alone, chiefly the white-pine, that had tempted any but the hunter to precede us on this route.

Waite's farm, thirteen miles from the Point, is an extensive and elevated clearing, from which we got a fine view of the river, rippling and gleaming far beneath us. My companions had formerly had a good view of Ktaadn and the other mountains here, but to-day it was so smoky that we could see nothing of them. We could overlook an immense country of uninter-rupted forest, stretching away up the East Branch toward Canada on the north and north-west, and toward the Aroostook valley on the northeast; and imagine what wild life was stir-ring in its midst. Here was quite a field of corn for this region, whose peculiar dry scent we per-ceived a third of a mile off, before we saw it.

Eighteen miles from the Point brought us in sight of McCauslin's, or "Uncle George's," as he was familiarly called by my companions, to whom he was well known, where we intended to

break our long fast. His house was in the midst
of an extensive clearing of intervale, at the
mouth of the Little Schoodic River, on the opposite or north bank of the Penobscot. So we
collected on a point of the shore, that we might
be seen, and fired our gun as a signal, which
brought out his dogs forthwith, and thereafter
their master, who in due time took us across in
his batteau. This clearing was bounded abruptly, on all sides but the river, by the naked
stems of the forest, as if you were to cut only a
few feet square in the midst of a thousand acres
of mowing, and set down a thimble therein.
He had a whole heaven and horizon to himself,
and the sun seemed to be journeying over his
clearing only the livelong day. Here we concluded to spend the night, and wait for the Indians, as there was no stopping-place so convenient above. He had seen no Indians pass, and
this did not often happen without his knowledge.
He thought that his dogs sometimes gave notice
of the approach of Indians half an hour before
they arrived.

McCauslin was a Kennebec man, of Scotch
descent, who had been a waterman twenty-two
years, and had driven on the lakes and head-
waters of the Penobscot five or six springs in
succession, but was now settled here to raise
supplies for the lumberers and for himself. He

entertained us a day or two with true Scotch
hospitality, and would accept no recompense for
it.   A man of a dry wit and shrewdness, and a
general intelligence which I had not looked for
in the backwoods.   In fact, the deeper you penetrate into the woods, the more intelligent, and,
in one sense, less countrified do you find the inhabitants; for always the pioneer has been a
traveler, and, to some extent, a man of the
world; and, as the distances with which he is
familiar are greater, so is his information more
general and far reaching than the villagers.   If
I were to look for a narrow, uninformed, and
countrified mind, as opposed to the intelligence
and refinement which are thought to emanate
from cities, it would be among the rusty inhabitants of an old-settled country, on farms all run
out and gone to seed with life-everlasting, in
the towns about Boston, even on the high-road
in Concord, and not in the backwoods of Maine.

Supper was got before our eyes in the ample
kitchen, by a fire which would have roasted an
ox; many whole logs, four feet long, were con-
sumed to boil our tea-kettle, — birch, or beech,
or maple, the same summer and winter; and the
dishes were soon smoking on the table, late the
arm-chair, against the wall, from which one of
the party was expelled.   The arms of the chair
formed the frame on which the table rested;

and, when the round top was turned up against
the wall, it formed the back of the chair, and
was no more in the way than the wall itself.
This, we noticed, was the prevailing fashion in
these log-houses, in order to economize in room.
There were piping-hot wheaten cakes, the flour
having been brought up the river in batteaux,
— no Indian bread, for the upper part of Maine,
it will be remembered, is a wheat country, —
and ham, eggs, and potatoes, and milk and
cheese, the produce of the farm; and also shad
and salmon, tea sweetened with molasses, and
sweet cakes, in contradistinction to the hot cakes
not sweetened, the one white, the other yellow,
to wind up with. Such we found was the prevailing fare, ordinary and extraordinary, along
this river. Mountain cranberries (*Vaccinium
Vitis-Idœa*), stewed and sweetened, were the
common dessert. Everything here was in profusion, and the best of its kind. Butter was in
such plenty that it was commonly used, before
it was salted, to grease boots with.

In the night we were entertained by the sound
of rain-drops on the cedar-splints which covered
the roof, and awaked the next morning with a
drop or two in our eyes. It had set in for a
storm, and we made up our minds not to forsake
such comfortable quarters with this prospect,
but wait for Indians and fair weather. It

rained and drizzled and gleamed by turns, the livelong day. What we did there, how we killed the time would perhaps be idle to tell; how many times we buttered our boots, and how often a drowsy one was seen to sidle off to the bedroom. When it held up, I strolled up and down the bank, and gathered the harebell and cedar - berries, which grew there; or else we tried by turns the long-handled axe on the logs before the door. The axe-helves here were made to chop standing on the log, — a primitive log of course, — and were, therefore, nearly a foot longer than with us. One while we walked over the farm and visited his well-filled barns with McCauslin. There were one other man and two women only here. He kept horses, cows, oxen, and sheep. I think he said that he was the first to bring a plough and a cow so far; and he might have added the last, with only two exceptions. The potato-rot had found him out here, too, the previous year, and got half or two thirds of his crop, though the seed was of his own raising. Oats, grass, and potatoes were his staples; but he raised, also, a few carrots and turnips, and "a little corn for the hens," for this was all that he dared risk, for fear that it would not ripen. Melons, squashes, sweet-corn, beans, tomatoes, and many other vegetables, could not be ripened there.

The very few settlers along this stream were obviously tempted by the cheapness of the land mainly. When I asked McCauslin why more settlers did not come in, he answered, that one reason was, they could not buy the land, it belonged to individuals or companies who were afraid that their wild lands would be settled, and so incorporated into towns, and they be taxed for them; but to settling on the States' land there was no such hindrance. For his own part, he wanted no neighbors, — he didn't wish to see any road by his house. Neighbors, even the best, were a trouble and expense, especially on the score of cattle and fences. They might live across the river, perhaps, but not on the same side.

The chickens here were protected by the dogs. As McCauslin said, "The old one took it up first, and she taught the pup, and now they had got it into their heads that it wouldn't do to have anything of the bird kind on the premises." A hawk hovering over was not allowed to alight, but barked off by the dogs circling underneath; and a pigeon, or a "yellow-hammer," as they called the pigeon-woodpecker, on a dead limb or stump, was instantly expelled. It was the main business of their day, and kept them constantly coming and going. One would rush out of the house on the least alarm given by the other.

When it rained hardest, we returned to the house, and took down a tract from the shelf. There was the "Wandering Jew," cheap edition, and fine print, the "Criminal Calendar," and "Parish's Geography," and flash novels two or three. Under the pressure of circumstances, we read a little in these. With such aid, the press is not so feeble an engine, after all. This house, which was a fair specimen of those on this river, was built of huge logs, which peeped out everywhere, and were chinked with clay and moss. It contained four or five rooms. There were no sawed boards, or shingles, or clapboards, about it; and scarcely any tool but the axe had been used in its construction. The partitions were made of long clapboard-like splints, of spruce or cedar, turned to a delicate salmon color by the smoke. The roof and sides were covered with the same, instead of shingles and clapboards, and some of a much thicker and larger size were used for the floor. These were all so straight and smooth, that they answered the purpose admirably, and a careless observer would not have suspected that they were not sawed and planed. The chimney and hearth were of vast size, and made of stone. The broom was a few twigs of arbor-vitæ tied to a stick; and a pole was suspended over the hearth, close to the ceilings, to dry stockings and clothes on. I noticed that the floor was full of small, dingy holes, as if made with a gimlet, but which were, in fact, made by the spikes, nearly an inch long, which the lumberers wear in their boots to prevent their slipping on wet logs. Just above McCauslin's, there is a rocky rapid, where logs jam in the spring; and many "drivers" are there collected, who frequent his house for supplies; these were their tracks which I saw.

At sundown McCauslin pointed away over the forest, across the river, to signs of fair weather amid the clouds, — some evening redness there. For even there the points of compass held; and there was a quarter of the heavens appropriated to sunrise and another to sunset.

The next morning, the weather proving fair enough for our purpose, we prepared to start, and, the Indians having failed us, persuaded McCauslin, who was not unwilling to revisit the scenes of his driving, to accompany us in their stead, intending to engage one other boatman on the way. A strip of cotton cloth for a tent, a couple of blankets, which would suffice for the whole party, fifteen pounds of hard bread, ten pounds of "clear" pork, and a little tea, made up "Uncle George's" pack. The last three articles were calculated to be provision enough for six men for a week, with what we might pick up. A tea-kettle, a frying-pan, and an axe, to be obtained at the last house, would complete our outfit.

We were soon out of McCauslin's clearing, and in the ever green woods again. The obscure trail made by the two settlers above, which even the woodman is sometimes puzzled to discern, erelong crossed a narrow, open strip in the woods overrun with weeds, called the Burnt Land, where a fire had raged formerly, stretching northward nine or ten miles, to Millinocket Lake. At the end of three miles, we reached Shad Pond, or Noliseemack, an expansion of the river. Hodge, the Assistant State Geologist, who passed through this on the 25th of June, 1837, says, "We pushed our boat through an acre or more of buck-beans, which had taken root at the bottom, and bloomed above the surface in the greatest profusion and beauty." Thomas Fowler's house is four miles from McCauslin's, on the shore of the pond, at the mouth of the Millinocket River, and eight miles from the lake of the same name, on the latter stream. This lake affords a more direct course to Ktaadn, but we preferred to follow the Penobscot and the Pamadumcook lakes. Fowler was just completing a new log-hut, and was sawing out a window through the logs, nearly two feet thick, when we arrived. He had begun to paper his house with spruce-bark, turned inside out, which had a good effect, and was in keeping with the circumstances. Instead of water we got here a draught of beer, which, it was allowed, would be better; clear and thin, but strong and stringent as the cedar-sap. It was as if we sucked at the very teats of Nature's pine-clad bosom in these parts, — the sap of all Millinocket botany commingled, — the topmost, most fantastic, and spiciest sprays of the primitive wood, and whatever invigorating and stringent gum or essence it afforded steeped and dissolved in it, — a lumberer's drink, which would acclimate and naturalize a man at once, — which would make him see green, and, if he slept, dream that he heard the wind sough among the pines. Here was a fife, praying to be played on, through which we breathed a few tuneful strains, — brought hither to tame wild beasts. As we stood upon the pile of chips by the door, fish-hawks were sailing overhead; and here, over Shad Pond, might daily be witnessed the tyranny of the bald-eagle over that bird. Tom pointed away over the lake to a bald-eagle's nest, which was plainly visible more than a mile off, on a pine, high above the surrounding forest, and was frequented from year to year by the same pair, and held sacred by him. There were these two houses only there, his low hut and the eagles' airy cart-load of fagots. Thomas Fowler, too, was persuaded to join us, for two men were necessary to manage the batteau, which was soon to be our carriage, and these men needed to be cool and skillful for the navigation of the Penobscot. Tom's pack was soon made, for he had not far to look for his waterman's boots, and a red flannel shirt. This is the favorite color with lumbermen; and red flannel is reputed to possess some mysterious virtues, to be most healthful and convenient in respect to perspiration. In every gang there will be a large proportion of red birds. We took here a poor and leaky batteau, and began to pole up the Millinocket two miles, to the elder Fowler's, in order to avoid the Grand Falls of the Penobscot, intending to exchange our batteau there for a better. The Millinocket is a small, shallow, and sandy stream, full of what I took to be lamprey-eels' or suckers' nests, and lined with musquash cabins, but free from rapids, according to Fowler, excepting at its outlet from the lake. He was at this time engaged in cutting the native grass — rush-grass and meadow-clover, as he called it — on the meadows and small, low islands of this stream. We noticed flattened places in the grass on either side, where, he said, a moose had laid down the night before, adding, that there were thousands in these meadows.

Old Fowler's, on the Millinocket, six miles from McCauslin's, and twenty-four from the Point, is the last house. Gibson's, on the Sowadnehunk, is the only clearing above, but that had proved a failure, and was long since deserted. Fowler is the oldest inhabitant of these woods. He formerly lived a few miles from here, on the south side of the West Branch, where he built his house sixteen years ago, the first house built above the Five Islands. Here our new batteau was to be carried over the first portage of two miles, round the Grand Falls of the Penobscot, on a horse-sled made of saplings, to jump the numerous rocks in the way; but we had to wait a couple of hours for them to catch the horses, which were pastured at a distance, amid the stumps, and had wandered still farther off. The last of the salmon for this season had just been caught, and were still fresh in pickle, from which enough was extracted to fill our empty kettle, and so graduate our introduction to simpler forest fare. The week before they had lost nine sheep here out of their first flock, by the wolves. The surviving sheep came round the house, and seemed frightened, which induced them to go and look for the rest, when they found seven dead and lacerated, and two still alive. These last they carried to the house, and, as Mrs. Fowler said, they were merely scratched in the throat, and had no more visible wound than would be produced by the prick of a pin. She sheared off the wool from their throats, and washed them, and put on some salve, and turned them out, but in a few moments they were missing, and had not been found since. In fact, they were all poisoned, and those that were found swelled up at once, so that they saved neither skin nor wool. This realized the old fables of the wolves and the sheep, and convinced me that that ancient hostility still existed. Verily, the shepherd-boy did not need to sound a false alarm this time. There were steel traps by the door, of various sizes, for wolves, otter, and bears, with large claws instead of teeth, to catch in their sinews. Wolves are frequently killed with poisoned bait.

At length, after we had dined here on the usual backwoods fare, the horses arrived, and we hauled our batteau out of the water, and lashed it to its wicker carriage, and, throwing in our packs, walked on before, leaving the boatmen and driver, who was Tom's brother, to manage the concern. The route, which led through the wild pasture where the sheep were killed, was in some places the roughest ever traveled by horses, over rocky hills, where the

sled bounced and slid along, like a vessel pitching in a storm; and one man was as necessary
to stand at the stern, to prevent the boat from
being wrecked, as a helmsman in the roughest
sea. The philosophy of our progress was something like this: when the runners struck a rock
three or four feet high, the sled bounced back
and upwards at the same time; but, as the
horses never ceased pulling, it came down on
the top of the rock, and so we got over. This
portage probably followed the trail of an ancient
Indian carry round these falls. By two o'clock
we, who had walked on before, reached the river
above the falls, not far from the outlet of
Quakish Lake, and waited for the batteau to
come up. We had been here but a short time,
when a thunder-shower was seen coming up
from the west, over the still invisible lakes, and
that pleasant wilderness which we were so eager
to become acquainted with; and soon the heavy
drops began to patter on the leaves around us.
I had just selected the prostrate trunk of a huge
pine, five or six feet in diameter, and was crawling under it, when, luckily, the boat arrived.
It would have amused a sheltered man to witness
the manner in which it was unlashed, and
whirled over, while the first water-spout burst
upon us. It was no sooner in the hands of the
eager company than it was abandoned to the

first revolutionary impulse, and to gravity, to
adjust it; and they might have been seen all
stooping to its shelter, and wriggling under like
so many eels, before it was fairly deposited on
the ground.   When all were under, we propped
up the lee side, and busied ourselves there whittling thole-pins for rowing, when we should
reach the lakes; and made the woods ring, between the claps of thunder, with such boat-songs
as we could remember.   The horses stood sleek
and shining with the rain, all drooping and
crestfallen, while deluge after deluge washed
over us; but the bottom of a boat may be relied
on for a tight roof.   At length, after two hours'
delay at this place, a streak of fair weather appeared in the northwest, whither our course now
lay, promising a serene evening for our voyage;
and the driver returned with his horses, while
we made haste to launch our boat, and commence our voyage in good earnest.

There were six of us, including the two boatmen.   With our packs heaped up near the
bows, and ourselves disposed as baggage to trim
the boat, with instructions not to move in case
we should strike a rock, more than so many
barrels of pork, we pushed out into the first
rapid, a slight specimen of the stream we had to
navigate.   With Uncle George in the stern,
and Tom in the bows, each using a spruce pole

about twelve feet long, pointed with iron,[1] and poling on the same side, we shot up the rapids like a salmon, the water rushing and roaring around, so that only a practiced eye could distinguish a safe course, or tell what was deep water and what rocks, frequently grazing the latter on one or both sides, with a hundred as narrow escapes as ever the Argo had in passing through the Symplegades. I, who had had some experience in boating, had never experienced any half so exhilarating before. We were lucky to have exchanged our Indians, whom we did not know, for these men, who, together with Tom's brother, were reputed the best boatmen on the river, and were at once indispensable pilots and pleasant companions. The canoe is smaller, more easily upset, and sooner worn out; and the Indian is said not to be so skillful in the management of the batteau. He is, for the most part, less to be relied on, and more disposed to sulks and whims. The utmost familiarity with dead streams, or with the ocean, would not prepare a man for this peculiar navigation; and the most skillful boatman anywhere else would here be obliged to take out his boat and carry round a hundred times, still with great risk, as well as delay, where the practiced batteau-man poles up with comparative

---

[1] The Canadians call it *picquer de fond*.

ease and safety. The hardy "voyageur" pushes
with incredible perseverance and success quite
up to the foot of the falls, and then only carries
round some perpendicular ledge, and launches
again in

" The torrent's smoothness, ere it dash below,"

to struggle with the boiling rapids above. The
Indians say that the river once ran both ways,
one half up and the other down, but that, since
the white man came, it all runs down, and now
they must laboriously pole their canoes against
the stream, and carry them over numerous portages. In the summer, all stores — the grind-
stone and the plough of the pioneer, flour, pork,
and utensils for the explorer, — must be con-
veyed up the river in batteaux; and many a
cargo and many a boatman is lost in these
waters. In the winter, however, which is very
equable and long, the ice is the great highway,
and the loggers' team penetrates to Chesuncook
Lake, and still higher up, even two hundred
miles above Bangor. Imagine the solitary sled-
track running far up into the snowy and evergreen wilderness, hemmed in closely for a hundred miles by the forest, and again stretching
straight across the broad surfaces of concealed
lakes!

We were soon in the smooth water of the

Quakish Lake, and took our turns at rowing and paddling across it. It is a small, irregular, but handsome lake, shut in on all sides by the forest, and showing no traces of man but some low boom in a distant cove, reserved for spring use. The spruce and cedar on its shores, hung with gray lichens, looked at a distance like the ghosts of trees. Ducks were sailing here and there on its surface, and a solitary loon, like a more living wave, — a vital spot on the lake's surface, — laughed and frolicked, and showed its straight leg, for our amusement. Joe Merry Mountain appeared in the northwest, as if it were looking down on this lake especially; and we had our first, but a partial view of Ktaadn, its summit veiled in clouds, like a dark isthmus in that quarter, connecting the heavens with the earth. After two miles of smooth rowing across this lake, we found ourselves in the river again, which was a continuous rapid for one mile, to the dam, requiring all the strength and skill of our boatmen to pole up it.

This dam is a quite important and expensive work for this country, whither cattle and horses cannot penetrate in the summer, raising the whole river ten feet, and flooding, as they said, some sixty square miles by means of the innumerable lakes with which the river connects. It is a lofty and solid structure, with sloping piers, some distance above, made of frames of logs filled with stones, to break the ice.[1] Here every log pays toll as it passes through the sluices.

We filed into the rude loggers' camp at this place, such as I have described, without ceremony, and the cook, at that moment the sole occupant, at once set about preparing tea for his visitors. His fireplace, which the rain had converted into a mud-puddle, was soon blazing again, and we sat down on the log benches around it to dry us. On the well-flattened and somewhat faded beds of arbor-vitæ leaves, which stretched on either hand under the eaves behind us, lay an odd leaf of the Bible, some genealogical chapter out of the Old Testament; and, half buried by the leaves, we found Emerson's Address on West India Emancipation, which had been left here formerly by one of our company, and *had made two converts to the Liberty party here*, as I was told; also, an odd number of the Westminster Review, for 1834, and a pamphlet entitled History of the Erection of the Monument on the grave of Myron Holly. This was the readable or reading matter in a lumberer's camp in the Maine woods, thirty miles from a

---

[1] Even the Jesuit missionaries, accustomed to the St. Lawrence and other rivers of Canada, in their first expeditions to the Abenaquinois, speak of rivers *ferrées de rochers*, shod with rocks. See also No. 10 *Relations*, for 1647, p. 185.

road, which would be given up to the bears in a fortnight. These things were well thumbed and soiled. This gang was headed by one John Morrison, a good specimen of a Yankee; and was necessarily composed of men not bred to the business of dam-building, but who were Jacks-at-all-trades, handy with the axe, and other simple implements, and well skilled in wood and water craft. We had hot cakes for our supper even here, white as snowballs, but without butter, and the never-failing sweet cakes, with which we filled our pockets, foreseeing that we should not soon meet with the like again. Such delicate puff-balls seemed a singular diet for backwoodsmen. There was also tea without milk, sweetened with molasses. And so, exchanging a word with John Morrison and his gang when we had returned to the shore, and also exchanging our batteau for a better still, we made haste to improve the little daylight that remained. This camp, exactly twenty-nine miles from Mattawamkeag Point by the way we had come, and about one hundred from Bangor by the river, was the last human habitation of any kind in this direction. Beyond, there was no trail, and the river and lakes, by batteaux and canoes, was considered the only practicable route. We were about thirty miles by the river from the summit of Ktaadn, which was in sight, though not more than twenty, perhaps, in a straight line.

It being about the full of the moon, and a warm and pleasant evening, we decided to row five miles by moonlight to the head of the North Twin Lake, lest the wind should rise on the morrow. After one mile of river, or what the boatmen call "thoroughfare," — for the river becomes at length only the connecting link between the lakes, — and some slight rapid which had been mostly made smooth water by the dam, we entered the North Twin Lake just after sundown, and steered across for the river "thoroughfare," four miles distant. This is a noble sheet of water, where one may get the impression which a new country and a "lake of the woods" are fitted to create. There was the smoke of no log-hut nor camp of any kind to greet us, still less was any lover of nature or musing traveler watching our batteau from the distant hills; not even the Indian hunter was there, for he rarely climbs them, but hugs the river like ourselves. No face welcomed us but the fine fantastic sprays of free and happy evergreen trees, waving one above another in their ancient home. At first the red clouds hung over the western shore as gorgeously as if over a city, and the lake lay open to the light with even a civilized aspect, as if expecting trade and commerce, and towns and villas. We could distinguish the inlet to the South Twin, which is said to be the larger, where the shore was misty and blue, and it was worth the while to look thus through a narrow opening across the entire expanse of a concealed lake to its own yet more dim and distant shore. The shores rose gently to ranges of low hills covered with forests; and though, in fact, the most valuable white-pine timber, even about this lake, had been culled out, this would never have been suspected by the voyager. The impression, which indeed corresponded with the fact, was, as if we were upon a high table-land between the States and Canada, the northern side of which is drained by the St. John and Chaudière, the southern by the Penobscot and Kennebec. There was no bold mountainous shore, as we might have expected, but only isolated hills and mountains rising here and there from the plateau. The country is an archipelago of lakes, — the lake-country of New England. Their levels vary but a few feet, and the boatmen, by short portages, or by none at all, pass easily from one to another. They say that at very high water the Penobscot and the Kennebec flow into each other, or at any rate, that you may lie with your face in the one and your toes in the other. Even the Penobscot and St. John have been connected by a canal, so that the lumber of the Allegash, instead of going down the St. John, comes down the Penobscot; and the Indian's tradition, that the Penobscot once ran both ways for his convenience, is, in one sense, partially realized to-day.

None of our party but McCauslin had been above this lake, so we trusted to him to pilot us, and we could not but confess the importance of a pilot on these waters. While it is river, you will not easily forget which way is up stream; but when you enter a lake, the river is completely lost, and you scan the distant shores in vain to find where it comes in. A stranger is, for the time at least, lost, and must set about a voyage of discovery first of all to find the river. To follow the windings of the shore when the lake is ten miles, or even more, in length, and of an irregularity which will not soon be mapped, is a wearisome voyage, and will spend his time and his provisions. They tell a story of a gang of experienced woodmen sent to a location on this stream, who were thus lost in the wilderness of lakes. They cut their way through thickets, and carried their baggage and their boats over from lake to lake, sometimes several miles. They carried into Millinocket Lake, which is on another stream, and is ten miles square, and contains a hundred islands.

They explored its shores thoroughly, and then carried into another, and another, and it was a week of toil and anxiety before they found the Penobscot River again, and then their provisions were exhausted, and they were obliged to return.

While Uncle George steered for a small island near the head of the lake, now just visible, like a speck on the water, we rowed by turns swiftly over its surface, singing such boat-songs as we could remember. The shores seemed at an indefinite distance in the moonlight. Occasionally we paused in our singing and rested on our oars, while we listened to hear if the wolves howled, for this is a common serenade, and my companions affirmed that it was the most dismal and unearthly of sounds; but we heard none this time. If we did not *hear*, however, we did *listen*, not without a reasonable expectation; that at least I have to tell, — only some utterly uncivilized, big-throated owl hooted loud and dismally in the drear and boughy wilderness, plainly not nervous about his solitary life, nor afraid to hear the echoes of his voice there. We remembered also that possibly moose were silently watching us from the distant coves, or some surly bear or timid caribou had been startled by our singing. It was with new emphasis that we sang there the Canadian boat-song, —

"Row, brothers, row, the stream runs fast,
    The Rapids are near and the daylight 's past! " —

which describes precisely our own adventure,
and was inspired by the experience of a similar
kind of life, — for the rapids were ever near,
and the daylight long past; the woods on shore
looked dim, and many an Utawas' tide here
emptied into the lake.

"Why should we yet our sail unfurl?
    There is not a breath the blue wave to curl!
    But, when the wind blows off the shore,
    Oh, sweetly we 'll rest our weary oar."

"Utawas' tide! this trembling moon
    Shall see us float o'er thy surges soon."

At last we glided past the "green isle,"
which had been our landmark, all joining in the
chorus; as if by the watery links of rivers and
of lakes we were about to float over unmeasured
zones of earth, bound on unimaginable adventures, —

"Saint of this green isle! hear our prayers,
    Oh, grant us cool heavens and favoring airs!"

About nine o'clock we reached the river, and
ran our boat into a natural haven between some
rocks, and drew her out on the sand. This
camping-ground McCauslin had been familiar
with in his lumbering days, and he now struck
it unerringly in the moonlight, and we heard the
sound of the rill which would supply us with

cool water emptying into the lake. The first
business was to make a fire, an operation which
was a little delayed by the wetness of the fuel
and the ground, owing to the heavy showers of
the afternoon. The fire is the main comfort of
the camp, whether in summer or winter, and is
about as ample at one season as at another. It
is as well for cheerfulness as for warmth and
dryness. It forms one side of the camp; one
bright side at any rate. Some were dispersed
to fetch in dead trees and boughs, while Uncle
George felled the birches and beeches which
stood convenient, and soon we had a fire some
ten feet long by three or four high, which rapidly dried the sand before it. This was calculated to burn all night. We next proceeded to
pitch our tent; which operation was performed
by sticking our two spike-poles into the ground
in a slanting direction, about ten feet apart, for
rafters, and then drawing our cotton cloth over
them, and tying it down at the ends, leaving it
open in front, shed-fashion. But this evening
the wind carried the sparks on to the tent and
burned it. So we hastily drew up the batteau
just within the edge of the woods before the fire,
and propping up one side three or four feet
high, spread the tent on the ground to lie on;
and with the corner of a blanket, or what more
or less we could get to put over us, lay down

with our heads and bodies under the boat, and our feet and legs on the sand toward the fire. At first we lay awake, talking of our course, and finding ourselves in so convenient a posture for studying the heavens, with the moon and stars shining in our faces, our conversation naturally turned upon astronomy, and we recounted by turns the most interesting discoveries in that science. But at length we composed ourselves seriously to sleep. It was interesting, when awakened at midnight, to watch the grotesque and fiend-like forms and motions of some one of the party, who, not being able to sleep, had got up silently to arouse the fire, and add fresh fuel, for a change; now stealthily lugging a dead tree from out the dark, and heaving it on, now stirring up the embers with his fork, or tiptoeing about to observe the stars, watched, perchance, by half the prostrate party in breathless silence; so much the more intense because they were awake, while each supposed his neighbor sound asleep. Thus aroused, I, too, brought fresh fuel to the fire, and then rambled along the sandy shore in the moonlight, hoping to meet a moose come down to drink, or else a wolf. The little rill tinkled the louder, and peopled all the wilderness for me; and the glassy smoothness of the sleeping lake, laving the shores of a new world, with the dark, fan-

tastic rocks rising here and there from its surface, made a scene not easily described. It has
left such an impression of stern, yet gentle,
wildness on my memory as will not soon be
effaced. Not far from midnight we were one
after another awakened by rain falling on our
extremities; and as each was made aware of the
fact by cold or wet, he drew a long sigh and
then drew up his legs, until gradually we had
all sidled round from lying at right angles with
the boat, till our bodies formed an acute angle
with it, and were wholly protected. When
next we awoke, the moon and stars were shining
again, and there were signs of dawn in the east.
I have been thus particular in order to convey
some idea of a night in the woods.

We had soon launched and loaded our boat,
and, leaving our fire blazing, were off again before breakfast. The lumberers rarely trouble
themselves to put out their fires, such is the
dampness of the primitive forest; and this is
one cause, no doubt, of the frequent fires in
Maine, of which we hear so much on smoky
days in Massachusetts. The forests are held
cheap after the white-pine has been culled out;
and the explorers and hunters pray for rain
only to clear the atmosphere of smoke. The
woods were so wet to-day, however, that there
was no danger of our fire spreading. After

poling up half a mile of river, or thoroughfare, we rowed a mile across the foot of Pamadum-cook Lake, which is the name given on the map to this whole chain of lakes, as if there was but one, though they are, in each instance, distinctly separated by a reach of the river, with its narrow and rocky channel and its rapids. This lake, which is one of the largest, stretched northwest ten miles, to hills and mountains in the distance. McCauslin pointed to some distant, and as yet inaccessible, forests of white-pine, on the sides of a mountain in that direction. The Joe Merry Lakes, which lay between us and Moosehead, on the west, were recently, if they are not still, "surrounded by some of the best timbered land in the State." By another thoroughfare we passed into Deep Cove, a part of the same lake, which makes up two miles, toward the northeast, and rowing two miles across this, by another short thoroughfare, entered Ambejijis Lake.

At the entrance to a lake we sometimes observed what is technically called "fencing stuff," or the unhewn timbers of which booms are formed, either secured together in the water, or laid up on the rocks and lashed to trees, for spring use. But it was always startling to discover so plain a trail of civilized man there. I remember that I was strangely affected, when we were returning, by the sight of a ring-bolt well drilled into a rock, and fastened with lead, at the head of this solitary Ambejijis Lake.

It was easy to see that driving logs must be an exciting as well as arduous and dangerous business. All winter long the logger goes on piling up the trees which he has trimmed and hauled in some dry ravine at the head of a stream, and then in the spring he stands on the bank and whistles for Rain and Thaw, ready to wring the perspiration out of his shirt to swell the tide, till suddenly, with a whoop and halloo from him, shutting his eyes, as if to bid fare-well to the existing state of things, a fair pro-portion of his winter's work goes scrambling down the country, followed by his faithful dogs, Thaw and Rain and Freshet and Wind, the whole pack in full cry, toward the Orono Mills. Every log is marked with the owner's name, cut in the sapwood with an axe or bored with an auger, so deep as not to be worn off in the driv-ing, and yet not so as to injure the timber; and it requires considerable ingenuity to invent new and simple marks where there are so many owners. They have quite an alphabet of their own, which only the practised can read. One of my companions read off from his memoran-dum book some marks of his own logs, among which there were crosses, belts, crow's feet, gir-

dles, etc., as, "Y — girdle — crow-foot," and
various other devices. When the logs have
run the gauntlet of innumerable rapids and
falls, each on its own account, with more or less
jamming and bruising, those bearing various
owners' marks being mixed up together, — since
all must take advantage of the same freshet, —
they are collected together at the heads of the
lakes, and surrounded by a boom fence of floating logs, to prevent their being dispersed by
the wind, and are thus towed all together, like
a flock of sheep, across the lake, where there is
no current, by a windlass, or boom-head, such
as we sometimes saw standing on an island or
headland, and, if circumstances permit, with
the aid of sails and oars. Sometimes, notwithstanding, the logs are dispersed over many
miles of lake surface in a few hours by winds
and freshets, and thrown up on distant shores,
where the driver can pick up only one or two
at a time, and return with them to the thoroughfare; and before he gets his flock well through
Ambejijis or Pamadumcook, he makes many a
wet and uncomfortable camp on the shore. He
must be able to navigate a log as if it were a
canoe, and be as indifferent to cold and wet as
a muskrat. He uses a few efficient tools, — a
lever commonly of rock-maple, six or seven feet
long, with a stout spike in it, strongly ferruled

on, and a long spike-pole, with a screw at the
end of the spike to make it hold. The boys
along shore learn to walk on floating logs as
city boys on sidewalks. Sometimes the logs
are thrown up on rocks in such positions as to
be irrecoverable but by another freshet as high
or they jam together at rapids and falls, and
accumulate in vast piles, which the driver must
start at the risk of his life. Such is the lumber
business, which depends on many accidents, as
the early freezing of the rivers, that the teams
may get up in season, a sufficient freshet in the
spring, to fetch the logs down, and many
others.[1] I quote Michaux on Lumbering on
the Kennebec, then the source of the best white-
pine lumber carried to England. "The persons engaged in this branch of industry are
generally emigrants from New Hampshire. . . .
In the summer they unite in small companies,
and traverse these vast solitudes in every direction, to ascertain the places in which the pines
abound. After cutting the grass and convert-

---

[1] "A steady current or pitch of water is preferable to one
either rising or diminishing; as, when rising rapidly, the
water at the middle of the river is considerably higher than
at the shores, — so much so as to be distinctly perceived by
the eye of a spectator on the banks, presenting an appearance
like a turnpike road. The lumber, therefore, is always sure
to incline from the centre of the channel toward either shore."
— Springer.

ing it into hay for the nourishment of the cattle
to be employed in their labor, they return home.
In the beginning of the winter they enter the
forests again, establish themselves in huts covered with the bark of the canoe-birch, or the
arbor-vitæ; and, though the cold is so intense
that the mercury sometimes remains for several
weeks from 40° to 50° [Fahr.] below the point
of congelation, they persevere, with unabated
courage, in their work." According to Springer,
the company consists of choppers, swampers, —
who make roads, — barker and loader, teamster, and cook. "When the trees are felled,
they cut them into logs from fourteen to eighteen feet long, and, by means of their cattle,
which they employ with great dexterity, drag
them to the river, and, after stamping on them
a mark of property, roll them on its frozen
bosom. At the breaking of the ice, in the
spring, they float down with the current. . . .
The logs that are not drawn the first year,"
adds Michaux, "are attacked by large worms,
which form holes about two lines in diameter,
in every direction; but, if stripped of their
bark, they will remain uninjured for thirty
years."

Ambejijis, this quiet Sunday morning, struck
me as the most beautiful lake we had seen. It
is said to be one of the deepest. We had the

fairest view of Joe Merry, Double Top, and Ktaadn, from its surface. The summit of the latter had a singularly flat, table-land appearance, like a short highway, where a demigod might be let down to take a turn or two in an afternoon, to settle his dinner. We rowed a mile and a half to near the head of the lake, and, pushing through a field of lily-pads, landed, to cook our breakfast, by the side of a large rock, known to McCauslin. Our breakfast consisted of tea, with hardbread and pork, and fried salmon, which we ate with forks neatly whittled from alder-twigs, which grew there, off strips of birch-bark for plates. The tea was black tea, without milk to color or sugar to sweeten it, and two tin dippers were our tea-cups. This beverage is as indispensable to the loggers as to any gossiping old women in the land, and they, no doubt, derive great comfort from it. Here was the site of an old logger's camp, remembered by McCauslin, now overgrown with weeds and bushes. In the midst of a dense underwood we noticed a whole brick, on a rock, in a small run, clean and red and square as in a brick-yard, which had been brought thus far formerly for tamping. Some of us afterward regretted that we had not carried this on with us to the top of the mountain, to be left there for our mark. It would certainly have

been a simple evidence of civilized man. Mc-
Causlin said that large wooden crosses, made of
oak, still sound, were sometimes found standing
in this wilderness, which were set up by the first
Catholic missionaries who came through to the
Kennebec.

In the next nine miles, which were the extent
of our voyage, and which it took us the rest of
the day to get over, we rowed across several
small lakes, poled up numerous rapids and
thoroughfares, and carried over four portages.
I will give the names and distances, for the benefit of future tourists. First, after leaving
Ambejijis Lake, we had a quarter of a mile of
rapids to the portage, or carry of ninety rods
around Ambejijis Falls; then a mile and a half
through Passamagamet Lake, which is narrow
and river-like, to the falls of the same name, —
Ambejijis stream coming in on the right; then
two miles through Katepskonegan Lake to the
portage of ninety rods around Katepskonegan
Falls, which name signifies "carrying-place," —
Passamagamet stream coming in on the left;
then three miles through Pockwockomus Lake,
a slight expansion of the river, to the portage of
forty rods around the falls of the same name,
— Katepskonegan stream coming in on the left;
then three quarters of a mile through Aboljacarmegus Lake, similar to the last, to the por-

tage of forty rods around the falls of the same name; then half a mile of rapid water to the Sowadnehunk dead-water, and the Aboljack-nagesic stream.

This is generally the order of names as you ascend the river: First, the lake, or, if there is no expansion, the dead-water; then the falls; then the stream emptying into the lake, or river above, all of the same name. First we came to Passamagamet Lake, then to Passamagamet Falls, then to Passamagamet stream, emptying in. This order and identity of names, it will be perceived, is quite philosophical, since the dead-water or lake is always at least partially pro-duced by the stream emptying in above; and the first fall below, which is the outlet of that lake, and where that tributary water makes its first plunge, also naturally bears the same name.

At the portage around Ambejijis Falls I ob-served a pork-barrel on the shore, with a hole eight or nine inches square cut in one side, which was set against an upright rock; but the bears, without turning or upsetting the barrel, had gnawed a hole in the opposite side, which looked exactly like an enormous rat-hole, big enough to put their heads in; and at the bottom of the barrel were still left a few mangled and slabbered slices of pork. It is usual for the lumberers to leave such supplies as they cannot

conveniently carry along with them at carries or
camps, to which the next comers do not scruple
to help themselves, they being the property,
commonly, not of an individual, but a company,
who can afford to deal liberally.

I will describe particularly how we got over
some of these portages and rapids, in order that
the reader may get an idea of the boatman's
life.   At Ambejijis Falls, for instance, there
was the roughest path imaginable cut through
the woods; at first up hill, at an angle of nearly
forty-five degrees, over rocks and logs without
end.   This was the manner of the portage.   We
first carried over our baggage, and deposited it
on the shore at the other end; then, returning
to the batteau, we dragged it up the hill by the
painter, and onward, with frequent pauses, over
half the portage.   But this was a bungling way,
and would soon have worn out the boat.   Commonly, three men walk over with a batteau
weighing from three to five or six hundred
pounds on their heads and shoulders, the tallest
standing under the middle of the boat, which is
turned over, and one at each end, or else there
are two at the bows.   More cannot well take
hold at once.   But this requires some practice,
as well as strength, and is in any case extremely
laborious, and wearing to the constitution, to
follow.   We were, on the whole, rather an in-

valid party, and could render our boatmen but little assistance. Our two men at length took the batteau upon their shoulders, and, while two of us steadied it, to prevent it from rocking and wearing into their shoulders, on which they placed their hats folded, walked bravely over the remaining distance, with two or three pauses. In the same manner they accomplished the other portages. With this crushing weight they must climb and stumble along over fallen trees and slippery rocks of all sizes, where those who walked by the sides were continually brushed off, such was the narrowness of the path. But we were fortunate not to have to cut our path in the first place. Before we launched our boat, we scraped the bottom smooth again, with our knives, where it had rubbed on the rocks, to save friction.

To avoid the difficulties of the portage, our men determined to "warp up" the Passama-gamet Falls; so while the rest walked over the portage with the baggage, I remained in the batteau, to assist in warping up. We were soon in the midst of the rapids, which were more swift and tumultuous than any we had poled up, and had turned to the side of the stream for the purpose of warping, when the boatmen, who felt some pride in their skill, and were ambitious to do something more than usual,

for my benefit, as I surmised, took one more
view of the rapids, or rather the falls; and, in
answer to our question, whether we could n't
get up there, the other answered that he guessed
he 'd try it. So we pushed again into the midst
of the stream, and began to struggle with the
current. I sat in the middle of the boat to trim
it, moving slightly to the right or left as it
grazed a rock. With an uncertain and waver-
ing motion we wound and bolted our way up,
until the bow was actually raised two feet above
the stern at the steepest pitch; and then, when
everything depended upon his exertions, the
bowman's pole snapped in two; but before he
had time to take the spare one, which I reached
him, he had saved himself with the fragment
upon a rock; and so we got up by a hair's
breadth; and Uncle George exclaimed that that
was never done before, and he had not tried it
if he had not known whom he had got in the
bow, nor he in the bow, if he had not known
him in the stern. At this place there was a
regular portage cut through the woods, and our
boatmen had never known a batteau to ascend
the falls. As near as I can remember, there
was a perpendicular fall here, at the worst place
of the whole Penobscot River, two or three feet
at least. I could not sufficiently admire the
skill and coolness with which they performed

this feat, never speaking to each other. The bowman, not looking behind, but knowing exactly what the other is about, works as if he worked alone. Now sounding in vain for a bottom in fifteen feet of water, while the boat falls back several rods, held straight only with the greatest skill and exertion; or, while the sternman obstinately holds his ground, like a turtle, the bowman springs from side to side with wonderful suppleness and dexterity, scanning the rapids and the rocks with a thousand eyes; and now, having got a bite at last, with a lusty shove, which makes his pole bend and quiver, and the whole boat tremble, he gains a few feet upon the river. To add to the danger, the poles are liable at any time to be caught between the rocks, and wrenched out of their hands, leaving them at the mercy of the rapids, — the rocks, as it were, lying in wait, like so many alligators, to catch them in their teeth, and jerk them from your hands, before you have stolen an effectual shove against their palates. The pole is set close to the boat, and the prow is made to overshoot, and just turn the corners of the rocks, in the very teeth of the rapids. Nothing but the length and lightness, and the slight draught of the batteau, enables them to make any headway. The bowman must quickly choose his course; there is no time to deliberate.

Frequently the boat is shoved between rocks where both sides touch, and the waters on either hand are a perfect maelstrom.

Half a mile above this two of us tried our hands at poling up a slight rapid; and we were just surmounting the last difficulty, when an unlucky rock confounded our calculations; and while the batteau was sweeping round irrecoverably amid the whirlpool, we were obliged to resign the poles to more skillful hands.

Katepskonegan is one of the shallowest and weediest of the lakes, and looked as if it might abound in pickerel. The falls of the same name, where we stopped to dine, are considerable and quite picturesque. Here Uncle George had seen trout caught by the barrelful; but they would not rise to our bait at this hour. Half-way over this carry, thus far in the Maine wilderness on its way to the Provinces, we noticed a large, flaming, Oak Hall hand-bill, about two feet long, wrapped round the trunk of a pine, from which the bark had been stripped, and to which it was fast glued by the pitch. This should be recorded among the advantages of this mode of advertising, that so, possibly, even the bears and wolves, moose, deer, otter, and beaver, not to mention the Indian, may learn where they can fit themselves according to the latest fashion, or, at least, recover some of their

own lost garments. We christened this the Oak
Hall carry.

The forenoon was as serene and placid on this
wild stream in the woods, as we are apt to imagine that Sunday in summer usually is in
Massachusetts. We were occasionally startled
by the scream of a bald-eagle, sailing over the
stream in front of our batteau; or of the fish-
hawks, on whom he levies his contributions.
There were, at intervals, small meadows of a
few acres on the sides of the stream, waving
with uncut grass, which attracted the attention
of our boatmen, who regretted that they were
not nearer to their clearings, and calculated how
many stacks they might cut. Two or three
men sometimes spend the summer by themselves,
cutting the grass in these meadows, to sell to
the loggers in the winter, since it will fetch a
higher price on the spot than in any market in
the State. On a small isle, covered with this
kind of rush, or cut grass, on which we landed
to consult about our further course, we noticed
the recent track of a moose, a large, roundish
hole in the soft, wet ground, evincing the great
size and weight of the animal that made it.
They are fond of the water, and visit all these
island-meadows, swimming as easily from island
to island as they make their way through the
thickets on land. Now and then we passed

what McCauslin called a pokelogan, an Indian term for what the drivers might have reason to call a poke-logs-in, an inlet that leads nowhere. If you get in, you have got to get out again the same way. These, and the frequent "run-rounds" which come into the river again, would embarrass an inexperienced voyager not a little.

The carry around Pockwockomus Falls was exceedingly rough and rocky, the batteau having to be lifted directly from the water up four or five feet on to a rock, and launched again down a similar bank. The rocks on this portage were covered with the *dents* made by the spikes in the lumberers' boots while staggering over under the weight of their batteaux; and you could see where the surface of some large rocks on which they had rested their batteaux was worn quite smooth with use. As it was, we had carried over but half the usual portage at this place for this stage of the water, and launched our boat in the smooth wave just curving to the fall, prepared to struggle with the most violent rapid we had to encounter. The rest of the party walked over the remainder of the portage, while I remained with the boatmen to assist in warping up. One had to hold the boat while the others got in to prevent it from going over the falls. When we had pushed up the rapids as far as possible, keeping close to the shore, Tom seized the painter and leaped out upon a rock just visible in the water, but he lost his footing, notwithstanding his spiked boots, and was instantly amid the rapids; but recovering himself by good luck, and reaching another rock, he passed the painter to me, who had followed him, and took his place again in the bows. Leaping from rock to rock in the shoal water, close to the shore, and now and then getting a bite with the rope round an upright one, I held the boat while one reset his pole, and then all three forced it upward against any rapid. This was "warping up." When a part of us walked round at such a place, we generally took the precaution to take out the most valuable part of the baggage for fear of being swamped.

As we poled up a swift rapid for half a mile above Aboljacarmegus Falls, some of the party read their own marks on the huge logs which lay piled up high and dry on the rocks on either hand, the relics probably of a jam which had taken place here in the Great Freshet in the spring. Many of these would have to wait for another great freshet, perchance, if they lasted so long, before they could be got off. It was singular enough to meet with property of theirs which they had never seen, and where they had never been before, thus detained by freshets and rocks when on its way to them.   Methinks that must be where all my property lies, cast up on the rocks on some distant and unexplored stream, and waiting for an unheard-of freshet to fetch it down.   O make haste, ye gods, with your winds and rains, and start the jam before it rots!

The last half mile carried us to the Sowadne-hunk dead-water, so called from the stream of the same name, signifying "running between mountains," an important tributary which comes in a mile above.   Here we decided to camp, about twenty miles from the Dam, at the mouth of Murch Brook and the Aboljacknagesic, mountain streams, broad off from Ktaadn, and about a dozen miles from its summit, having made fifteen miles this day.

We had been told by McCauslin that we should here find trout enough; so, while some prepared the camp, the rest fell to fishing. Seizing the birch poles which some party of Indians, or white hunters, had left on the shore, and baiting our hooks with pork, and with trout, as soon as they were caught, we cast our lines into the mouth of the Aboljacknagesic, a clear, swift, shallow stream, which came in from Ktaadn.   Instantly a shoal of white chivin (*Leucisci pulchelli*), silvery roaches, cousin-trout, or what not, large and small, prowling thereabouts, fell upon our bait, and one after another were landed amidst the bushes. Anon their cousins, the true trout, took their turn, and alternately the speckled trout, and the silvery roaches, swallowed the bait as fast as we could throw in; and the finest specimens of both that I have ever seen, the largest one weighing three pounds, were heaved upon the shore, though at first in vain, to wriggle down into the water again, for we stood in the boat; but soon we learned to remedy this evil; for one, who had lost his hook, stood on shore to catch them as they fell in a perfect shower around him, — sometimes, wet and slippery, full in his face and bosom, as his arms were outstretched to receive them. While yet alive, before their tints had faded, they glistened like the fairest flowers, the product of primitive rivers; and he could hardly trust his senses, as he stood over them, that these jewels should have swam away in that Aboljacknagesic water for so long, so many dark ages; — these bright fluviatile flowers, seen of Indians only, made beautiful, the Lord only knows why, to swim there! I could understand better for this, the truth of mythology, the fables of Proteus, and all those beautiful sea-monsters, — how all history, indeed, put to a terrestrial use, is mere history; but put to a celestial, is mythology always.

But there is the rough voice of Uncle George, who commands at the frying-pan, to send over what you've got, and then you may stay till morning. The pork sizzles and cries for fish. Luckily for the foolish race, and this particularly foolish generation of trout, the night shut down at last, not a little deepened by the dark side of Ktaadn, which, like a permanent shadow, reared itself from the eastern bank. Lescarbot, writing in 1609, tells us that the Sieur Champdoré, who, with one of the people of the Sieur de Monts, ascended some fifty leagues up the St. John in 1608, found the fish so plenty, "qu'en mettant la chaudière sur le feu ils en avoient pris suffisamment pour eux dîsner avant que l'eau fust chaude." Their descendants here are no less numerous. So we accompanied Tom into the woods to cut cedar-twigs for our bed. While he went ahead with the axe and lopped off the smallest twigs of the flat-leaved cedar, the arbor-vitæ of the gardens, we gathered them up, and returned with them to the boat, until it was loaded. Our bed was made with as much care and skill as a roof is shingled; beginning at the foot, and laying the twig end of the cedar upward, we advanced to the head, a course at a time, thus successively covering the stub-ends, and producing a soft and level bed. For us six it was about ten feet long by

six in breadth. This time we lay under our
tent, having pitched it more prudently with ref-
erence to the wind and the flame, and the usual
huge fire blazed in front. Supper was eaten off
a large log, which some freshet had thrown up.
This night we had a dish of arbor-vitæ, or cedar-
tea, which the lumberer sometimes uses when
other herbs fail,—

> " A quart of arbor-vitæ,
> To make him strong and mighty,"

but I had no wish to repeat the experiment. It
had too medicinal a taste for my palate. There
was the skeleton of a moose here, whose bones
some Indian hunters had picked on this very
spot.

In the night I dreamed of trout-fishing; and,
when at length I awoke, it seemed a fable that
this painted fish swam there so near my couch,
and rose to our hooks the last evening, and I
doubted if I had not dreamed it all. So I arose
before dawn to test its truth, while my companions were still sleeping. There stood Ktaadn
with distinct and cloudless outline in the moonlight; and the rippling of the rapids was the
only sound to break the stillness. Standing on
the shore, I once more cast my line into the
stream, and found the dream to be real and the
fable true. The speckled trout and silvery
roach, like flying-fish, sped swiftly through the

moonlight air, describing bright arcs on the dark side of Ktaadn, until moonlight, now fading into daylight, brought satiety to my mind, and the minds of my companions, who had joined me.

By six o'clock, having mounted our packs and a good blanketful of trout, ready dressed, and swung up such baggage and provision as we wished to leave behind upon the tops of saplings, to be out of the reach of bears, we started for the summit of the mountain, distant, as Uncle George said the boatmen called it, about four miles, but as I judged, and as it proved, nearer fourteen. He had never been any nearer the mountain than this, and there was not the slightest trace of man to guide us farther in this direction. At first, pushing a few rods up the Aboljacknagesic, or "open-land stream," we fastened our batteau to a tree, and traveled up the north side, through burnt lands, now partially overgrown with young aspens and other shrubbery; but soon, recrossing this stream, where it was about fifty or sixty feet wide, upon a jam of logs and rocks, — and you could cross it by this means almost anywhere, — we struck at once for the highest peak, over a mile or more of comparatively open land, still very gradually ascending the while. Here it fell to my lot, as the oldest mountain-climber, to take the lead.

So, scanning the woody side of the mountain, which lay still at an indefinite distance, stretched out some seven or eight miles in length before us, we determined to steer directly for the base of the highest peak, leaving a large slide, by which, as I have since learned, some of our predecessors ascended, on our left. This course would lead us parallel to a dark seam in the forest, which marked the bed of a torrent, and over a slight spur, which extended southward from the main mountain, from whose bare summit we could get an outlook over the country, and climb directly up the peak, which would then be close at hand. Seen from this point, a bare ridge at the extremity of the open land, Ktaadn presented a different aspect from any mountain I have seen, there being a greater proportion of naked rock rising abruptly from the forest; and we looked up at this blue barrier as if it were some fragment of a wall which anciently bounded the earth in that direction. Setting the compass for a northeast course, which was the bearing of the southern base of the highest peak, we were soon buried in the woods.

We soon began to meet with traces of bears and moose, and those of rabbits were everywhere visible. The tracks of moose, more or less recent, to speak literally, covered every square rod on the sides of the mountain; and these animals are probably more numerous there now than ever before, being driven into this wilderness, from all sides, by the settlements. The track of a full-grown moose is like that of a cow, or larger, and of the young, like that of a calf. Sometimes we found ourselves traveling in faint paths, which they had made, like cow-paths in the woods, only far more indistinct, being rather openings, affording imperfect vistas through the dense underwood, than trodden paths; and everywhere the twigs had been browsed by them, clipped as smoothly as if by a knife. The bark of trees was stripped up by them to the height of eight or nine feet, in long, narrow strips, an inch wide, still showing the distinct marks of their teeth. We expected nothing less than to meet a herd of them every moment, and our Nimrod held his shooting-iron in readiness; but we did not go out of our way to look for them, and, though numerous, they are so wary that the unskillful hunter might range the forest a long time before he could get sight of one. They are sometimes dangerous to encounter, and will not turn out for the hunter, but furiously rush upon him and trample him to death, unless he is lucky enough to avoid them by dodging round a tree. The largest are nearly as large as a horse, and weigh sometimes one thousand pounds; and it is said that they can step over a five-foot gate in their ordinary walk. They are described as exceedingly awk-ward-looking animals, with their long legs and short bodies, making a ludicrous figure when in full run, but making great headway, neverthe-less. It seemed a mystery to us how they could thread these woods, which it required all our suppleness to accomplish, — climbing, stooping, and winding, alternately. They are said to drop their long and branching horns, which usually spread five or six feet, on their backs, and make their way easily by the weight of their bodies. Our boatmen said, but I know not with how much truth, that their horns are apt to be gnawed away by vermin while they sleep. Their flesh, which is more like beef than veni-son, is common in Bangor market.

We had proceeded on thus seven or eight miles, till about noon, with frequent pauses to refresh the weary ones, crossing a considerable mountain stream, which we conjectured to be Murch Brook, at whose mouth we had camped, all the time in woods, without having once seen the summit, and rising very gradually, when the boatmen beginning to despair a little, and fearing that we were leaving the mountain on one side of us, for they had not entire faith in the compass, McCauslin climbed a tree, from the top of which he could see the peak, when it appeared that we had not swerved from a right line, the compass down below still ranging with his arm, which pointed to the summit. By the side of a cool mountain rill, amid the woods, where the water began to partake of the purity and transparency of the air, we stopped to cook some of our fishes, which we had brought thus far in order to save our hard bread and pork, in the use of which we had put ourselves on short allowance. We soon had a fire blazing, and stood around it, under the damp and sombre forest of firs and birches, each with a sharpened stick, three or four feet in length, upon which he had spitted his trout, or roach, previously well gashed and salted, our sticks radiating like the spokes of a wheel from one centre, and each crowding his particular fish into the most desirable exposure, not with the truest regard always to his neighbor's rights. Thus we regaled ourselves, drinking meanwhile at the spring, till one man's pack, at least, was considerably lightened, when we again took up our line of march.

At length we reached an elevation sufficiently bare to afford a view of the summit, still distant and blue, almost as if retreating from us. A torrent, which proved to be the same we had crossed, was seen tumbling down in front, literally from out of the clouds. But this glimpse at our whereabouts was soon lost, and we were buried in the woods again. The wood was chiefly yellow birch, spruce, fir, mountain-ash, or round-wood, as the Maine people call it, and moose - wood. It was the worst kind of traveling; sometimes like the densest scrub - oak patches with us. The cornel, or bunch-berries, were very abundant, as well as Solomon's seal and mooseberries. Blueberries were distributed along our whole route; and in one place the bushes were drooping with the weight of the fruit, still as fresh as ever. It was the 7th of September. Such patches afforded a grateful repast, and served to bait the tired party forward. When any lagged behind, the cry of "blueberries" was most effectual to bring them up. Even at this elevation we passed through a moose-yard, formed by a large flat rock, four or five rods square, where they tread down the snow in winter. At length, fearing that if we held the direct course to the summit, we should not find any water near our camping-ground, we gradually swerved to the west, till, at four o'clock, we struck again the torrent which I have mentioned, and here, in view of the summit, the weary party decided to camp that night.

While my companions were seeking a suita-

ble spot for this purpose, I improved the little
daylight that was left in climbing the mountain
alone. We were in a deep and narrow ravine,
sloping up to the clouds, at an angle of nearly
forty-five degrees, and hemmed in by walls of
rock, which were at first covered with low trees,
then with impenetrable thickets of scraggy
birches and spruce-trees, and with moss, but
at last bare of all vegetation but lichens, and
almost continually draped in clouds. Following up the course of the torrent which occupied
this, — and I mean to lay some emphasis on this
word *up*, — pulling myself up by the side of
perpendicular falls of twenty or thirty feet, by
the roots of firs and birches, and then, perhaps,
walking a level rod or two in the thin stream,
for it took up the whole road, ascending by
huge steps, as it were, a giant's stairway, down
which a river flowed, I had soon cleared the
trees, and paused on the successive shelves, to
look back over the country. The torrent was
from fifteen to thirty feet wide, without a tributary, and seemingly not diminishing in breadth
as I advanced; but still it came rushing and
roaring down, with a copious tide, over and
amidst masses of bare rock, from the very
clouds, as though a waterspout had just burst
over the mountain. Leaving this at last, I began to work my way, scarcely less arduous than

Satan's anciently through Chaos, up the nearest, though not the highest peak. At first
scrambling on all fours over the tops of ancient
black spruce-trees (*Abies nigra*), old as the
flood, from two to ten or twelve feet in height,
their tops flat and spreading, and their foliage
blue, and nipped with cold, as if for centuries
they had ceased growing upward against the
bleak sky, the solid cold. I walked some good
rods erect upon the tops of these trees, which
were overgrown with moss and mountain-cranberries. It seemed that in the course of time
they had filled up the intervals between the
huge rocks, and the cold wind had uniformly
leveled all over. Here the principle of vegetation was hard put to it. There was apparently a belt of this kind running quite round the
mountain, though, perhaps, nowhere so remarkable as here. Once slumping through, I looked
down ten feet, into a dark and cavernous region, and saw the stem of a spruce, on whose
top I stood, as on a mass of coarse basket-work,
fully nine inches in diameter at the ground.
These holes were bears' dens, and the bears
were even then at home. This was the sort of
garden I made my way *over*, for an eighth of a
mile, at the risk, it is true, of treading on some
of the plants, not seeing any path *through* it, —
certainly the most treacherous and porous country I ever traveled.

"Nigh foundered on he fares,
Treading the crude consistence, half on foot,
Half flying."

But nothing could exceed the toughness of the twigs, — not one snapped under my weight, for they had slowly grown. Having slumped, scrambled, rolled, bounced, and walked, by turns, over this scraggy country, I arrived upon a side-hill, or rather side-mountain, where rocks, gray, silent rocks, were the flocks and herds that pastured, chewing a rocky cud at sunset. They looked at me with hard gray eyes, without a bleat or a low. This brought me to the skirt of a cloud, and bounded my walk that night. But I had already seen that Maine country when I turned about, waving, flowing, rippling, down below.

When I returned to my companions, they had selected a camping-ground on the torrent's edge, and were resting on the ground; one was on the sick list, rolled in a blanket, on a damp shelf of rock. It was a savage and dreary scenery enough; so wildly rough, that they looked long to find a level and open space for the tent. We could not well camp higher, for want of fuel; and the trees here seemed so evergreen and sappy, that we almost doubted if they would acknowledge the influence of fire; but fire prevailed at last, and blazed here, too,

like a good citizen of the world. Even at this
height we met with frequent traces of moose, as
well as of bears. As here was no cedar, we
made our bed of coarser feathered spruce; but
at any rate the feathers were plucked from the
live tree. It was, perhaps, even a more grand
and desolate place for a night's lodging than
the summit would have been, being in the neighborhood of those wild trees, and of the torrent.
Some more aerial and finer-spirited winds rushed
and roared through the ravine all night, from
time to time arousing our fire, and dispersing
the embers about. It was as if we lay in the
very nest of a young whirlwind. At midnight,
one of my bed-fellows, being startled in his
dreams by the sudden blazing up to its top of
a fir-tree, whose green boughs were dried by the
heat, sprang up, with a cry, from his bed,
thinking the world on fire, and drew the whole
camp after him.

In the morning, after whetting our appetite
on some raw pork, a wafer of hard bread, and
a dipper of condensed cloud or waterspout, we
all together began to make our way up the falls,
which I have described; this time choosing the
right hand, or highest peak, which was not the
one I had approached before. But soon my
companions were lost to my sight behind the
mountain ridge in my rear, which still seemed

ever retreating before me, and I climbed alone
over huge rocks, loosely poised, a mile or more,
still edging toward the clouds; for though the
day was clear elsewhere, the summit was concealed by mist. The mountain seemed a vast
aggregation of loose rocks, as if some time it
had rained rocks, and they lay as they fell on
the mountain sides, nowhere fairly at rest, but
leaning on each other, all rocking-stones, with
cavities between, but scarcely any soil or
smoother shelf. They were the raw materials
of a planet dropped from an unseen quarry,
which the vast chemistry of nature would anon
work up, or work down, into the smiling and
verdant plains and valleys of earth. This was
an undone extremity of the globe; as in lignite,
we see coal in the process of formation.

At length I entered within the skirts of the
cloud which seemed forever drifting over the
summit, and yet would never be gone, but was
generated out of that pure air as fast as it
flowed away; and when, a quarter of a mile
farther, I reached the summit of the ridge,
which those who have seen in clearer weather
say is about five miles long, and contains a
thousand acres of table-land, I was deep within
the hostile ranks of clouds, and all objects were
obscured by them. Now the wind would blow
me out a yard of clear sunlight, wherein I

stood; then a gray, dawning light was all it
could accomplish, the cloud-line ever rising and
falling with the wind's intensity. Sometimes it
seemed as if the summit would be cleared in a
few moments, and smile in sunshine; but what
was gained on one side was lost on another. It
was like sitting in a chimney and waiting for the
smoke to blow away. It was, in fact, a cloud
factory, — these were the cloud-works, and the
wind turned them off done from the cool, bare
rocks. Occasionally, when the windy columns
broke in to me, I caught sight of a dark, damp
crag to the right or left; the mist driving cease-
lessly between it and me. It reminded me of
the creations of the old epic and dramatic poets,
of Atlas, Vulcan, the Cyclops, and Prometheus.
Such was Caucasus and the rock where Prometheus was bound. Æschylus had no doubt
visited such scenery as this. It was vast, Titanic, and such as man never inhabits. Some
part of the beholder, even some vital part, seems
to escape through the loose grating of his ribs as
he ascends. He is more lone than you can imagine. There is less of substantial thought and
fair understanding in him than in the plains
where men inhabit. His reason is dispersed
and shadowy, more thin and subtile, like the
air. Vast, Titanic, inhuman Nature has got
him at disadvantage, caught him alone, and pil-

fers him of some of his divine faculty. She does not smile on him as in the plains. She seems to say sternly, Why came ye here before your time. This ground is not prepared for you. Is it not enough that I smile in the valleys? I have never made this soil for thy feet, this air for thy breathing, these rocks for thy neighbors. I cannot pity nor fondle thee here, but forever relentlessly drive thee hence to where I *am* kind. Why seek me where I have not called thee, and then complain because you find me but a stepmother? Shouldst thou freeze or starve, or shudder thy life away, here is no shrine, nor altar, nor any access to my ear.

> "Chaos and ancient Night, I come no spy
> With purpose to explore or to disturb
> The secrets of your realm, but . . .
> .   .   .   .   .   as my way
> Lies through your spacious empire up to light."

The tops of mountains are among the unfinished parts of the globe, whither it is a slight insult to the gods to climb and pry into their secrets, and try their effect on our humanity. Only daring and insolent men, perchance, go there. Simple races, as savages, do not climb mountains, — their tops are sacred and mysterious tracts never visited by them. Pomola is always angry with those who climb to the summit of Ktaadn.

According to Jackson, who, in his capacity of geological surveyor of the State, has accurately measured it, — the altitude of Ktaadn is 5300 feet, or a little more than one mile above the level of the sea, — and he adds, "It is then evidently the highest point in the State of Maine, and is the most abrupt granite mountain in New England." The peculiarities of that spacious table-land on which I was standing, as well as the remarkable semi-circular precipice or basin on the eastern side, were all concealed by the mist. I had brought my whole pack to the top, not knowing but I should have to make my descent to the river, and possibly to the settled portion of the State alone, and by some other route, and wishing to have a complete outfit with me. But at length, fearing that my companions would be anxious to reach the river before night, and knowing that the clouds might rest on the mountain for days, I was compelled to descend. Occasionally, as I came down, the wind would blow me a vista open, through which I could see the country eastward, boundless forests, and lakes, and streams, gleaming in the sun, some of them emptying into the East Branch. There were also new mountains in sight in that direction. Now and then some small bird of the sparrow family would flit away before me, unable to command its course,

like a fragment of the gray rock blown off by
the wind.

I found my companions where I had left
them, on the side of the peak, gathering the
mountain-cranberries, which filled every crevice
between the rocks, together with blueberries,
which had a spicier flavor the higher up they
grew, but were not the less agreeable to our
palates. When the country is settled, and
roads are made, these cranberries will perhaps
become an article of commerce. From this elevation, just on the skirts of the clouds, we could
overlook the country, west and south, for a hundred miles. There it was, the State of Maine,
which we had seen on the map, but not much
like that, — immeasurable forest for the sun to
shine on, that eastern *stuff* we hear of in Massachusetts. No clearing, no house. It did not
look as if a solitary traveler had cut so much
as a walking-stick there. Countless lakes, —
Moosehead in the southwest, forty miles long by
ten wide, like a gleaming silver platter at the
end of the table; Chesuncook, eighteen long by
three wide, without an island; Millinocket, on
the south, with its hundred islands; and a hundred others without a name; and mountains,
also, whose names, for the most part, are known
only to the Indians. The forest looked like a
firm grass sward, and the effect of these lakes

in its midst has been well compared, by one who has since visited this same spot, to that of a "mirror broken into a thousand fragments, and wildly scattered over the grass, reflecting the full blaze of the sun." It was a large farm for somebody, when cleared. According to the Gazetteer, which was printed before the boundary question was settled, this single Penobscot county, in which we were, was larger than the whole State of Vermont, with its fourteen counties; and this was only a part of the wild lands of Maine. We are concerned now, however, about natural, not political limits. We were about eighty miles, as the bird flies, from Bangor, or one hundred and fifteen, as we had ridden, and walked, and paddled. We had to console ourselves with the reflection that this view was probably as good as that from the peak, as far as it went; and what were a mountain without its attendant clouds and mists? Like ourselves, neither Bailey nor Jackson had obtained a clear view from the summit.

Setting out on our return to the river, still at an early hour in the day, we decided to follow the course of the torrent, which we supposed to be Murch Brook, as long as it would not lead us too far out of our way. We thus traveled about four miles in the very torrent itself, continually crossing and recrossing it, leaping from rock to rock, and jumping with the stream down falls of seven or eight feet, or sometimes sliding down on our backs in a thin sheet of water. This ravine had been the scene of an extraordinary freshet in the spring, apparently accompanied by a slide from the mountain. It must have been filled with a stream of stones and water, at least twenty feet above the present level of the torrent. For a rod or two, on either side of its channel, the trees were barked and splintered up to their tops, the birches bent over, twisted, and sometimes finely split, like a stable-broom; some, a foot in diameter, snapped off, and whole clumps of trees bent over with the weight of rocks piled on them. In one place we noticed a rock, two or three feet in diameter, lodged nearly twenty feet high in the crotch of a tree. For the whole four miles, we saw but one rill emptying in, and the volume of water did not seem to be increased from the first. We traveled thus very rapidly with a downward impetus, and grew remarkably expert at leaping from rock to rock, for leap we must, and leap we did, whether there was any rock at the right distance or not. It was a pleasant picture when the foremost turned about and looked up the winding ravine, walled in with rocks and the green forest, to see, at intervals of a rod or two, a red-shirted or green-jacketed mountaineer against the white torrent, leaping down the channel with his pack on his back, or pausing upon a convenient rock in the midst of the torrent to mend a rent in his clothes, or un- strap the dipper at his belt to take a draught of the water. At one place we were startled by seeing, on a little sandy shelf by the side of the stream, the fresh print of a man's foot, and for a moment realized how Robinson Crusoe felt in a similar case; but at last we remembered that we had struck this stream on our way up, though we could not have told where, and one had descended into the ravine for a drink. The cool air above and the continual bathing of our bodies in mountain water, alternate foot, sitz, douche, and plunge baths, made this walk exceedingly refreshing, and we had traveled only a mile or two, after leaving the torrent, before every thread of our clothes was as dry as usual, owing perhaps to a peculiar quality in the atmosphere.

After leaving the torrent, being in doubt about our course, Tom threw down his pack at the foot of the loftiest spruce-tree at hand, and shinned up the bare trunk some twenty feet, and then climbed through the green tower, lost to our sight, until he held the topmost spray in his hand.[1] McCauslin, in his younger days,

[1] " The spruce-tree," says Springer in '51, " is generally se-

had marched through the wilderness with a body
of troops, under General Somebody, and with
one other man did all the scouting and spying
service. The General's word was, "Throw
down the top of that tree," and there was no
tree in the Maine woods so high that it did not
lose its top in such a case. I have heard a
story of two men being lost once in these woods,
nearer to the settlements than this, who climbed
the loftiest pine they could find, some six feet
in diameter at the ground, from whose top they
discovered a solitary clearing and its smoke.
When at this height, some two hundred feet
from the ground, one of them became dizzy, and
fainted in his companion's arms, and the latter
had to accomplish the descent with him, alternately fainting and reviving, as best he could.
To Tom we cried, Where away does the summit
bear? where the burnt lands? The last he
could only conjecture; he descried, however, a
little meadow and pond, lying probably in our

lected, principally for the superior facilities which its numerous limbs afford the climber. To gain the first limbs of this
tree, which are from twenty to forty feet from the ground, a
smaller tree is undercut and lodged against it, clambering up
which the top of the spruce is reached. In some cases, when
a very elevated position is desired, the spruce-tree is lodged
against the trunk of some lofty pine, up which we ascend to
a height twice that of the surrounding forest."

To indicate the direction of pines, one throws down a
branch, and a man on the ground takes the bearing.

course, which we concluded to steer for. On
reaching this secluded meadow, we found fresh
tracks of moose on the shore of the pond, and
the water was still unsettled as if they had fled
before us. A little farther, in a dense thicket,
we seemed to be still on their trail. It was a
small meadow, of a few acres, on the mountain
side, concealed by the forest, and perhaps
never seen by a white man before, where one
would think that the moose might browse and
bathe, and rest in peace. Pursuing this course,
we soon reached the open land, which went sloping down some miles toward the Penobscot.

Perhaps I most fully realized that this was
primeval, untamed, and forever untamable
Nature, or whatever else men call it, while
coming down this part of the mountain. We
were passing over "Burnt Lands," burnt by
lightning, perchance, though they showed no recent marks of fire, hardly so much as a charred
stump, but looked rather like a natural pasture
for the moose and deer, exceedingly wild and
desolate, with occasional strips of timber crossing them, and low poplars springing up, and
patches of blueberries here and there. I found
myself traversing them familiarly, like some
pasture run to waste, or partially reclaimed by
man; but when I reflected what man, what brother or sister or kinsman of our race made it

and claimed it, I expected the proprietor to rise up and dispute my passage. It is difficult to conceive of a region uninhabited by man. We habitually presume his presence and influence everywhere. And yet we have not seen pure Nature, unless we have seen her thus vast and drear and inhuman, though in the midst of cities. Nature was here something savage and awful, though beautiful. I looked with awe at the ground I trod on, to see what the Powers had made there, the form and fashion and material of their work. This was that Earth of which we have heard, made out of Chaos and Old Night. Here was no man's garden, but the unhandseled globe. It was not lawn, nor pasture, nor mead, nor woodland, nor lea, nor arable, nor waste land. It was the fresh and natural surface of the planet Earth, as it was made forever and ever, — to be the dwelling of man, we say, — so Nature made it, and man may use it if he can. Man was not to be associated with it. It was Matter, vast, terrific, — not his Mother Earth that we have heard of, not for him to tread on, or be buried in, — no, it were being too familiar even to let his bones lie there, — the home, this, of Necessity and Fate. There was clearly felt the presence of a force not bound to be kind to man. It was a place for heathenism and superstitious rites, —

to be inhabited by men nearer of kin to the rocks and to wild animals than we. We walked over it with a certain awe, stopping, from time to time, to pick the blueberries which grew there, and had a smart and spicy taste. Perchance where *our* wild pines stand, and leaves lie on their forest floor, in Concord, there were once reapers, and husbandmen planted grain; but here not even the surface had been scarred by man, but it was a specimen of what God saw fit to make this world. What is it to be admitted to a museum, to see a myriad of particular things, compared with being shown some star's surface, some hard matter in its home! I stand in awe of my body, this matter to which I am bound has become so strange to me. I fear not spirits, ghosts, of which I am one, — *that* my body might, — but I fear bodies, I tremble to meet them. What is this Titan that has possession of me? Talk of mysteries! Think of our life in nature, — daily to be shown matter, to come in contact with it, — rocks, trees, wind on our cheeks! the *solid* earth! the *actual* world! the *common sense!* *Contact! Contact! Who* are we? *where* are we?

Erelong we recognized some rocks and other features in the landscape which we had purposely impressed on our memories, and, quickening our pace, by two o'clock we reached the

batteau.[1] Here we had expected to dine on
trout, but in this glaring sunlight they were
slow to take the bait, so we were compelled to
make the most of the crumbs of our hard bread
and our pork, which were both nearly exhausted.
Meanwhile we deliberated whether we should go
up the river a mile farther, to Gibson's clearing, on the Sowadnehunk, where there was a
deserted log-hut, in order to get a half-inch
auger, to mend one of our spike-poles with.
There were young spruce-trees enough around
us, and we had a spare spike, but nothing to
make a hole with. But as it was uncertain
whether we should find any tools left there, we
patched up the broken pole, as well as we could,
for the downward voyage, in which there would
be but little use for it. Moreover, we were unwilling to lose any time in this expedition, lest
the wind should rise before we reached the larger
lakes, and detain us; for a moderate wind pro-
duces quite a sea on these waters, in which a
batteau will not live for a moment; and on one
occasion McCauslin had been delayed a week at
the head of the North Twin, which is only four
miles across. We were nearly out of provisions, and ill prepared in this respect for what

[1] The bears had not touched things on our possessions.
They sometimes tear a batteau to pieces for the sake of the
tar with which it is besmeared.

might possibly prove a week's journey round
by the shore, fording innumerable streams, and
threading a trackless forest, should any accident
happen to our boat.

It was with regret that we turned our backs
on Chesuncook, which McCauslin had formerly
logged on, and the Allegash lakes. There were
still longer rapids and portages above; among
the last the Rippogenus Portage, which he described as the most difficult on the river, and
three miles long. The whole length of the
Penobscot is two hundred and seventy-five miles,
and we are still nearly one hundred miles from
its source. Hodge, the assistant State Geologist, passed up this river in 1837, and by a
portage of only one mile and three quarters
crossed over into the Allegash, and so went
down that into the St. John, and up the Mada-
waska to the Grand Portage across to the St.
Lawrence. His is the only account that I
know of an expedition through to Canada in
this direction. He thus describes his first sight
of the latter river, which, to compare small
things with great, is like Balboa's first sight of
the Pacific from the mountains of the Isthmus
of Darien. "When we first came in sight of
the St. Lawrence," he says, "from the top of a
high hill, the view was most striking, and much
more interesting to me from having been shut

up in the woods for the two previous months. Directly before us lay the broad river, extending across nine or ten miles, its surface broken by a few islands and reefs, and two ships riding at anchor near the shore. Beyond, extended ranges of uncultivated hills, parallel with the river. The sun was just going down behind them, and gilding the whole scene with its parting rays.''

About four o'clock, the same afternoon, we commenced our return voyage, which would require but little if any poling. In shooting rapids the boatmen use large and broad paddles, instead of poles, to guide the boat with. Though we glided so swiftly, and often smoothly, down, where it had cost us no slight effort to get up, our present voyage was attended with far more danger; for if we once fairly struck one of the thousand rocks by which we were surrounded the boat would be swamped in an instant. When a boat is swamped under these circumstances, the boatmen commonly find no difficulty in keeping afloat at first, for the current keeps both them and their cargo up for a long way down the stream; and if they can swim, they have only to work their way gradually to the shore. The greatest danger is of being caught in an eddy behind some larger rock, where the water rushes up stream faster than elsewhere it does down, and being carried round and round under the surface till they are drowned. McCauslin pointed out some rocks which had been the scene of a fatal accident of this kind. Sometimes the body is not thrown out for several hours. He himself had performed such a circuit once, only his legs being visible to his companions; but he was fortunately thrown out in season to recover his breath.[1] In shooting the rapids, the boatman has this problem to solve: to choose a circuitous and safe course amid a thousand sunken rocks, scattered over a quarter or half a mile, at the same time that he is moving steadily on at the rate of fifteen miles an hour. Stop he cannot; the only question is, where will he go? The bowman chooses the course with all his eyes about him, striking broad off with his paddle, and drawing the boat by main force into her course. The sternman faithfully follows the bow.

We were soon at the Aboljacarmegus Falls. Anxious to avoid the delay, as well as the labor, of the portage here, our boatmen went forward first to reconnoitre, and concluded to let

[1] I cut this from a newspaper. "On the 11th (instant?) [May, '49], on Rappogenes Falls, Mr. John Delantee, of Orono, Me., was drowned while running logs. He was a citizen of Orono, and was twenty-six years of age. His companions found his body, enclosed it in bark, and buried it in the solemn woods."

the batteau down the falls, carrying the baggage only over the portage. Jumping from rock to rock until nearly in the middle of the stream, we were ready to receive the boat and let her down over the first fall, some six or seven feet perpendicular. The boatmen stand upon the edge of a shelf of rock, where the fall is perhaps nine or ten feet perpendicular, in from one to two feet of rapid water, one on each side of the boat, and let it slide gently over, till the bow is run out ten or twelve feet in the air; then, letting it drop squarely, while one holds the painter, the other leaps in, and his companion following, they are whirled down the rapids to a new fall, or to smooth water. In a very few minutes they had accomplished a passage in safety, which would be as foolhardy for the un- skillful to attempt as the descent of Niagara itself. It seemed as if it needed only a little familiarity, and a little more skill, to navigate down such falls as Niagara itself with safety. At any rate, I should not despair of such men in the rapids above Table-Rock, until I saw them actually go over the falls, so cool, so col- lected, so fertile in resources are they. One might have thought that these were falls, and that falls were not to be waded through with im- punity, like a mud-puddle. There was really danger of their losing their sublimity in losing their power to harm us. Familiarity breeds contempt. The boatman pauses, perchance, on some shelf beneath a table-rock under the fall, standing in some cove of back-water two feet deep, and you hear his rough voice come up through the spray, coolly giving directions how to launch the boat this time.

Having carried round Pockwockomus Falls, our oars soon brought us to the Katepskonegan, or Oak Hall carry, where we decided to camp half-way over, leaving our batteau to be carried over in the morning on fresh shoulders. One shoulder of each of the boatmen showed a red spot as large as one's hand, worn by the batteau on this expedition; and this shoulder, as it did all the work, was perceptibly lower than its fellow, from long service. Such toil soon wears out the strongest constitution. The drivers are accustomed to work in the cold water in the spring, rarely ever dry; and if one falls in all over he rarely changes his clothes till night, if then, even. One who takes this precaution is called by a particular nickname, or is turned off. None can lead this life who are not almost amphibious. McCauslin said soberly, what is at any rate a good story to tell, that he had seen where six men were wholly under water at once, at a jam, with their shoulders to handspikes. If the log did not start, then they had to put out their heads to breathe. The driver works as long as he can see, from dark to dark, and at night has not time to eat his supper and dry his clothes fairly, before he is asleep on his cedar bed. We lay that night on the very bed made by such a party, stretching our tent over the poles which were still standing, but re-shingling the damp and faded bed with fresh leaves.

In the morning we carried our boat over and launched it, making haste lest the wind should rise. The boatmen ran down Passamagamet, and soon after Ambejijis Falls, while we walked round with the baggage. We made a hasty breakfast at the head of Ambejijis Lake on the remainder of our pork, and were soon rowing across its smooth surface again, under a pleasant sky, the mountain being now clear of clouds in the northeast. Taking turns at the oars, we shot rapidly across Deep Cove, the foot of Pamadumcook, and the North Twin, at the rate of six miles an hour, the wind not being high enough to disturb us, and reached the Dam at noon. The boatmen went through one of the log sluices in the batteau, where the fall was ten feet at the bottom, and took us in below. Here was the longest rapid in our voyage, and perhaps the running this was as dangerous and arduous a task as any. Shooting down sometimes at the rate, as we judged, of fifteen miles an hour, if we struck a rock we were split from end to end in an instant. Now like a bait bobbing for some river monster, amid the eddies, now darting to this side of the stream, now to that, gliding swift and smooth near to our destruction, or striking broad off with the paddle and drawing the boat to right or left with all our might, in order to avoid a rock. I suppose that it was like running the rapids of the Sault Sainte Marie, at the outlet of Lake Superior, and our boatmen probably displayed no less dexterity than the Indians there do. We soon ran through this mile, and floated in Quakish Lake.

After such a voyage, the troubled and angry waters, which once had seemed terrible and not to be trifled with, appeared tamed and subdued; they had been bearded and worried in their channels, pricked and whipped into submission with the spike-pole and paddle, gone through and through with impunity, and all their spirit and their danger taken out of them, and the most swollen and impetuous rivers seemed but playthings henceforth. I began, at length, to understand the boatman's familiarity with, and contempt for, the rapids. "Those Fowler boys," said Mrs. McCauslin, "are perfect ducks for the water." They had run down to Lincoln, according to her, thirty or forty miles, in a batteau, in the night, for a doctor, when it was so dark that they could not see a rod before them, and the river was swollen so as to be almost a continuous rapid, so that the doctor *cried*, when they brought him up by daylight, "Why, Tom, how did you see to steer?" "We did n't steer much, — only kept her straight." And yet they met with no accident. It is true, the more difficult rapids are higher up than this.

When we reached the Millinocket opposite to Tom's house, and were waiting for his folks to set us over, for we had left our batteau above the Grand Falls, we discovered two canoes, with two men in each, turning up this stream from Shad Pond, one keeping the opposite side of a small island before us, while the other approached the side where we were standing, examining the banks carefully for muskrats as they came along. The last proved to be Louis Neptune and his companion, now, at last, on their way up to Chesuncook after moose; but they were so disguised that we hardly knew them. At a little distance they might have been taken for Quakers, with their broad-brimmed hats and overcoats with broad capes, the spoils of Bangor, seeking a settlement in this Sylvania, — or, nearer at hand, for fashionable gentlemen the morning after a spree. Met face to face, these Indians in their native woods looked like the sinister and slouching fellows whom you meet picking up strings and paper in the streets of a city. There is, in fact, a remarkable and unexpected resemblance between the degraded savage and the lowest classes in a great city. The one is no more a child of nature than the other. In the progress of degradation the distinction of races is soon lost. Neptune at first was only anxious to know what we "kill," seeing some partridges in the hands of one of the party, but we had assumed too much anger to permit of a reply. We thought Indians had some honor before. But — "Me been sick. Oh, me unwell now. You make bargain, then me go." They had in fact been delayed so long by a drunken frolic at the Five Islands, and they had not yet recovered from its effects. They had some young musquash in their canoes, which they dug out of the banks with a hoe, for food, not for their skins, for musquash are their principal food on these expeditions. So they went on up the Millinocket, and we kept down the bank of the Penobscot, after recruiting ourselves with a draught of Tom's beer, leaving Tom at his home.

Thus a man shall lead his life away here on the edge of the wilderness, on Indian Millinocket stream, in a new world, far in the dark of a continent, and have a flute to play at evening here, while his strains echo to the stars, amid the howling of wolves; shall live, as it were, in the primitive age of the world, a primitive man. Yet he shall spend a sunny day, and in this century be my contemporary; perchance shall read some scattered leaves of literature, and sometimes talk with me. Why read history, then, if the ages and the generations are now? He lives three thousand years deep into time, an age not yet described by poets. Can you well go further back in history than this? Ay! ay! — for there turns up but now into the mouth of Millinocket stream a still more ancient and primitive man, whose history is not brought down even to the former. In a bark vessel sewn with the roots of the spruce, with hornbeam paddles, he dips his way along. He is but dim and misty to me, obscured by the æons that lie between the bark canoe and the batteau. He builds no house of logs, but a wigwam of skins. He eats no hot bread and sweet cake, but musquash and moose meat and the fat of bears. He glides up the Millinocket and is lost to my sight, as a more distant and misty cloud is seen flitting by behind a nearer, and is lost in space. So he goes about his destiny, the red face of man.

After having passed the night, and buttered

our boots for the last time, at Uncle George's, whose dogs almost devoured him for joy at his return, we kept on down the river the next day, about eight miles on foot, and then took a batteau, with a man to pole it, to Mattawamkeag, ten more. At the middle of that very night, to make a swift conclusion to a long story, we dropped our buggy over the half-finished bridge at Oldtown, where we heard the confused din and clink of a hundred saws, which never rest, and at six o'clock the next morning one of the party was steaming his way to Massachusetts.

What is most striking in the Maine wilderness is the continuousness of the forest, with fewer open intervals or glades than you had imagined. Except the few burnt lands, the narrow intervals on the rivers, the bare tops of the high mountains, and the lakes and streams, the forest is uninterrupted. It is even more grim and wild than you had anticipated, a damp and intricate wilderness, in the spring everywhere wet and miry. The aspect of the country, indeed, is universally stern and savage, excepting the distant views of the forest from hills, and the lake prospects, which are mild and civilizing in a degree. The lakes are something which you are unprepared for; they lie up so high, exposed to the light, and the forest is diminished to a fine fringe on their edges, with here and there a blue mountain, like amethyst jewels set around some jewel of the first water, — so anterior, so superior, to all the changes that are to take place on their shores, even now civil and refined, and fair as they can ever be. These are not the artificial forests of an English king, — a royal preserve merely. Here prevail no forest laws but those of nature. The aborigines have never been dispossessed, nor nature disforested.

It is a country full of evergreen trees, of mossy silver birches and watery maples, the ground dotted with insipid, small, red berries, and strewn with damp and moss-grown rocks, — a country diversified with innumerable lakes and rapid streams, peopled with trout and various species of *leucisci*, with salmon, shad, and pickerel, and other fishes; the forest resounding at rare intervals with the note of the chickadee, the blue-jay, and the woodpecker, the scream of the fish-hawk and the eagle, the laugh of the loon, and the whistle of ducks along the solitary streams; at night, with the hooting of owls and howling of wolves; in summer, swarming with myriads of black flies and mosquitoes, more formidable than wolves to the white man. Such is the home of the moose, the bear, the caribou, the wolf, the beaver, and the Indian. Who shall describe the inexpressible tenderness and immortal life of the grim forest, where Nature, though it be mid-winter, is ever in her spring, where the moss-grown and decaying trees are not old, but seem to enjoy a perpetual youth; and blissful, innocent Nature, like a serene infant, is too happy to make a noise, except by a few tinkling, lisping birds and trickling rills?

What a place to live, what a place to die and be buried in! There certainly men would live forever, and laugh at death and the grave. There they could have no such thoughts as are associated with the village graveyard, — that make a grave out of one of those moist evergreen hummocks!

> Die and be buried who will,
> I mean to live here still;
> My nature grows ever more young
> The primitive pines among.

I am reminded by my journey how exceedingly new this country still is. You have only to travel for a few days into the interior and back parts even of many of the old States, to come to that very America which the Northmen, and Cabot, and Gosnold, and Smith, and Raleigh visited. If Columbus was the first to discover the islands, Americus Vespucius and Cabot, and the Puritans, and we their descendants, have discovered only the shores of America. While the republic has already acquired

a history world-wide, America is still unsettled
and unexplored. Like the English in New
Holland, we live only on the shores of a continent even yet, and hardly know where the rivers
come from which float our navy. The very
timber and boards and shingles of which our
houses are made grew but yesterday in a wilderness where the Indian still hunts and the
moose runs wild. New York has her wilderness
within her own borders; and though the sailors
of Europe are familiar with the soundings of
her Hudson, and Fulton long since invented the
steamboat on its waters, an Indian is still necessary to guide her scientific men to its head-
waters in the Adirondack country.

Have we even so much as discovered and settled the shores? Let a man travel on foot along
the coast, from the Passamaquoddy to the Sa-
bine, or to the Rio Bravo, or to wherever the
end is now, if he is swift enough to overtake it,
faithfully following the windings of every inlet
and of every cape, and stepping to the music of
the surf, — with a desolate fishing-town once a
week, and a city's port once a month to cheer
him, and putting up at the light-houses, when
there are any, — and tell me if it looks like a
discovered and settled country, and not rather,
for the most part, like a desolate island, and
No-Man's Land.

We have advanced by leaps to the Pacific, and left many a lesser Oregon and California unexplored behind us. Though the railroad and the telegraph have been established on the shores of Maine, the Indian still looks out from her interior mountains over all these to the sea. There stands the city of Bangor, fifty miles up the Penobscot, at the head of navigation for vessels of the largest class, the principal lumber depot on this continent, with a population of twelve thousand, like a star on the edge of night, still hewing at the forests of which it is built, already overflowing with the luxuries and refinement of Europe, and sending its vessels to Spain, to England, and to the West Indies for its groceries, — and yet only a few axe-men have gone "up river," into the howling wilderness which feeds it. The bear and deer are still found within its limits; and the moose, as he swims the Penobscot, is entangled amid its shipping, and taken by foreign sailors in its harbor. Twelve miles in the rear, twelve miles of railroad, are Orono and the Indian Island, the home of the Penobscot tribe, and then commence the batteau and the canoe, and the military road; and sixty miles above, the country is virtually unmapped and unexplored, and there still waves the virgin forest of the New World.

CHESUNCOOK

AT five P. M., September 13, 1853, I left Boston, in the steamer, for Bangor, by the outside course. It was a warm and still night, — warmer, probably, on the water than on the land, — and the sea was as smooth as a small lake in summer, merely rippled. The passengers went singing on the deck, as in a parlor, till ten o'clock. We passed a vessel on her beam-ends on a rock just outside the islands, and some of us thought that she was the "rapt ship" which ran

" on her side so low
That she drank water, and her keel ploughed air,"

not considering that there was no wind, and that she was under bare poles. Now we have left the islands behind and are off Nahant. We behold those features which the discoverers saw, apparently unchanged. Now we see the Cape Ann lights, and now pass near a small village-like fleet of mackerel-fishers at anchor, probably off Gloucester. They salute us with a shout from their low decks; but I understand their "Good evening" to mean, "Don't run against me, sir." From the wonders of the deep we go below to yet deeper sleep. And then the absurdity of being waked up in the night by a man who wants the job of blacking your boots! It is more inevitable than sea-sickness, and may have something to do with it. It is like the ducking you get on crossing the line the first time. I trusted that these old customs were abolished. They might with the same propriety insist on blacking your face. I heard of one man who complained that somebody had stolen his boots in the night; and when he found them, he wanted to know what they had done to them, — they had spoiled them, — he never put that stuff on them; and the bootblack narrowly escaped paying damages.

Anxious to get out of the whale's belly, I rose early, and joined some old salts, who were smoking by a dim light on a sheltered part of the deck. We were just getting into the river. They knew all about it, of course. I was proud to find that I had stood the voyage so well, and was not in the least digested. We brushed up and watched the first signs of dawn through an open port; but the day seemed to hang fire. We inquired the time; none of my companions had a chronometer. At length an African prince rushed by, observing, "Twelve o'clock, gentlemen!" and blew out the light. It was moonrise. So I slunk down into the monster's bowels again.

The first land we make is Monhegan Island, before dawn, and next St. George's Islands, seeing two or three lights. Whitehead, with its bare rocks and funereal bell, is interesting. Next I remember that the Camden Hills attracted my eyes, and afterward the hills about Frankfort. We reached Bangor about noon.

When I arrived, my companion that was to be had gone up river, and engaged an Indian, Joe Aitteon, a son of the Governor, to go with us to Chesuncook Lake. Joe had conducted two white men a-moose-hunting in the same direction the year before. He arrived by cars at Bangor that evening, with his canoe and a companion, Sabattis Solomon, who was going to leave Bangor the following Monday with Joe's father, by way of the Penobscot, and join Joe in moose-hunting at Chesuncook when we had done with him. They took supper at my friend's house and lodged in his barn, saying that they should fare worse than that in the woods. They only made Watch bark a little, when they came to the door in the night for water, for he does not like Indians.

The next morning Joe and his canoe were put on board the stage for Moosehead Lake, sixty and odd miles distant, an hour before we started in an open wagon. We carried hard bread, pork, smoked beef, tea, sugar, etc., seemingly enough for a regiment; the sight of which brought together reminded me by what ignoble means we had maintained our ground hitherto. We went by the Avenue Road, which is quite straight and very good, northwestward toward Moosehead Lake, through more than a dozen flourishing towns, with almost every one its academy, — not one of which, however, is on my General Atlas, published, alas! in 1824; so much are they before the age, or I behind it! The earth must have been considerably lighter to the shoulders of General Atlas then.

It rained all this day and till the middle of the next forenoon, concealing the landscape almost entirely; but we had hardly got out of the streets of Bangor before I began to be exhilarated by the sight of the wild fir and spruce tops, and those of other primitive evergreens, peering through the mist in the horizon. It was like the sight and odor of cake to a schoolboy. He who rides and keeps the beaten track studies the fences chiefly. Near Bangor, the fence-posts, on account of the frost's heaving them in the clayey soil, were not planted in the ground, but were mortised into a transverse horizontal beam lying on the surface. Afterwards, the prevailing fences were log ones, with sometimes a Virginia fence, or else rails slanted over crossed stakes, — and these zigzagged or played leap-frog all the way to the lake, keeping just ahead of us. After getting out of the Penobscot valley, the country was unexpectedly level, or consisted of very even and equal swells, for twenty or thirty miles, never rising above the general level, but affording, it is said, a very good prospect in clear weather, with frequent views of Ktaadn, — straight roads and long hills. The houses were far apart, commonly small and of one story, but framed. There was very little land under cultivation, yet the forest did not often border the road. The stumps were frequently as high as one's head, showing the depth of the snows. The white hay-caps, drawn over small stacks of beans or corn in the fields on account of the rain, were a novel sight to me. We saw large flocks of pigeons, and several times came within a rod or two of partridges in the road. My companion said that in one journey out of Bangor he and his son had shot sixty partridges from his buggy. The mountain-ash was now very handsome, as also the wayfarer's-tree or hobble-bush, with its ripe purple berries mixed with red. The Canada thistle, an introduced plant, was the prevailing weed all the way to the lake, — the roadside in many places, and fields not long cleared, being densely filled with it as with a crop, to the exclusion of everything else. There were also whole fields full of ferns, now rusty and withering, which in older countries are commonly confined to wet ground. There were very few flowers, even allowing for the lateness of the season. It chanced that I saw no asters in bloom along the road for fifty miles, though they were so abundant then in Massachusetts, — except in one place one or two of the Aster acuminatus, — and no golden-rods till within twenty miles of Monson, where I saw a three-ribbed one. There were many late buttercups, however, and the two fire-weeds, Erechthites and Epilobium, commonly where there had been a burning, and at last the pearly everlasting. I noticed occasionally very long troughs which supplied the road with water, and my companion said that three dollars annually were granted by the State to one man in each school-district, who provided and maintained a suitable water-trough by the roadside, for the use of travelers, — a piece of intelligence as refreshing to me as the water itself. That legislature did not sit in vain. It was an Oriental act, which made me wish that I was still farther down East, — another Maine law, which I hope we may get in Massachusetts. That State is banishing barrooms from its highways, and conducting the mountain springs thither.

The country was first decidedly mountainous
in Garland, Sangerville, and onwards, twenty-
five or thirty miles from Bangor.   At Sangerville, where we stopped at mid-afternoon to
warm and dry ourselves, the landlord told us
that he had found a wilderness where we found
him.   At a fork in the road between Abbot and
Monson, about twenty miles from Moosehead
Lake, I saw a guide-post surmounted by a pair
of moose horns, spreading four or five feet, with
the word "Monson" painted on one blade, and
the name of some other town on the other.
They are sometimes used for ornamental hat-
trees, together with deer's horns, in front en-
tries; but, after the experience which I shall
relate, I trust that I shall have a better excuse
for killing a moose than that I may hang my hat
on his horns.   We reached Monson, fifty miles
from Bangor, and thirteen from the lake, after
dark.

At four o'clock the next morning, in the dark,
and still in the rain, we pursued our journey.
Close to the academy in this town they have
erected a sort of gallows for the pupils to practice on.   I thought that they might as well
hang at once all who need to go through such
exercises in so new a country, where there is
nothing to hinder their living an outdoor life.
Better omit Blair, and take the air.   The coun-

try about the south end of the lake is quite mountainous, and the road began to feel the effects of it. There is one hill which, it is calculated, it takes twenty-five minutes to ascend. In many places the road was in that condition called *repaired*, having just been whittled into the required semi-cylindrical form with the shovel and scraper, with all the softest inequalities in the middle, like a hog's back with the bristles up, and Jehu was expected to keep astride of the spine. As you looked off each side of the bare sphere into the horizon, the ditches were awful to behold, — a vast hollowness, like that between Saturn and his ring. At a tavern hereabouts the hostler greeted our horse as an old acquaintance, though he did not remember the driver. He said that he had taken care of that little mare for a short time, a year or two before, at the Mount Kineo House, and thought she was not in as good condition as then. Every man to his trade. I am not acquainted with a single horse in the world, not even the one that kicked me.

Already we had thought that we saw Moosehead Lake from a hilltop, where an extensive fog filled the distant lowlands, but we were mistaken. It was not till we were within a mile or two of its south end that we got our first view of it, — a suitably wild-looking sheet of water, sprinkled with small, low islands, which were covered with shaggy spruce and other wild wood, — seen over the infant port of Greenville with mountains on each side and far in the north, and a steamer's smoke-pipe rising above a roof. A pair of moose horns ornamented a corner of the public house where we left our horse, and a few rods distant lay the small steamer Moosehead, Captain King. There was no village, and no summer road any farther in this direction, — but a winter road, that is, one passable only when deep snow covers its inequalities, from Greenville up the east side of the lake to Lily Bay, about twelve miles.

I was here first introduced to Joe. He had ridden all the way on the outside of the stage, the day before, in the rain, giving way to ladies, and was well wetted. As it still rained, he asked if we were going to "put it through." He was a good-looking Indian, twenty-four years old, apparently of unmixed blood, short and stout, with a broad face and reddish complexion, and eyes, methinks, narrower and more turned up at the outer corners than ours, answering to the description of his race. Beside his underclothing, he wore a red flannel shirt, woolen pants, and a black Kossuth hat, the ordinary dress of the lumberman, and, to a considerable extent, of the Penobscot Indian. When,

afterward, he had occasion to take off his shoes
and stockings, I was struck with the smallness
of his feet. He had worked a good deal as a
lumberman, and appeared to identify himself
with that class. He was the only one of the
party who possessed an india - rubber jacket.
The top strip or edge of his canoe was worn
nearly through by friction on the stage.

At eight o'clock the steamer, with her bell
and whistle, scaring the moose, summoned us on
board. She was a well-appointed little boat,
commanded by a gentlemanly captain, with
patent life-seats and metallic life-boat, and dinner on board, if you wish. She is chiefly used
by lumberers for the transportation of themselves, their boats, and supplies, but also by
hunters and tourists. There was another
steamer, named Amphitrite, laid up close by;
but, apparently, her name was not more trite
than her hull. There were also two or three
large sail-boats in port. These beginnings of
commerce on a lake in the wilderness are very
interesting, — these larger white birds that come
to keep company with the gulls. There were
but few passengers, and not one female among
them: a St. Francis Indian, with his canoe and
moose-hides; two explorers for lumber; three
men who landed at Sandbar Island, and a gentleman who lives on Deer Island, eleven miles

up the lake, and owns also Sugar Island, between which and the former the steamer runs; these, I think, were all beside ourselves. In the saloon was some kind of musical instrument — cherubim or seraphim — to soothe the angry waves; and there, very properly, was tacked up the map of the public lands of Maine and Massachusetts, a copy of which I had in my pocket.

The heavy rain confining us to the saloon awhile, I discoursed with the proprietor of Sugar Island on the condition of the world in Old Testament times. But at length, leaving this subject as fresh as we found it, he told me that he had lived about this lake twenty or thirty years, and yet had not been to the head of it for twenty-one years. He faces the other way. The explorers had a fine new birch on board, larger than ours, in which they had come up the Piscataquis from Howland, and they had had several messes of trout already. They were going to the neighborhood of Eagle and Chamberlain lakes, or the head-waters of the St. John, and offered to keep us company as far as we went. The lake to-day was rougher than I found the ocean, either going or returning, and Joe remarked that it would swamp his birch. Off Lily Bay it is a dozen miles wide, but it is much broken by islands. The scenery is not merely wild, but varied and interesting; mountains were seen, farther or nearer, on all sides but the northwest, their summits now lost in the clouds; but Mount Kineo is the principal feature of the lake, and more exclusively belongs to it. After leaving Greenville, at the foot, which is the nucleus of a town some eight or ten years old, you see but three or four houses for the whole length of the lake, or about forty miles, three of them the public houses at which the steamer is advertised to stop, and the shore is an unbroken wilderness. The prevailing wood seemed to be spruce, fir, birch, and rock-maple. You could easily distinguish the hard wood from the soft, or "black growth," as it is called, at a great distance, — the former being smooth, round-topped, and light green, with a bowery and cultivated look.

Mount Kineo, at which the boat touched, is a peninsula with a narrow neck, about midway the lake on the east side. The celebrated precipice is on the east or land side of this, and is so high and perpendicular that you can jump from the top, many hundred feet, into the water, which makes up behind the point. A man on board told us that an anchor had been sunk ninety fathoms at its base before reaching bottom! Probably it will be discovered erelong that some Indian maiden jumped off it for love once, for true love never could have found a path more to its mind. We passed quite close to the rock here, since it is a very bold shore, and I observed marks of a rise of four or five feet on it. The St. Francis Indian expected to take in his boy here, but he was not at the landing. The father's sharp eyes, however, detected a canoe with his boy in it far away under the mountain, though no one else could see it. "Where is the canoe?" asked the captain, "I don't see it;" but he held on, nevertheless, and by and by it hove in sight.

We reached the head of the lake about noon. The weather had, in the mean while, cleared up, though the mountains were still capped with clouds. Seen from this point, Mount Kineo, and two other allied mountains ranging with it northeasterly, presented a very strong family likeness, as if all cast in one mould. The steamer here approached a long pier projecting from the northern wilderness, and built of some of its logs, — and whistled, where not a cabin nor a mortal was to be seen. The shore was quite low, with flat rocks on it, overhung with black ash, arbor-vitæ, etc., which at first looked as if they did not care a whistle for us. There was not a single cabman to cry "Coach!" or inveigle us to the United States Hotel. At length a Mr. Hinckley, who has a camp at the other end of the "carry," appeared with a truck drawn by an ox and a horse over a rude log-railway through the woods. The next thing was to get our canoe and effects over the carry from this lake, one of the heads of the Kennebec, into the Penobscot River. This railway from the lake to the river occupied the middle of a clearing two or three rods wide and perfectly straight through the forest. We walked across while our baggage was drawn behind. My companion went ahead to be ready for partridges, while I followed, looking at the plants.

This was an interesting botanical locality for one coming from the South to commence with; for many plants which are rather rare, and one or two which are not found at all, in the eastern part of Massachusetts, grew abundantly between the rails, — as Labrador tea, Kalmia glauca, Canada blueberry (which was still in fruit, and a second time in bloom), Clintonia and Linnæa borealis, which last a lumberer called *moxon*, creeping snowberry, painted trillium, large-flowered bellwort, etc. I fancied that the Aster radula, Diplopappus umbellatus, Solidago lanceolatus, red trumpet-weed, and many others which were conspicuously in bloom on the shore of the lake and on the carry, had a peculiarly wild and primitive look there. The spruce and fir trees crowded to the track on each side to welcome us, the arbor-vitæ, with its changing leaves, prompted us to make haste, and the sight of the canoe-birch gave us spirits to do so. Sometimes an evergreen just fallen lay across the track with its rich burden of cones, looking, still, fuller of life than our trees in the most favorable positions. You did not expect to find such *spruce* trees in the wild woods, but they evidently attend to their toilets each morning even there. Through such a front-yard did we enter that wilderness.

There was a very slight rise above the lake, — the country appearing like, and perhaps being partly a swamp, — and at length a gradual descent to the Penobscot, which I was surprised to find here a large stream, from twelve to fifteen rods wide, flowing from west to east, or at right angles with the lake, and not more than two and a half miles from it. The distance is nearly twice too great on the Map of the Public Lands, and on Colton's Map of Maine, and Russell Stream is placed too far down. Jackson makes Moosehead Lake to be nine hundred and sixty feet above high water in Portland harbor. It is higher than Chesuncook, for the lumberers consider the Penobscot, where we struck it, twenty-five feet lower than Moosehead, — though eight miles above it is said to be the highest, so that the water can be made to flow either way, and the river falls a good deal between here and Chesuncook. The carry-man called this about one hundred and forty miles above Bangor by the river, or two hundred from the ocean, and fifty-five miles below Hilton's, on the Canada road, the first clearing above, which is four and a half miles from the source of the Penobscot.

At the north end of the carry, in the midst of a clearing of sixty acres or more, there was a log camp of the usual construction, with something more like a house adjoining, for the accommodation of the carry-man's family and passing lumberers. The bed of withered fir-twigs smelled very sweet, though really very dirty. There was also a store-house on the bank of the river, containing pork, flour, iron, batteaux, and birches, locked up.

We now proceeded to get our dinner, which always turned out to be tea, and to pitch canoes, for which purpose a large iron pot lay permanently on the bank. This we did in company with the explorers. Both Indians and whites use a mixture of rosin and grease for this purpose, that is, for the pitching, not the dinner. Joe took a small brand from the fire and blew the heat and flame against the pitch on his birch, and so melted and spread it. Sometimes he put his mouth over the suspected spot and sucked, to see if it admitted air; and at one place, where we stopped, he set his canoe high on crossed stakes, and poured water into it. I narrowly watched his motions, and listened attentively to his observations, for we had employed an Indian mainly that I might have an opportunity to study his ways. I heard him swear once, mildly, during this operation, about his knife being as dull as a hoe, — an accomplishment which he owed to his intercourse with the whites; and he remarked, "We ought to have some tea before we start; we shall be hungry before we kill that moose."

At mid-afternoon we embarked on the Penobscot. Our birch was nineteen and a half feet long by two and a half at the widest part, and fourteen inches deep within, both ends alike, and painted green, which Joe thought affected the pitch and made it leak. This, I think, was a middling-sized one. That of the explorers was much larger, though probably not much longer. This carried us three with our baggage, weighing in all between five hundred and fifty and six hundred pounds. We had two heavy, though slender, rock-maple paddles, one of them of bird's-eye maple. Joe placed birch-bark on the bottom for us to sit on, and slanted cedar splints against the cross-bars to protect our backs, while he himself sat upon a cross-bar in the stern. The baggage occupied the middle or widest part of the canoe. We also paddled by turns in the bows, now sitting with our legs extended, now sitting upon our legs, and now rising upon our knees; but I found none of these positions endurable, and was reminded of the complaints of the old Jesuit missionaries of the torture they endured from long confinement in constrained positions in canoes, in their long voyages from Quebec to the Huron country; but afterwards I sat on the cross-bars, or stood up, and experienced no inconvenience.

It was dead water for a couple of miles. The river had been raised about two feet by the rain, and lumberers were hoping for a flood sufficient to bring down the logs that were left in the spring. Its banks were seven or eight feet high, and densely covered with white and black spruce, — which, I think, must be the commonest trees thereabouts, — fir, arbor-vitæ, canoe, yellow, and black birch, rock, mountain, and a few red maples, beech, black and mountain ash, the large-toothed aspen, many civil looking elms, now imbrowned, along the stream, and at first a few hemlocks also. We had not gone far before I was startled by seeing what I thought was an Indian encampment, covered with a red flag, on the bank, and exclaimed, "Camp!" to my comrades. I was slow to discover that it was a red maple changed by the

frost.   The immediate shores were also densely
covered with the speckled alder, red osier,
shrubby-willows or sallows, and the like.   There
were a few yellow lily pads still left, half-
drowned, along the sides, and sometimes a
white one.   Many fresh tracks of moose were
visible where the water was shallow, and on the
shore, and the lily stems were freshly bitten off
by them.

After paddling about two miles, we parted
company with the explorers, and turned up
Lobster Stream, which comes in on the right,
from the southeast.   This was six or eight rods
wide, and appeared to run nearly parallel with
the Penobscot.   Joe said that it was so called
from small fresh-water lobsters found in it.   It
is the Matahumkeag of the maps.   My companion wished to look for moose signs, and intended, if it proved worth the while, to camp
up that way, since the Indian advised it.   On
account of the rise of the Penobscot the water
ran up this stream quite to the pond of the same
name, one or two miles.   The Spencer Mountains, east of the north end of Moosehead Lake,
were now in plain sight in front of us.   The
kingfisher flew before us, the pigeon woodpecker
was seen and heard, and nuthatches and chicka-
dees close at hand.   Joe said that they called
the chickadee *kecunnilessu* in his language.   I

will not vouch for the spelling of what possibly
was never spelt before, but I pronounced after
him till he said it would do. We passed close
to a woodcock, which stood perfectly still on
the shore, with feathers puffed up, as if sick.
This Joe said they called *nipsquecohossus*. The
kingfisher was *skuscumonsuck ;* bear was *wassus ;* Indian Devil, *lunxus ;* the mountain-ash,
upahsis. This was very abundant and beautiful. Moose tracks were not so fresh along this
stream, except in a small creek about a mile up
it, where a large log had lodged in the spring,
marked "W-cross-girdle-crow-foot." We saw
a pair of moose horns on the shore, and I asked
Joe if a moose had shed them; but he said there
was a head attached to them, and I knew that
they did not shed their heads more than once in
their lives.

After ascending about a mile and a half, to
within a short distance of Lobster Lake, we returned to the Penobscot. Just below the mouth
of the Lobster we found quick water, and the
river expanded to twenty or thirty rods in width.
The moose tracks were quite numerous and
fresh here. We noticed in a great many places
narrow and well-trodden paths by which they
had come down to the river, and where they had
slid on the steep and clayey bank. Their tracks
were either close to the edge of the **stream, those**

of the calves distinguishable from the others, or in shallow water; the holes made by their feet in the soft bottom being visible for a long time. They were particularly numerous where there was a small bay, or pokelogan, as it is called, bordered by a strip of meadow, or separated from the river by a low peninsula covered with coarse grass, wool-grass, etc., wherein they had waded back and forth and eaten the pads. We detected the remains of one in such a spot. At one place, where we landed to pick up a summer duck, which my companion had shot, Joe peeled a canoe-birch for bark for his hunting-horn. He then asked if we were not going to get the other duck, for his sharp eyes had seen another fall in the bushes a little farther along, and my companion obtained it. I now began to notice the bright red berries of the tree-cranberry, which grows eight or ten feet high, mingled with the alders and cornel along the shore. There was less hard wood than at first.

After proceeding a mile and three quarters below the mouth of the Lobster, we reached, about sundown, a small island at the head of what Joe called the Moosehorn Dead-water (the Moosehorn, in which he was going to hunt that night, coming in about three miles below), and on the upper end of this we decided to camp. On a point at the lower end lay the carcass of a

moose killed a month or more before. We concluded merely to prepare our camp, and leave
our baggage here, that all might be ready when
we returned from moose-hunting. Though I
had not come a-hunting, and felt some compunc-
tions about accompanying the hunters, I wished
to see a moose near at hand, and was not sorry
to learn how the Indian managed to kill one. I
went as reporter or chaplain to the hunters, —
and the chaplain has been known to carry a gun
himself. After clearing a small space amid the
dense spruce and fir trees, we covered the damp
ground with a shingling of fir-twigs, and, while
Joe was preparing his birch horn and pitching
his canoe, — for this had to be done whenever
we stopped long enough to build a fire, and was
the principal labor which he took upon himself
at such times, — we collected fuel for the night,
large, wet, and rotting logs, which had lodged at
the head of the island, for our hatchet was too
small for effective chopping; but we did not
kindle a fire, lest the moose should smell it.
Joe set up a couple of forked stakes, and prepared half a dozen poles, ready to cast one of
our blankets over in case it rained in the night,
which precaution, however, was omitted the next
night. We also plucked the ducks which had
been killed for breakfast.

While we were thus engaged in the twilight,

we heard faintly, from far down the stream, what sounded like two strokes of a wood-chopper's axe, echoing dully through the grim solitude.   We are wont to liken many sounds, heard at a distance in the forest, to the stroke of an axe, because they resemble each other under those circumstances, and that is the one we commonly hear there.   When we told Joe of this, he exclaimed, "By George, I'll bet that was a moose!   They make a noise like that." These sounds affected us strangely, and by their very resemblance to a familiar one, where they probably had so different an origin, enhanced the impression of solitude and wildness.

At starlight we dropped down the stream, which was a dead-water for three miles, or as far as the Moosehorn; Joe telling us that we must be very silent, and he himself making no noise with his paddle, while he urged the canoe along with effective impulses.   It was a still night, and suitable for this purpose, — for if there is wind, the moose will smell you, — and Joe was very confident that he should get some. The harvest moon had just risen, and its level rays began to light up the forest on our right, while we glided downward in the shade on the same side, against the little breeze that was stirring.   The lofty, spiring tops of the spruce and fir were very black against the sky, and more distinct than by day, close bordering this broad avenue on each side; and the beauty of the scene, as the moon rose above the forest, it would not be easy to describe. A bat flew over our heads, and we heard a few faint notes of birds from time to time, perhaps the myrtle-bird for one, or the sudden plunge of a mus-quash, or saw one crossing the stream before us, or heard the sound of a rill emptying in, swollen by the recent rain. About a mile below the island, when the solitude seemed to be growing more complete every moment, we suddenly saw the light and heard the crackling of a fire on the bank, and discovered the camp of the two explorers; they standing before it in their red shirts, and talking aloud of the adventures and profits of the day. They were just then speaking of a bargain, in which, as I understood, somebody had cleared twenty-five dollars. We glided by without speaking, close under the bank, within a couple of rods of them; and Joe, taking his horn, imitated the call of the moose, till we suggested that they might fire on us. This was the last we saw of them, and we never knew whether they detected or suspected us.

I have often wished since that I was with them. They search for timber over a given section, climbing hills and often high trees to look off, — explore the streams by which it is to be driven, and the like, — spend five or six weeks in the woods, they two alone, a hundred miles or more from any town, — roaming about, and sleeping on the ground where night overtakes them, — depending chiefly on the provisions they carry with them, though they do not decline what game they come across, — and then in the fall they return and make report to their employers, determining the number of teams that will be required the following winter. Experienced men get three or four dollars a day for this work. It is a solitary and adventurous life, and comes nearest to that of the trapper of the West, perhaps. They work ever with a gun as well as an axe, let their beards grow, and live without neighbors, not on an open plain, but far within a wilderness.

This discovery accounted for the sounds which we had heard, and destroyed the prospect of seeing moose yet awhile. At length, when we had left the explorers far behind, Joe laid down his paddle, drew forth his birch - horn, — a straight one, about fifteen inches long and three or four wide at the mouth, tied round with strips of the same bark, — and, standing up, imitated the call of the moose, — *ugh-ugh-ugh*, or *oo-oo-oo-oo*, and then a prolonged *oo-o-o-o-o-o-o-o*, and listened attentively for several minutes. We asked him what kind of noise he expected to hear. He said that if a moose heard it, he guessed we should find out; we should hear him coming half a mile off; he would come close to, perhaps into, the water, and my companion must wait till he got fair sight, and then aim just behind the shoulder.

The moose venture out to the river-side to feed and drink at night. Earlier in the season the hunters do not use a horn to call them out, but steal upon them as they are feeding along the sides of the stream, and often the first notice they have of one is the sound of the water dropping from its muzzle. An Indian whom I heard imitate the voice of the moose, and also that of the caribou and the deer, using a much longer horn than Joe's, told me that the first could be heard eight or ten miles, sometimes; it was a loud sort of bellowing sound, clearer and more sonorous than the lowing of cattle, — the caribou's a sort of snort, — and the small deer's like that of a lamb.

At length we turned up the Moosehorn, where the Indians at the carry had told us that they killed a moose the night before. This is a very meandering stream, only a rod or two in width, but comparatively deep, coming in on the right, fitly enough named Moosehorn, whether from its windings or its inhabitants. It was bordered here and there by narrow meadows between the stream and the endless forest, affording favorable places for the moose to feed, and to call them out on. We proceeded half a mile up this, as through a narrow, winding canal, where the tall, dark spruce and firs and arbor-vitæ towered on both sides in the moonlight, forming a perpendicular forest-edge of great height, like the spires of a Venice in the forest. In two places stood a small stack of hay on the bank, ready for the lumberer's use in the winter, looking strange enough there. We thought of the day when this might be a brook winding through smooth-shaven meadows on some gentleman's grounds; and seen by moonlight then, excepting the forest that now hems it in, how little changed it would appear!

Again and again Joe called the moose, placing the canoe close by some favorable point of meadow for them to come out on, but listened in vain to hear one come rushing through the woods, and concluded that they had been hunted too much thereabouts. We saw, many times, what to our imaginations looked like a gigantic moose, with his horns peering from out the forest edge; but we saw the forest only, and not its inhabitants, that night. So at last we turned about. There was now a little fog on the water, though it was a fine, clear night above. There were very few sounds to break the stillness of

the forest. Several times we heard the hooting
of a great horned-owl, as at home, and told Joe
that he would call out the moose for him, for he
made a sound considerably like the horn, — but
Joe answered, that the moose had heard that
sound a thousand times, and knew better; and
oftener still we were startled by the plunge of a
musquash. Once, when Joe had called again,
and we were listening for moose, we heard,
come faintly echoing, or creeping from far,
through the moss-clad aisles, a dull, dry, rushing sound, with a solid core to it, yet as if half
smothered under the grasp of the luxuriant and
fungus-like forest, like the shutting of a door in
some distant entry of the damp and shaggy wilderness. If we had not been there, no mortal
had heard it. When we asked Joe in a whisper
what it was, he answered, "Tree fall." There
is something singularly grand and impressive in
the sound of a tree falling in a perfectly calm
night like this, as if the agencies which over-
throw it did not need to be excited, but worked
with a subtle, deliberate, and conscious force,
like a boa-constrictor, and more effectively then
than even in a windy day. If there is any such
difference, perhaps it is because trees with the
dews of the night on them are heavier than by
day.

Having reached the camp, about ten o'clock,

we kindled our fire and went to bed. Each of us had a blanket, in which he lay on the fir-twigs, with his extremities toward the fire, but nothing over his head. It was worth the while to lie down in a country where you could afford such great fires; that was one whole side, and the bright side, of our world. We had first rolled up a large log some eighteen inches through and ten feet long, for a backlog, to last all night, and then piled on the trees to the height of three or four feet, no matter how green or damp. In fact, we burned as much wood that night as would, with economy and an air-tight stove, last a poor family in one of our cities all winter. It was very agreeable, as well as independent, thus lying in the open air, and the fire kept our uncovered extremities warm enough. The Jesuit missionaries used to say, that, in their journeys with the Indians in Canada, they lay on a bed which had never been shaken up since the creation, unless by earth-quakes. It is surprising with what impunity and comfort one who has always lain in a warm bed in a close apartment, and studiously avoided drafts of air, can lie down on the ground without a shelter, roll himself in a blanket, and sleep before a fire, in a frosty, autumn night, just after a long rain-storm, and even come soon to enjoy and value the fresh air.

I lay awake awhile, watching the ascent of the sparks through the firs, and sometimes their descent in half-extinguished cinders on my blanket. They were as interesting as fireworks, going up in endless, successive crowds, each after an explosion, in an eager, serpentine course, some to five or six rods above the tree-tops before they went out. We do not suspect how much our chimneys have concealed; and now air-tight stoves have come to conceal all the rest. In the course of the night, I got up once or twice and put fresh logs on the fire, making my companions curl up their legs.

When we awoke in the morning (Saturday, September 17), there was considerable frost whitening the leaves. We heard the sound of the chickadee, and a few faintly lisping birds, and also of ducks in the water about the island. I took a botanical account of stock of our domains before the dew was off, and found that the ground hemlock, or American yew, was the prevailing under-shrub. We breakfasted on tea, hard bread, and ducks.

Before the fog had fairly cleared away we paddled down the stream again, and were soon past the mouth of the Moosehorn. These twenty miles of the Penobscot, between Moosehead and Chesuncook lakes, are comparatively smooth, and a great part dead-water; but from time to time it is shallow and rapid, with rocks or gravel beds, where you can wade across. There is no expanse of water, and no break in the forest, and the meadow is a mere edging here and there. There are no hills near the river nor within sight, except one or two distant mountains seen in a few places. The banks are from six to ten feet high, but once or twice rise gently to higher ground. In many places the forest on the bank was but a thin strip, letting the light through from some alder swamp or meadow behind. The conspicuous berry-bearing bushes and trees along the shore were the red osier, with its whitish fruit, hobble-bush, mountain-ash, tree-cranberry, choke-cherry, now ripe, alternate cornel, and naked viburnum. Following Joe's example, I ate the fruit of the last, and also of the hobble-bush, but found them rather insipid and seedy. I looked very narrowly at the vegetation, as we glided along close to the shore, and frequently made Joe turn aside for me to pluck a plant, that I might see by comparison what was primitive about my native river. Horehound, horsemint, and the sensitive fern grew close to the edge, under the willows and alders, and wool-grass on the islands, as along the Assabet River in Concord. It was too late for flowers, except a few asters, goldenrods, etc. In several places we noticed the

slight frame of a camp, such as we had prepared
to set up, amid the forest by the river-side,
where some lumberers or hunters had passed a
night, — and sometimes steps cut in the muddy
or clayey bank in front of it.

We stopped to fish for trout at the mouth of
a small stream called Ragmuff, which came in
from the west, about two miles below the Moosehorn. Here were the ruins of an old lumber-
ing-camp, and a small space, which had formerly been cleared and burned over, was now
densely overgrown with the red cherry and raspberries. While we were trying for trout, Joe,
Indian-like, wandered off up the Ragmuff on
his own errands, and when we were ready to
start was far beyond call. So we were compelled to make a fire and get our dinner here,
not to lose time. Some dark reddish birds,
with grayer females (perhaps purple finches),
and myrtle-birds in their summer dress, hopped
within six or eight feet of us and our smoke.
Perhaps they smelled the frying pork. The
latter bird, or both, made the lisping notes
which I had heard in the forest. They suggested that the few small birds found in the
wilderness are on more familiar terms with the
lumberman and hunter than those of the orchard
and clearing with the farmer. I have since
found the Canada jay, and partridges, both the

black and the common, equally tame there, as if
they had not yet learned to mistrust man entirely. The chickadee, which is at home alike
in the primitive woods and in our wood-lots,
still retains its confidence in the towns to a
remarkable degree.

Joe at length returned, after an hour and a
half, and said that he had been two miles up
the stream exploring, and had seen a moose, but,
not having the gun, he did not get him. We
made no complaint, but concluded to look out
for Joe the next time. However, this may
have been a mere mistake, for we had no reason
to complain of him afterwards. As we continued down the stream, I was surprised to hear
him whistling "O Susanna," and several other
such airs, while his paddle urged us along.
Once he said, "Yes, sir-ee." His common word
was "Sartain." He paddled, as usual, on one
side only, giving the birch an impulse by using
the side as a fulcrum. I asked him how the
ribs were fastened to the side rails. He answered, "I don't know, I never noticed."
Talking with him about subsisting wholly on
what the woods yielded, game, fish, berries, etc.,
I suggested that his ancestors did so; but he
answered that he had been brought up in such a
way that he could not do it. "Yes," said he,
"that's the way they got a living, like wild fel-

lows, wild as bears. By George! I sha'n't go into the woods without provision, — hard bread, pork, etc." He had brought on a barrel of hard bread and stored it at the carry for his hunting. However, though he was a Governor's son, he had not learned to read.

At one place below this, on the east side, where the bank was higher and drier than usual, rising gently from the shore to a slight elevation, some one had felled the trees over twenty or thirty acres, and left them drying in order to burn. This was the only preparation for a house between the Moosehead carry and Chesuncook, but there was no hut nor inhabitants there yet. The pioneer thus selects a site for his house, which will, perhaps, prove the germ of a town.

My eyes were all the while on the trees, distinguishing between the black and white spruce and the fir. You paddle along in a narrow canal through an endless forest, and the vision I have in my mind's eye, still, is of the small, dark, and sharp tops of tall fir and spruce trees, and pagoda-like arbor-vitæs, crowded together on each side, with various hard woods intermixed. Some of the arbor-vitæs were at least sixty feet high. The hard woods, occasionally occurring exclusively, were less wild to my eye. I fancied them ornamental grounds, with farm-

houses in the rear. The canoe and yellow birch,
beech, maple, and elm are Saxon and Norman,
but the spruce and fir, and pines generally, are
Indian. The soft engravings which adorn the
annuals give no idea of a stream in such a wilderness as this. The rough sketches in Jackson's Reports on the Geology of Maine answer
much better. At one place we saw a small
grove of slender sapling white-pines, the only
collection of pines that I saw on this voyage.
Here and there, however, was a full-grown, tall,
and slender, but defective one, what lumbermen
call a *konchus* tree, which they ascertain with
their axes, or by the knots. I did not learn
whether this word was Indian or English. It
reminded me of the Greek κόγχη, a conch or
shell, and I amused myself with fancying that
it might signify the dead sound which the trees
yield when struck. All the rest of the pines
had been driven off.

How far men go for the material of their
houses! The inhabitants of the most civilized
cities, in all ages, send into far, primitive forests, beyond the bounds of their civilization,
where the moose and bear and savage dwell, for
their pine boards for ordinary use. And, on
the other hand, the savage soon receives from
cities iron arrow-points, hatchets, and guns, to
point his savageness with.

The solid and well-defined fir-tops, like sharp and regular spear-heads, black against the sky, gave a peculiar, dark, and sombre look to the forest. The spruce-tops have a similar but more ragged outline, — their shafts also merely feathered below. The firs were somewhat oftener regular and dense pyramids. I was struck by this universal spiring upward of the forest evergreens. The tendency is to slender, spiring tops, while they are narrower below. Not only the spruce and fir, but even the arbor-vitæ and white-pine, unlike the soft, spreading, second-growth, of which I saw none; all spire upwards, lifting a dense spear - head of cones to the light and air, at any rate, while their branches straggle after as they may; as Indians lift the ball over the heads of the crowd in their desperate game. In this they resemble grasses, as also palms somewhat. The hemlock is commonly a tent-like pyramid from the ground to its summit.

After passing through some long rips, and by a large island, we reached an interesting part of the river called the Pine Stream Dead-Water, about six miles below Ragmuff, where the river expanded to thirty rods in width and had many islands in it, with elms and canoe-birches, now yellowing, along the shore, and we got our first sight of Ktaadn.

Here, about two o'clock, we turned up a small branch three or four rods wide, which comes in on the right from the south, called Pine Stream, to look for moose signs. We had gone but a few rods before we saw very recent signs along the water's edge, the mud lifted up by their feet being quite fresh, and Joe declared that they had gone along there but a short time before. We soon reached a small meadow on the east side, at an angle in the stream, which was, for the most part, densely covered with alders. As we were advancing along the edge of this, rather more quietly than usual, perhaps, on account of the freshness of the signs, — the design being to camp up this stream, if it promised well, — I heard a slight crackling of twigs deep in the alders, and turned Joe's attention to it; whereupon he began to push the canoe back rapidly; and we had receded thus half a dozen rods, when we suddenly spied two moose standing just on the edge of the open part of the meadow which we had passed, not more than six or seven rods distant, looking round the alders at us. They made me think of great frightened rabbits, with their long ears and half-inquisitive, half-frightened looks; the true denizens of the forest (I saw at once), filling a vacuum which now first I discovered had not been filled for me, — *moose*-men, *wood-eaters*,

the word is said to mean, — clad in a sort of
Vermont gray, or homespun. Our Nimrod,
owing to the retrograde movement, was now the
farthest from the game; but being warned of
its neighborhood, he hastily stood up, and,
while we ducked, fired over our heads one barrel at the foremost, which alone he saw, though
he did not know what kind of creature it was;
whereupon this one dashed across the meadow
and up a high bank on the northeast, so rapidly
as to leave but an indistinct impression of its
outlines on my mind. At the same instant, the
other, a young one, but as tall as a horse,
leaped out into the stream, in full sight, and
there stood cowering for a moment, or rather its
disproportionate lowness behind gave it that
appearance, and uttering two or three trumpet-
ing squeaks. I have an indistinct recollection
of seeing the old one pause an instant on the
top of the bank in the woods, look toward its
shivering young, and then dash away again.
The second barrel was leveled at the calf, and
when we expected to see it drop in the water,
after a little hesitation, it, too, got out of the
water, and dashed up the hill, though in a
somewhat different direction. All this was the
work of a few seconds, and our hunter, having
never seen a moose before, did not know but
they were deer, for they stood partly in the

water, nor whether he had fired at the same one twice or not. From the style in which they went off, and the fact that he was not used to standing up and firing from a canoe, I judged that we should not see anything more of them. The Indian said that they were a cow and her calf, — a yearling, or perhaps two years old, for they accompany their dams so long; but, for my part, I had not noticed much difference in their size. It was but two or three rods across the meadow to the foot of the bank, which, like all the world thereabouts, was densely wooded; but I was surprised to notice, that, as soon as the moose had passed behind the veil of the woods, there was no sound of footsteps to be heard from the soft, damp moss which carpets that forest, and long before we landed, perfect silence reigned. Joe said, "If you wound 'em moose, me sure get 'em."

We all landed at once. My companion re-loaded; the Indian fastened his birch, threw off his hat, adjusted his waistband, seized the hatchet, and set out. He told me afterward, casually, that before we landed he had seen a drop of blood on the bank, when it was two or three rods off. He proceeded rapidly up the bank and through the woods, with a peculiar, elastic, noiseless, and stealthy tread, looking to right and left on the ground, and stepping in

the faint tracks of the wounded moose, now and
then pointing in silence to a single drop of blood
on the handsome, shining leaves of the Clintonia borealis, which, on every side, covered
the ground, or to a dry fern-stem freshly
broken, all the while chewing some leaf or else
the spruce gum. I followed, watching his motions more than the trail of the moose. After
following the trail about forty rods in a pretty
direct course, stepping over fallen trees and
winding between standing ones, he at length
lost it, for there were many other moose tracks
there, and, returning once more to the last
blood-stain, traced it a little way and lost it
again, and, too soon, I thought, for a good hunter, gave it up entirely. He traced a few steps,
also, the tracks of the calf; but, seeing no blood,
soon relinquished the search.

I observed, while he was tracking the moose,
a certain reticence or moderation in him. He
did not communicate several observations of interest which he made, as a white man would have
done, though they may have leaked out afterward. At another time, when we heard a slight
crackling of twigs and he landed to reconnoitre, he stepped lightly and gracefully, stealing
through the bushes with the least possible noise,
in a way in which no white man does, — as it
were, finding a place for his foot each time.

About half an hour after seeing the moose, we pursued our voyage up Pine Stream, and soon, coming to a part which was very shoal and also rapid, we took out the baggage, and proceeded to carry it round, while Joe got up with the canoe alone. We were just completing our portage and I was absorbed in the plants, admiring the leaves of the Aster macrophyllus, ten inches wide, and plucking the seeds of the great round-leaved orchis, when Joe exclaimed from the stream that he had killed a moose. He had found the cow-moose lying dead, but quite warm, in the middle of the stream, which was so shallow that it rested on the bottom, with hardly a third of its body above water. It was about an hour after it was shot, and it was swollen with water. It had run about a hundred rods and sought the stream again, cutting off a slight bend. No doubt a better hunter would have tracked it to this spot at once. I was surprised at its great size, horse-like, but Joe said it was not a large cow-moose. My companion went in search of the calf again. I took hold of the ears of the moose, while Joe pushed his canoe down-stream toward a favorable shore, and so we made out, though with some difficulty, its long nose frequently sticking in the bottom, to drag it into still shallower water. It was a brownish black, or perhaps a dark iron-gray, on the back and sides, but lighter beneath and in front. I took the cord which served for the canoe's painter, and with Joe's assistance measured it carefully, the greatest distances first, making a knot each time. The painter being wanted, I reduced these measures that night with equal care to lengths and fractions of my umbrella, beginning with the smallest measures, and untying the knots as I proceeded; and when we arrived at Chesuncook the next day, finding a two-foot rule there, I reduced the last to feet and inches; and, moreover, I made myself a two-foot rule of a thin and narrow strip of black ash, which would fold up conveniently to six inches. All this pains I took because I did not wish to be obliged to say merely that the moose was very large. Of the various dimensions which I obtained I will mention only two. The distance from the tips of the hoofs of the fore-feet, stretched out, to the top of the back between the shoulders, was seven feet and five inches. I can hardly believe my own measure, for this is about two feet greater than the height of a tall horse. [Indeed, I am now satisfied that this measurement was incorrect, but the other measures given here I can warrant to be correct, having proved them in a more recent visit to those woods.] The extreme length was eight feet and two

inches. Another cow-moose, which I have since
measured in those woods with a tape, was just
six feet from the tip of the hoof to the shoulders,
and eight feet long as she lay.

When afterward I asked an Indian at the
carry how much taller the male was, he answered, "Eighteen inches," and made me observe the height of a cross-stake over the fire,
more than four feet from the ground, to give me
some idea of the depth of his chest. Another
Indian, at Oldtown, told me that they were nine
feet high to the top of the back, and that one
which he tried weighed eight hundred pounds.
The length of the spinal projections between the
shoulders is very great. A white hunter, who
was the best authority among hunters that I
could have, told me that the male was *not* eighteen inches taller than the female; yet he agreed
that he was sometimes nine feet high to the top
of the back, and weighed a thousand pounds.
Only the male has horns, and they rise two feet
or more above the shoulders, — spreading three
or four, and sometimes six feet, — which would
make him in all, sometimes, eleven feet high!
According to this calculation, the moose is as
tall, though it may not be as large, as the great
Irish elk, Megaceros Hibernicus, of a former
period, of which Mantell says that it "very far
exceeded in magnitude any living species, the

skeleton " being "upward of ten feet high from the ground to the highest point of the antlers." Joe said, that, though the moose shed the whole horn annually, each new horn has an additional prong; but I have noticed that they sometimes have more prongs on one side than on the other. I was struck with the delicacy and tenderness of the hoofs, which divide very far up, and the one half could be pressed very much behind the other, thus probably making the animal surer-footed on the uneven ground and slippery moss-covered logs of the primitive forest. They were very unlike the stiff and battered feet of our horses and oxen. The bare, horny part of the fore-foot was just six inches long, and the two portions could be separated four inches at the extremities.

The moose is singularly grotesque and awk-ward to look at. Why should it stand so high at the shoulders? Why have so long a head? Why have no tail to speak of? for in my exam-ination I overlooked it entirely. Naturalists say it is an inch and a half long. It reminded me at once of the camelopard, high before and low behind, — and no wonder, for, like it, it is fitted to browse on trees. The upper lip projected two inches beyond the lower for this purpose. This was the kind of man that was at home there; for, as near as I can learn, that has never been the residence, but rather the hunting-ground of the Indian. The moose will, perhaps, one day become extinct; but how naturally then, when it exists only as a fossil relic, and unseen as that, may the poet or sculptor invent a fabulous animal with similar branching and leafy horns, — a sort of fucus or lichen in bone, — to be the inhabitant of such a forest as this!

Here, just at the head of the murmuring rapids, Joe now proceeded to skin the moose with a pocket-knife, while I looked on; and a tragical business it was, — to see that still warm and palpitating body pierced with a knife, to see the warm milk stream from the rent udder, and the ghastly naked red carcass appearing from within its seemly robe, which was made to hide it. The ball had passed through the shoulder-blade diagonally and lodged under the skin on the opposite side, and was partially flattened. My companion keeps it to show to his grand-children. He has the shanks of another moose which he has since shot, skinned and stuffed, ready to be made into boots by putting in a thick leather sole. Joe said, if a moose stood fronting you, you must not fire, but advance toward him, for he will turn slowly and give you a fair shot. In the bed of this narrow, wild, and rocky stream, between two lofty walls of spruce and firs, a mere cleft in the forest which the stream had made, this work went on. At length Joe had stripped off the hide and dragged it trailing to the shore, declaring that it weighed a hundred pounds, though probably fifty would have been nearer the truth. He cut off a large mass of the meat to carry along, and another, together with the tongue and nose, he put with the hide on the shore to lie there all night, or till we returned. I was surprised that he thought of leaving this meat thus exposed by the side of the carcass, as the simplest course, not fearing that any creature would touch it; but nothing did. This could hardly have happened on the bank of one of our rivers in the eastern part of Massachusetts; but I suspect that fewer small wild animals are prowling there than with us. Twice, however, in this excursion, I had a glimpse of a species of large mouse.

This stream was so withdrawn, and the moose tracks were so fresh, that my companions, still bent on hunting, concluded to go farther up it and camp, and then hunt up or down at night. Half a mile above this, at a place where I saw the Aster puniceus and the beaked hazel, as we paddled along, Joe, hearing a slight rustling amid the alders, and seeing something black about two rods off, jumped up and whispered, "Bear!" but before the hunter had discharged his piece, he corrected himself to "Beaver!"

— "Hedgehog!" The bullet killed a large hedgehog more than two feet and eight inches long. The quills were rayed out and flattened on the hinder part of its back, even as if it had lain on that part, but were erect and long between this and the tail. Their points, closely examined, were seen to be finely bearded or barbed, and shaped like an awl, that is, a little concave, to give the barbs effect. After about a mile of still water, we prepared our camp on the right side, just at the foot of a considerable fall. Little chopping was done that night, for fear of scaring the moose. We had moose meat fried for supper. It tasted like tender beef, with perhaps more flavor, — sometimes like veal.

After supper, the moon having risen, we proceeded to hunt a mile up this stream, first "carrying" about the falls. We made a picturesque sight, wending single file along the shore, climbing over rocks and logs, — Joe, who brought up the rear, twirling his canoe in his hands as if it were a feather, in places where it was difficult to get along without a burden. We launched the canoe again from the ledge over which the stream fell, but after half a mile of still water, suitable for hunting, it became rapid again, and we were compelled to make our way along the shore, while Joe endeavored to get up in the birch alone, though it was still very difficult for

him to pick his way amid the rocks in the night.
We on the shore found the worst of walking, a
perfect chaos of fallen and drifted trees, and of
bushes projecting far over the water, and now
and then we made our way across the mouth of
a small tributary on a kind of network of alders.
So we went tumbling on in the dark, being on
the shady side, effectually scaring all the moose
and bears that might be thereabouts. At length
we came to a standstill, and Joe went forward
to reconnoitre; but he reported that it was still
a continuous rapid as far as he went, or half a
mile, with no prospect of improvement, as if it
were coming down from a mountain. So we
turned about, hunting back to the camp through
the still water. It was a splendid moonlight
night, and I, getting sleepy as it grew late, —
for I had nothing to do, — found it difficult to
realize where I was. This stream was much
more unfrequented than the main one, lumbering operations being no longer carried on in this
quarter. It was only three or four rods wide,
but the firs and spruce through which it trickled
seemed yet taller by contrast. Being in this
dreamy state, which the moonlight enhanced, I
did not clearly discern the shore, but seemed,
most of the time, to be floating through ornamental grounds, — for I associated the fir-tops
with such scenes; — very high up some Broad-

way, and beneath or between their tops, I
thought I saw an endless succession of porticoes
and columns, cornices and façades, verandas
and churches. I did not merely fancy this, but
in my drowsy state such was the illusion. I
fairly lost myself in sleep several times, still
dreaming of that architecture and the nobility
that dwelt behind and might issue from it; but
all at once I would be aroused and brought
back to a sense of my actual position by the
sound of Joe's birch-horn in the midst of all this
silence calling the moose, *ugh, ugh, oo-oo-oo-oo-
oo-oo*, and I prepared to hear a furious moose
come rushing and crashing through the forest,
and see him burst out on to the little strip of
meadow by our side.

But, on more accounts than one, I had had
enough of moose-hunting. I had not come to
the woods for this purpose, nor had I foreseen
it, though I had been willing to learn how the
Indian manœuvred; but one moose killed was
as good, if not as bad, as a dozen. The afternoon's tragedy, and my share in it, as it affected
the innocence, destroyed the pleasure of my
adventure. It is true, I came as near as is possible to come to being a hunter and miss it,
myself; and as it is, I think that I could spend
a year in the woods, fishing and hunting, just
enough to sustain myself, with satisfaction.

This would be next to living like a philosopher on the fruits of the earth which you had raised, which also attracts me. But this hunting of the moose merely for the satisfaction of killing him, — not even for the sake of his hide, — without making any extraordinary exertion or running any risk yourself, is too much like going out by night to some wood-side pasture and shooting your neighbor's horses. These are God's own horses, poor, timid creatures, that will run fast enough as soon as they smell you, though they *are* nine feet high. Joe told us of some hunters who a year or two before had shot down several oxen by night, somewhere in the Maine woods, mistaking them for moose. And so might any of the hunters; and what is the difference in the sport, but the name? In the former case, having killed one of God's and *your own* oxen, you strip off its hide, — because that is the common trophy, and, moreover, you have heard that it may be sold for moccasins, — cut a steak from its haunches, and leave the huge carcass to smell to heaven for you. It is no better, at least, than to assist at a slaughter-house.

This afternoon's experience suggested to me how base or coarse are the motives which commonly carry men into the. wilderness. The explorers and lumberers generally are all hirelings, paid so much a day for their labor, and as such they have no more love for wild nature than wood-sawyers have for forests. Other white men and Indians who come here are for the most part hunters, whose object is to slay as many moose and other wild animals as possible. But, pray, could .not one spend some weeks or years in the solitude of this vast wilderness with other employments than these — employments perfectly sweet and innocent and ennobling? For one that comes with a pencil to sketch or sing, a thousand come with an axe or rifle. What a coarse and imperfect use Indians and hunters make of Nature! No wonder that their race is so soon exterminated. I already, and for weeks afterward, felt my nature the coarser for this part of my woodland experience, and was reminded that our life should be lived as tenderly and daintily as one would pluck a flower.

With these thoughts, when we reached our camping-ground, I decided to leave my companions to continue moose-hunting down the stream, while I prepared the camp, though they requested me not to chop much nor make a large fire, for fear I should scare their game. In the midst of the damp fir-wood, high on the mossy bank, about nine o'clock of this bright moonlight night, I kindled a fire, when they were gone, and, sitting on the fir-twigs, within sound of the falls, examined by its light the botanical specimens which I had collected that afternoon, and wrote down some of the reflections which I have here expanded; or I walked along the shore and gazed up the stream, where the whole space above the falls was filled with mellow light. As I sat before the fire on my fir-twig seat, without walls above or around me, I remembered how far on every hand that wilderness stretched, before you came to cleared or cultivated fields, and wondered if any bear or moose was watching the light of my fire; for Nature looked sternly upon me on account of the murder of the moose.

Strange that so few ever come to the woods to see how the pine lives and grows and spires, lifting its evergreen arms to the light, — to see its perfect success; but most are content to behold it in the shape of many broad boards brought to market, and deem *that* its true success! But the pine is no more lumber than man is, and to be made into boards and houses is no more its true and highest use than the truest use of a man is to be cut down and made into manure. There is a higher law affecting our relation to pines as well as to men. A pine cut down, a dead pine, is no more a pine than a dead human carcass is a man. Can he who has discovered only some of the values of whalebone and whale oil be said to have discovered the true use of the whale? Can he who slays the elephant for his ivory be said to have "seen the elephant"? These are petty and accidental uses; just as if a stronger race were to kill us in order to make buttons and flageolets of our bones; for everything may serve a lower as well as a higher use. Every creature is better alive than dead, men and moose and pine-trees, and he who understands it aright will rather preserve its life than destroy it.

Is it the lumberman, then, who is the friend and lover of the pine, stands nearest to it, and understands its nature best? Is it the tanner who has barked it, or he who has boxed it for turpentine, whom posterity will fable to have been changed into a pine at last? No! no! it is the poet; he it is who makes the truest use of the pine, — who does not fondle it with an axe, nor tickle it with a saw, nor stroke it with a plane, — who knows whether its heart is false without cutting into it, — who has not bought the stumpage of the township on which it stands. All the pines shudder and heave a sigh when *that* man steps on the forest floor. No, it is the poet, who loves them as his own shadow in the air, and lets them stand. I have been into the lumber-yard, and the carpenter's shop, and the tannery, and the lampblack factory, and the turpentine clearing; but when at length I saw the tops of the pines waving and reflecting the light at a distance high over all the rest of the forest, I realized that the former were not the highest use of the pine. It is not their bones or hide or tallow that I love most. It is the living spirit of the tree, not its spirit of turpentine, with which I sympathize, and which heals my cuts. It is as immortal as I am, and perchance will go to as high a heaven, there to tower above me still.

Erelong, the hunters returned, not having seen a moose, but, in consequence of my suggestions, bringing a quarter of the dead one, which, with ourselves, made quite a load for the canoe.

After breakfasting on moose meat, we returned down Pine Stream on our way to Chesuncook Lake, which was about five miles distant. We could see the red carcass of the moose lying in Pine Stream when nearly half a mile off. Just below the mouth of this stream were the most considerable rapids between the two lakes, called Pine Stream Falls, where were large flat rocks washed smooth, and at this time you could easily wade across above them. Joe ran down alone while we walked over the portage, my companion collecting spruce gum for his friends at home, and I looking for flowers. Near the lake, which we were approaching with as much expectation as if it had been a university, — for it is not often that the stream of our life opens into such expansions, — were islands, and a low and meadowy shore with scattered trees, birches, white and yellow, slanted over the water, and maples, — many of the white birches killed, apparently by inundations. There was considerable native grass; and even a few cattle — whose movements we heard, though we did not see them, mistaking them at first for moose — were pastured there.

On entering the lake, where the stream runs southeasterly, and for some time before, we had a view of the mountains about Ktaadn (*Katahdinauquoh* one says they are called), like a cluster of blue fungi of rank growth, apparently twenty-five or thirty miles distant, in a southeast direction, their summits concealed by clouds. Joe called some of them the *Souadneunk* mountains. This is the name of a stream there, which another Indian told us meant "Running between mountains." Though some lower summits were afterward uncovered, we got no more complete view of Ktaadn while we were in the woods. The clearing to which we were bound was on the right of the mouth of the river, and was reached by going round a low

point, where the water was shallow to a great
distance from the shore.   Chesuncook Lake extends northwest and southeast, and is called
eighteen miles long and three wide, without an
island.   We had entered the northwest corner of
it, and when near the shore could see only part
way down it.   The principal mountains visible
from the land here were those already mentioned,
between southeast and east, and a few summits
a little west of north, but generally the north
and northwest horizon about the St. John and
the British boundary was comparatively level.

Ansell Smith's, the oldest and principal clearing about this lake, appeared to be quite a harbor for batteaux and canoes; seven or eight of
the former were lying about, and there was a
small scow for hay, and a capstan on a platform,
now high and dry, ready to be floated and an-
chored to tow rafts with.   It was a very primitive kind of harbor, where boats were drawn up
amid the stumps, — such a one, methought, as
the Argo might have been launched in.   There
were five other huts with small clearings on the
opposite side of the lake, all at this end and
visible from this point.   One of the Smiths told
me that it was so far cleared that they came
here to live and built the present house four
years before, though the family had been here
but a few months.

I was interested to see how a pioneer lived on this side of the country. His life is in some respects more adventurous than that of his brother in the West; for he contends with winter as well as the wilderness, and there is a greater interval of time at least between him and the army which is to follow. Here immigration is a tide which may ebb when it has swept away the pines; there it is not a tide, but an inundation, and roads and other improvements come steadily rushing after.

As we approached the log-house, a dozen rods from the lake, and considerably elevated above it, the projecting ends of the logs lapping over each other irregularly several feet at the corners gave it a very rich and picturesque look, far removed from the meanness of weather-boards. It was a very spacious, low building, about eighty feet long, with many large apartments. The walls were well clayed between the logs, which were large and round, except on the upper and under sides, and as visible inside as out, successive bulging cheeks gradually lessening upwards and tuned to each other with the axe, like Pandean pipes. Probably the musical forest gods had not yet cast them aside; they never do till they are split or the bark is gone. It was a style of architecture not described by Vitruvius, I suspect, though possibly hinted at in the biography of Orpheus; none of your frilled or fluted columns, which have cut such a false swell, and support nothing but a gable end and their builder's pretensions, — that is, with the multitude; and as for "ornamentation," one of those words with a dead tail which architects very properly use to describe their flourishes, there were the lichens and mosses and fringes of bark, which nobody troubled himself about. We certainly leave the handsomest paint and clapboards behind in the woods, when we strip off the bark and poison ourselves with white-lead in the towns. We get but half the spoils of the forest. For beauty, give me trees with the fur on. This house was designed and con-structed with the freedom of stroke of a for-ester's axe, without other compass and square than Nature uses. Wherever the logs were cut off by a window or door, that is, were not kept in place by alternate overlapping, they were held one upon another by very large pins, driven in diagonally on each side, where branches might have been, and then cut off so close up and down as not to project beyond the bulge of the log, as if the logs clasped each other in their arms. These logs were posts, studs, boards, clap-boards, laths, plaster, and nails, all in one. Where the citizen uses a mere sliver or board, the pioneer uses the whole trunk of a tree. The house had large stone chimneys, and was roofed with spruce-bark. The windows were imported, all but the casings. One end was a regular logger's camp, for the boarders, with the usual fir floor and log benches. Thus this house was but a slight departure from the hollow tree, which the bear still inhabits, — being a hollow made with trees piled up, with a coating of bark like its original.

The cellar was a separate building, like an ice-house, and it answered for a refrigerator at this season, our moose meat being kept there. It was a potato hole with a permanent roof. Each structure and institution here was so primitive that you could at once refer it to its source; but our buildings commonly suggest neither their origin nor their purpose. There was a large, and what farmers would call handsome, barn, part of whose boards had been sawed by a whip-saw; and the saw-pit, with its great pile of dust, remained before the house. The long split shingles on a portion of the barn were laid a foot to the weather, suggesting what kind of weather they have there. Grant's barn at Caribou Lake was said to be still larger, the biggest ox-nest in the woods, fifty feet by a hundred. Think of a monster barn in that primitive forest lifting its gray back above the tree-tops! Man makes very much such a nest for his domestic animals, of withered grass and fodder, as the squirrels and many other wild creatures do for themselves.

There was also a blacksmith's shop, where plainly a good deal of work was done. The oxen and horses used in lumbering operations were shod, and all the iron-work of sleds, etc., was repaired or made here. I saw them load a batteau at the Moosehead carry, the next Tuesday, with about thirteen hundredweight of bar iron for this shop. This reminded me how primitive and honorable a trade was Vulcan's. I do not hear that there was any carpenter or tailor among the gods. The smith seems to have preceded these and every other mechanic at Chesuncook as well as on Olympus, and his family is the most widely dispersed, whether he be christened John or Ansell.

Smith owned two miles down the lake by half a mile in width. There were about one hundred acres cleared here. He cut seventy tons of English hay this year on this ground, and twenty more on another clearing, and he uses it all himself in lumbering operations. The barn was crowded with pressed hay, and a machine to press it. There was a large garden full of roots, — turnips, beets, carrots, potatoes, etc., all of great size. They said that they were worth as much here as in New York. I suggested some currants for sauce, especially as they had no apple-trees set out, and showed how easily they could be obtained.

There was the usual long-handled axe of the primitive woods by the door, three and a half feet long, — for my new black-ash rule was in constant use, — and a large, shaggy dog, whose nose, report said, was full of porcupine quills. I can testify that he looked very sober. This is the usual fortune of pioneer dogs, for they have to face the brunt of the battle for their race, and act the part of Arnold Winkelried without intending it. If he should invite one of his town friends up this way, suggesting moose meat and unlimited freedom, the latter might pertinently inquire, "What is that sticking in your nose?" When a generation or two have used up all the enemies' darts, their successors lead a comparatively easy life. We owe to our fathers analogous blessings. Many old people receive pensions for no other reason, it seems to me, but as a compensation for having lived a long time ago. No doubt our town dogs still talk, in a snuffling way, about the days that tried dogs' noses. How they got a cat up there I do not know, for they are as shy as my aunt about entering a canoe. I wondered that she did not run up a tree on the way; but perhaps she was bewildered by the very crowd of opportunities.

Twenty or thirty lumberers, Yankee and Canadian, were coming and going, — Aleck among the rest, — and from time to time an Indian touched here. In the winter there are sometimes a hundred men lodged here at once. The most interesting piece of news that circulated among them appeared to be, that four horses belonging to Smith, worth seven hundred dollars, had passed by farther into the woods a week before.

The white-pine-tree was at the bottom or farther end of all this. It is a war against the pines, the only real Aroostook or Penobscot war. I have no doubt that they lived pretty much the same sort of life in the Homeric age, for men have always thought more of eating than of fighting; then, as now, their minds ran chiefly on the "hot bread and sweet cakes;" and the fur and lumber trade is an old story to Asia and Europe. I doubt if men ever made a trade of heroism. In the days of Achilles, even, they delighted in big barns, and perchance in pressed hay, and he who possessed the most valuable team was the best fellow.

We had designed to go on at evening up the Caucomgomoc, whose mouth was a mile or two distant, to the lake of the same name, about ten miles off; but some Indians of Joe's acquaintance, who were making canoes on the Caucomgomoc, came over from that side, and gave so poor an account of the moose-hunting, so many had been killed there lately, that my companions concluded not to go there. Joe spent this Sunday and the night with his acquaintances. The lumberers told me that there were many moose hereabouts, but no caribou or deer. A man from Oldtown had killed ten or twelve moose, within a year, so near the house that they heard all his guns. His name may have been Hercules, for aught I know, though I should rather have expected to hear the rattling of his club; but, no doubt, he keeps pace with the improvements of the age, and uses a Sharps' rifle now; probably he gets all his armor made and repaired at Smith's shop. One moose had been killed and another shot at within sight of the house within two years. I do not know whether Smith has yet got a poet to look after the cattle, which, on account of the early breaking up of the ice, are compelled to summer in the woods, but I would suggest this office to such of my acquaintances as love to write verses and go a-gunning.

After a dinner, at which apple-sauce was the greatest luxury to me, but our moose meat was oftenest called for by the lumberers, I walked across the clearing into the forest, southward, returning along the shore. For my dessert, I

helped myself to a large slice of the Chesuncook woods, and took a hearty draught of its
waters with all my senses. The woods were as
fresh and full of vegetable life as a lichen in
wet weather, and contained many interesting
plants; but unless they are of white-pine, they
are treated with as little respect here as a mil-
dew, and in the other case they are only the
more quickly cut down. The shore was of
coarse, flat, slate rocks, often in slabs, with the
surf beating on it. The rocks and bleached
drift-logs, extending some way into the shaggy
woods, showed a rise and fall of six or eight
feet, caused partly by the dam at the outlet.
They said that in winter the snow was three feet
deep on a level here, and sometimes four or five,
— that the ice on the lake was two feet thick,
clear, and four feet including the snow-ice.
Ice had already formed in vessels.

We lodged here this Sunday night in a comfortable bedroom, apparently the best one; and
all that I noticed unusual in the night — for I
still kept taking notes, like a spy in the camp
— was the creaking of the thin split boards,
when any of our neighbors stirred.

Such were the first rude beginnings of a
town. They spoke of the practicability of a
winter road to the Moosehead carry, which
would not cost much, and would connect them

with steam and staging and all the busy world. I almost doubted if the lake would be there, — the self-same lake, — preserve its form and identity, when the shores should be cleared and settled; as if these lakes and streams which explorers report never awaited the advent of the citizen.

The sight of one of these frontier houses, built of these great logs, whose inhabitants have unflinchingly maintained their ground many summers and winters in the wilderness, reminds me of famous forts, like Ticonderoga or Crown Point, which have sustained memorable sieges. They are especially winter-quarters, and at this season this one had a partially deserted look, as if the siege were raised a little, the snow-banks being melted from before it, and its garrison accordingly reduced. I think of their daily food as rations, — it is called "supplies;" a Bible and a great-coat are munitions of war, and a single man seen about the premises is a sentinel on duty. You expect that he will require the countersign, and will perchance take you for Ethan Allen, come to demand the surrender of his fort in the name of the Continental Congress. It is a sort of ranger service. Arnold's expedition is a daily experience with these settlers. They can prove that they were out at almost any time; and I think that all the first generation of them deserve a pension more than any that went to the Mexican war.

Early the next morning we started on our return up the Penobscot, my companion wishing to go about twenty-five miles above the Moose-head carry to a camp near the junction of the two forks, and look for moose there. Our host allowed us something for the quarter of the moose which we had brought, and which he was glad to get. Two explorers from Chamberlain Lake started at the same time that we did. Red flannel shirts should be worn in the woods, if only for the fine contrast which this color makes with the evergreens and the water. Thus I thought when I saw the forms of the explorers in their birch, poling up the rapids before us, far off against the forest. It is the surveyor's color also, most distinctly seen under all circumstances. We stopped to dine at Ragmuff, as before. My companion it was who wandered up the stream to look for moose this time, while Joe went to sleep on the bank, so that we felt sure of him; and I improved the opportunity to botanize and bathe. Soon after starting again, while Joe was gone back in the canoe for the frying-pan, which had been left, we picked a couple of quarts of tree-cranberries for a sauce.

I was surprised by Joe's asking me how far it was to the Moosehorn. He was pretty well

acquainted with this stream, but he had noticed
that I was curious about distances, and had several maps. He and Indians generally, with
whom I have talked, are not able to describe
dimensions or distances in our measures with
any accuracy. He could tell, perhaps, at what
time we should arrive, but not how far it was.
We saw a few wood-ducks, sheldrakes, and
black ducks, but they were not so numerous
there at that season as on our river at home.
We scared the same family of wood-ducks before
us, going and returning. We also heard the
note of one fish-hawk, somewhat like that of a
pigeon-woodpecker, and soon after saw him
perched near the top of a dead white-pine against
the island where we had first camped, while a
company of peetweets were twittering and tee-
tering about over the carcass of a moose on a low
sandy spit just beneath. We drove the fish-
hawk from perch to perch, each time eliciting a
scream or whistle, for many miles before us.
Our course being up-stream, we were obliged to
work much harder than before, and had frequent use for a pole. Sometimes all three of us
paddled together, standing up, small and heavily laden as the canoe was. About six miles
from Moosehead, we began to see the mountains
east of the north end of the lake, and at four
o'clock we reached the carry.

The Indians were still encamped here. There were three, including the St. Francis Indian who had come in the steamer with us. One of the others was called Sabattis. Joe and the St. Francis Indian were plainly clear Indian, the other two apparently mixed Indian and white; but the difference was confined to their features and complexion, for all that I could see. We here cooked the tongue of the moose for supper, — having left the nose, which is esteemed the choicest part, at Chesuncook, boiling, it being a good deal of trouble to prepare it. We also stewed our tree-cranberries (Viburnum opulus), sweetening them with sugar. The lumberers sometimes cook them with molasses. They were used in Arnold's expedition. This sauce was very grateful to us who had been confined to hard bread, pork, and moose meat, and, notwithstanding their seeds, we all three pronounced them equal to the common cranberry; but perhaps some allowance is to be made for our forest appetites. It would be worth the while to cultivate them, both for beauty and for food. I afterward saw them in a garden in Bangor. Joe said that they were called *ebeemenar*.

While we were getting supper, Joe commenced curing the moose-hide, on which I had sat a good part of the voyage, he having already cut most of the hair off with his knife at the

Caucomgomoc. He set up two stout forked
poles on the bank, seven or eight feet high, and
as much asunder east and west, and having cut
slits eight or ten inches long, and the same distance apart, close to the edge, on the sides of
the hide, he threaded poles through them, and
then, placing one of the poles on the forked
stakes, tied the other down tightly at the bottom. The two ends also were tied with cedar-
bark, their usual string, to the upright poles,
through small holes at short intervals. The
hide, thus stretched, and slanted a little to the
north, to expose its flesh side to the sun, measured, in the extreme, eight feet long by six high.
Where any flesh still adhered, Joe boldly scored
it with his knife to lay it open to the sun. It
now appeared somewhat spotted and injured by
the duck shot. You may see the old frames on
which hides have been stretched at many camp-
ing-places in these woods.

For some reason or other, the going to the
forks of the Penobscot was given up, and we
decided to stop here, my companion intending
to hunt down the stream at night. The Indians
invited us to lodge with them, but my companion inclined to go to the log-camp on the carry.
This camp was close and dirty, and had an ill
smell, and I preferred to accept the Indians'
offer, if we did not make a camp for ourselves;

for, though they were dirty, too, they were
more in the open air, and were much more
agreeable, and even refined company, than the
lumberers. The most interesting question entertained at the lumberers' camp was, which
man could "handle" any other on the carry;
and, for the most part, they possessed no qualities which you could not lay hands on. So we
went to the Indians' camp or wigwam.

It was rather windy, and therefore Joe concluded to hunt after midnight, if the wind went
down, which the other Indians thought it would
not do, because it was from the south. The
two mixed-bloods, however, went off up the
river for moose at dark, before we arrived at
their camp. This Indian camp was a slight,
patched-up affair, which had stood there several
weeks, built shed-fashion, open to the fire on the
west. If the wind changed, they could turn it
round. It was formed by two forked stakes
and a cross-bar, with rafters slanted from this to
the ground. The covering was partly an old
sail, partly birch-bark, quite imperfect, but securely tied on, and coming down to the ground
on the sides. A large log was rolled up at the
back side for a headboard, and two or three
moose-hides were spread on the ground with the
hair up. Various articles of their wardrobe
were tucked around the sides and corners, or

under the roof. They were smoking moose meat on just such a crate as is represented by With, in De Bry's "Collectio Peregrinationum," published in 1588, and which the natives of Brazil called *boucan* (whence buccaneer), on which were frequently shown pieces of human flesh drying along with the rest. It was erected in front of the camp over the usual large fire, in the form of an oblong square. Two stout forked stakes, four or five feet apart and five feet high, were driven into the ground at each end, and then two poles ten feet long were stretched across over the fire, and smaller ones laid transversely on these a foot apart. On the last hung large, thin slices of moose meat smoking and drying, a space being left open over the centre of the fire. There was the whole heart, black as a thirty-two pound ball, hanging at one corner. They said that it took three or four days to cure this meat, and it would keep a year or more. Refuse pieces lay about on the ground in different stages of decay, and some pieces also in the fire, half buried and sizzling in the ashes, as black and dirty as an old shoe. These last I at first thought were thrown away, but afterwards found that they were being cooked. Also a tremendous rib-piece was roasting before the fire, being impaled on an upright stake forced in and out between the ribs. There was a moose-hide stretched and curing on poles like ours, and quite a pile of cured skins close by. They had killed twenty-two moose within two months, but, as they could use but very little of the meat, they left the carcasses on the ground. Altogether it was about as savage a sight as was ever witnessed, and I was carried back at once three hundred years. There were many torches of birch-bark, shaped like straight tin horns, lying ready for use on a stump outside.

For fear of dirt, we spread our blankets over their hides, so as not to touch them anywhere. The St. Francis Indian and Joe alone were there at first, and we lay on our backs talking with them till midnight. They were very sociable, and, when they did not talk with us, kept up a steady chatting in their own language. We heard a small bird just after dark, which, Joe said, sang at a certain hour in the night, — at ten o'clock, he believed. We also heard the hylodes and tree-toads, and the lumberers singing in their camp a quarter of a mile off. I told them that I had seen pictured in old books pieces of human flesh drying on these crates; whereupon they repeated some tradition about the Mohawks eating human flesh, what parts they preferred, etc., and also of a battle with the Mohawks near Moosehead, in which many of the latter were killed; but I found that they

knew but little of the history of their race, and
could be entertained by stories about their ancestors as readily as any way.   At first I was
nearly roasted out, for I lay against one side
of the camp, and felt the heat reflected not only
from the birch-bark above, but from the side;
and again I remembered the sufferings of the
Jesuit missionaries, and what extremes of heat
and cold the Indians were said to endure.   I
struggled long between my desire to remain and
talk with them and my impulse to rush out and
stretch myself on the cool grass; and when I
was about to take the last step, Joe, hearing
my murmurs, or else being uncomfortable himself, got up and partially dispersed the fire.   I
suppose that that is Indian manners, — to defend yourself.

While lying there listening to the Indians, I
amused myself with trying to guess at their subject by their gestures, or some proper name introduced.   There can be no more startling evidence of their being a distinct and comparatively
aboriginal race than to hear this unaltered Indian language, which the white man cannot
speak nor understand.   We may suspect change
and deterioration in almost every other particular but the language which is so wholly unintelligible to us.   It took me by surprise, though
I had found so many arrow-heads, and convinced

me that the Indian was not the invention of historians and poets. It was a purely wild and
primitive American sound, as much as the bark-
ing of a *chickaree*, and I could not understand
a syllable of it; but Paugus, had he been there,
would have understood it. These Abenakis
gossiped, laughed, and jested, in the language
in which Eliot's Indian Bible is written, the
language which has been spoken in New England who shall say how long? These were the
sounds that issued from the wigwams of this
country before Columbus was born; they have
not yet died away; and, with remarkably few
exceptions, the language of their forefathers is
still copious enough for them. I felt that I
stood, or rather lay, as near to the primitive
man of America, that night, as any of its discoverers ever did.

In the midst of their conversation, Joe suddenly appealed to me to know how long Moosehead Lake was.

Meanwhile, as we lay there, Joe was making
and trying his horn, to be ready for hunting
after midnight. The St. Francis Indian also
amused himself with sounding it, or rather calling through it; for the sound is made with the
voice, and not by blowing through the horn.
The latter appeared to be a speculator in moose-
hides. He bought my companion's for two

dollars and a quarter, green. Joe said that it
was worth two and a half at Oldtown. Its chief
use is for moccasins. One or two of these Indians wore them. I was told that, by a recent
law of Maine, foreigners are not allowed to kill
moose there at any season; white Americans
can kill them only at a particular season, but
the Indians of Maine at all seasons. The St.
Francis Indian accordingly asked my companion
for a *wighiggin*, or bill, to show, since he was a
foreigner. He lived near Sorel. I found that
he could write his name very well, Tahmunt
Swasen. One Ellis, an old white man of Guil-
ford, a town through which we passed, not far
from the south end of Moosehead, was the most
celebrated moose-hunter of those parts. Indians and whites spoke with equal respect of
him. Tahmunt said that there were more moose
here than in the Adirondack country in New
York, where he had hunted; that three years
before there were a great many about, and there
were a great many now in the woods, but they
did not come out to the water. It was of no use
to hunt them at midnight, — they would not
come out then. I asked Sabattis, after he came
home, if the moose never attacked him. He answered that you must not fire many times, so
as to mad him. "I fire once and hit him in
the right place, and in the morning I find him.

He won't go far. But if you keep firing, you
mad him. I fired once five bullets, every one
through the heart, and he did not mind 'em at
all; it only made him more mad." I asked him
if they did not hunt them with dogs. He said
that they did so in winter, but never in the summer, for then it was of no use; they would run
right off straight and swiftly a hundred miles.

Another Indian said that the moose, once
scared, would run all day. A dog will hang to
their lips, and be carried along till he is swung
against a tree and drops off. They cannot run
on a "glaze," though they can run in snow four
feet deep; but the caribou can run on ice. They
commonly find two or three moose together.
They cover themselves with water, all but their
noses, to escape flies. He had the horns of
what he called "the black moose that goes in
low lands." These spread three or four feet.
The "red moose" was another kind, "running
on mountains," and had horns which spread six
feet. Such were his distinctions. Both can
move their horns. The broad flat blades are
covered with hair, and are so soft, when the animal is alive, that you can run a knife through
them. They regard it as a good or bad sign, if
the horns turn this way or that. His caribou
horns had been gnawed by mice in his wigwam,
but he thought that the horns neither of the

moose nor of the caribou were ever gnawed while
the creature was alive, as some have asserted.
An Indian, whom I met after this at Oldtown,
who had carried about a bear and other animals
of Maine to exhibit, told me that thirty years
ago there were not so many moose in Maine as
now; also, that the moose were very easily
tamed, and would come back when once fed,
and so would deer, but not caribou. The Indians of this neighborhood are about as familiar
with the moose as we are with the ox, having
associated with them for so many generations.
Father Rasles, in his Dictionary of the Abenaki
Language, gives not only a word for the male
moose (*aianbé*); and another for the female
(*hèrar*), but for the bone which is in the middle
of the heart of the moose (!), and for his left
hind-leg.

There were none of the small deer up there;
they are more common about the settlements.
One ran into the city of Bangor two years before, and jumped through a window of costly
plate glass, and then into a mirror, where it
thought it recognized one of its kind, and out
again, and so on, leaping over the heads of the
crowd, until it was captured. This the inhabitants speak of as the deer that went a-shopping.
The last-mentioned Indian spoke of the *lunxus*
or Indian devil (which I take to be the cougar,

and not the *Gulo luscus*), as the only animal in
Maine which man need fear; it would follow a
man, and did not mind a fire. He also said
that beavers were getting to be pretty numerous
again, where we went, but their skins brought
so little now that it was not profitable to hunt
them.

I had put the ears of our moose, which were
ten inches long, to dry along with the moose
meat over the fire, wishing to preserve them;
but Sabattis told me that I must skin and cure
them, else the hair would all come off. He observed that they made tobacco pouches of the
skins of their ears, putting the two together inside to inside. I asked him how he got fire;
and he produced a little cylindrical box of friction matches. He also had flints and steel, and
some punk, which was not dry; I think it was
from the yellow birch. "But suppose you upset, and all these and your powder get wet."
"Then," said he, "we wait till we get to where
there is some fire." I produced from my pocket
a little vial, containing matches, stoppled water-
tight, and told him, that, though we were upset,
we should still have some dry matches; at
which he stared without saying a word.

We lay awake thus a long while talking, and
they gave us the meaning of many Indian names
of lakes and streams in the vicinity, — especially

Tahmunt. I asked the Indian name of Moosehead Lake. Joe answered *Sebamook;* Tahmunt
pronounced it *Sebemook*. When I asked what
it meant, they answered, Moosehead Lake. At
length, getting my meaning, they alternately
repeated the word over to themselves, as a phi-
lologist might, — *Sebamook*, — *Sebamook*, —
now and then comparing notes in Indian; for
there was a slight difference in their dialects;
and finally Tahmunt said, "Ugh! I know," —
and he rose up partly on the moose-hide, —
"like as here is a place, and there is a place,"
pointing to different parts of the hide, "and
you take water from there and fill this, and it
stays here; that is *Sebamook*." I understood
him to mean that it was a reservoir of water
which did not run away, the river coming in on
one side and passing out again near the same
place, leaving a permanent bay. Another Indian said, that it meant Large Bay Lake, and
that *Sebago* and *Sebec*, the names of other
lakes, were kindred words, meaning large open
water. Joe said that *Seboois* meant Little
River. I observed their inability, often described, to convey an abstract idea. Having
got the idea, though indistinctly, they groped
about in vain for words with which to express
it. Tahmunt thought that the whites called it
Moosehead Lake, because Mount Kineo, which

commands it, is shaped like a moose's head, and
that Moose River was so called "because the
mountain points right across the lake to its
mouth." John Josselyn, writing about 1673,
says, "Twelve miles from Casco Bay, and passable for men and horses, is a lake, called by the
Indians Sebug. On the brink thereof, at one
end, is the famous rock, shaped like a moose
deer or helk, diaphanous, and called the Moose
Rock." He appears to have confounded Sebamook with Sebago, which is nearer, but has
no "diaphanous" rock on its shore.

I give more of their definitions, for what they
are worth, — partly *because* they differ sometimes from the commonly received ones. They
never analyzed these words before. After long
deliberation and repeating of the word, for it
gave much trouble, Tahmunt said that *Chesuncook* meant a place where many streams emptied
in (?), and he enumerated them, — Penobscot,
Umbazookskus, Cusabesex, Red Brook, etc. —
" *Caucomgomoc*, — what does that mean?"
"What are those large white birds?" he asked.
"Gulls," said I. "Ugh! Gull Lake." —
Pammadumcook, Joe thought, meant the Lake
with Gravelly Bottom or Bed. — *Kenduskeag*,
Tahmunt concluded at last, after asking if
birches went up it, for he said that he was not
much acquainted with it, meant something like

this: "You go up Penobscot till you come to *Kenduskeag*, and you go by, you don't turn up there. That is *Kenduskeag*." (?) Another Indian, however, who knew the river better, told us afterward that it meant Little Eel River. — *Mattawamkeag* was a place where two rivers meet. (?) — *Penobscot* was Rocky River. One writer says that this was "originally the name of only a section of the main channel, from the head of the tide-water to a short distance above Oldtown."

A very intelligent Indian, whom we afterward met, son-in-law of Neptune, gave us also these other definitions: *Umbazookskus*, Meadow Stream; *Millinoket*, Place of Islands; *Aboljacarmegus*, Smooth-Ledge Falls (and Dead-Water); *Aboljacarmeguscook*, the stream emptying in (the last was the word he gave when I asked about *Aboljacknagesic*, which he did not recognize); *Mattahumkeag*, Sand-Creek Pond; *Piscataquis*, Branch of a River.

I asked our hosts what *Musketaquid*, the Indian name of Concord, Massachusetts, meant; but they changed it to *Musketicook*, and repeated that, and Tahmunt said that it meant Dead Stream, which is probably true. *Cook* appears to mean stream, and perhaps *quid* signifies the place or ground. When I asked the meaning of the names of two of our hills, they answered that they were another language. As Tahmunt said that he traded at Quebec, my companion inquired the meaning of the word *Quebec,* about which there has been so much question. He did not know, but began to conjecture. He asked what those great ships were called that carried soldiers. "Men-of-war," we answered. "Well," he said, "when the English ships came up the river, they could not go any farther, it was so narrow there; they must go back, — go-back, — that's Que-bec." I mention this to show the value of his authority in the other cases.

Late at night the other two Indians came home from moose-hunting, not having been successful, aroused the fire again, lighted their pipes, smoked awhile, took something strong to drink, and ate some moose meat, and, finding what room they could, lay down on the moose-hides; and thus we passed the night, two white men and four Indians, side by side.

When I awoke in the morning the weather was drizzling. One of the Indians was lying outside, rolled in his blanket, on the opposite side of the fire, for want of room. Joe had neglected to awake my companion, and he had done no hunting that night. Tahmunt was making a cross-bar for his canoe with a singularly shaped knife, such as I have since seen other Indians using. The blade was thin, about three quarters of an inch wide, and eight or nine inches long, but curved out of its plane into a hook, which he said made it more convenient to shave with. As the Indians very far north and northwest use the same kind of knife, I suspect that it was made according to an aboriginal pattern, though some white artisans may use a similar one. The Indians baked a loaf of flour bread in a spider on its edge before the fire for their breakfast; and while my companion was making tea, I caught a dozen sizable fishes in the Penobscot, two kinds of sucker and one trout. After we had breakfasted by ourselves, one of our bed-fellows, who had also breakfasted, came along, and, being invited, took a cup of tea, and finally, taking up the common platter, licked it clean. But he was nothing to a white fellow, a lumberer, who was continually stuffing himself with the Indians' moose meat, and was the butt of his companions accordingly. He seems to have thought that it was a feast "to eat all." It is commonly said that the white man finally surpasses the Indian on his own ground, and it was proved true in this case. I cannot swear to his employment during the hours of darkness, but I saw him at it again as soon as it was light, though he came a quarter of a mile to his work.

The rain prevented our continuing any longer in the woods; so giving some of our provisions and utensils to the Indians, we took leave of them. This being the steamer's day, I set out for the lake at once.

I walked over the carry alone and waited at the head of the lake. An eagle, or some other large bird, flew screaming away from its perch by the shore at my approach. For an hour after I reached the shore there was not a human being to be seen, and I had all that wide prospect to myself. I thought that I heard the sound of the steamer before she came in sight on the open lake. I noticed at the landing, when the steamer came in, one of our bed-fellows, who had been a-moose-hunting the night before, now very sprucely dressed in a clean white shirt and fine black pants, a true Indian dandy, who had evidently come over the carry to show himself to any arrivers on the north shore of Moosehead Lake, just as New York dandies take a turn up Broadway and stand on the steps of a hotel.

Midway the lake we took on board two manly-looking middle-aged men, with their batteau, who had been exploring for six weeks as far as the Canada line, and had let their beards grow. They had the skin of a beaver, which they had recently caught, stretched on an oval hoop, though the fur was not good at that season. I talked with one of them, telling him that I had come all this distance partly to see where the white-pine, the Eastern stuff of which our houses are built, grew, but that on this and a previous excursion into another part of Maine I had found it a scarce tree; and I asked him where I must look for it. With a smile, he answered, that he could hardly tell me. However, he said that he had found enough to employ two teams the next winter in a place where there was thought to be none left. What was considered a "tip-top" tree now was not looked at twenty years ago, when he first went into the business; but they succeeded very well now with what was considered quite inferior timber then. The explorer used to cut into a tree higher and higher up, to see if it was false-hearted, and if there was a rotten heart as big as his arm, he let it alone; but now they cut such a tree, and sawed it all around the rot, and it made the very best of boards, for in such a case they were never shaky.

One connected with lumbering operations at Bangor told me that the largest pine belonging to his firm, cut the previous winter, "scaled" in the woods four thousand five hundred feet, and was worth ninety dollars in the log at the Bangor boom in Oldtown. They cut a road three and a half miles long for this tree alone.

He thought that the principal locality for the white-pine that came down the Penobscot now was at the head of the East Branch and the Allegash, about Webster Stream and Eagle and Chamberlain lakes. Much timber has been stolen from the public lands. (Pray, what kind of forest-warden is the Public itself?) I heard of one man who, having discovered some particularly fine trees just within the boundaries of the public lands, and not daring to employ an accomplice, cut them down, and by means of block and tackle, without cattle, tumbled them into a stream, and so succeeded in getting off with them without the least assistance. Surely, stealing pine-trees in this way is not so mean as robbing hen-roosts.

We reached Monson that night, and the next day rode to Bangor, all the way in the rain again, varying our route a little. Some of the taverns on this road, which were particularly dirty, were plainly in a transition state from the camp to the house.

The next forenoon we went to Oldtown. One slender old Indian on the Oldtown shore, who recognized my companion, was full of mirth and gestures, like a Frenchman. A Catholic priest crossed to the island in the same batteau with us. The Indian houses are framed, mostly of one story, and in rows one behind another, at the south end of the island, with a few scattered ones. I counted about forty, not including the church and what my companion called the council-house. The last, which I suppose is their town-house, was regularly framed and shingled like the rest. There were several of two stories, quite neat, with front-yards inclosed, and one at least had green blinds. Here and there were moose-hides stretched and drying about them. There were no cart-paths, nor tracks of horses, but foot-paths; very little land cultivated, but an abundance of weeds, indigenous and naturalized; more introduced weeds than useful vegetables, as the Indian is said to cultivate the vices rather than the virtues of the white man. Yet this village was cleaner than I expected, far cleaner than such Irish villages as I have seen. The children were not particularly ragged nor dirty. The little boys met us with bow in hand and arrow on string, and cried, "Put up a cent." Verily, the Indian has but a feeble hold on his bow now; but the curiosity of the white man is insatiable, and from the first he has been eager to witness this forest accomplishment. That elastic piece of wood with its feathered dart, so sure to be unstrung by contact with civilization, will serve for the type, the coat-of-arms of the savage.

Alas for the Hunter Race! the white man has driven off their game, and substituted a cent in its place. I saw an Indian woman washing at the water's edge. She stood on a rock, and, after dipping the clothes in the stream, laid them on the rock, and beat them with a short club. In the graveyard, which was crowded with graves, and overrun with weeds, I noticed an inscription in Indian, painted on a wooden grave-board. There was a large wooden cross on the island.

Since my companion knew him, we called on Governor Neptune, who lived in a little "ten-footer," one of the humblest of them all. Personalities are allowable in speaking of public men, therefore I will give the particulars of our visit. He was abed. When we entered the room, which was one half of the house, he was sitting on the side of the bed. There was a clock hanging in one corner. He had on a black frock-coat, and black pants, much worn, white cotton shirt, socks, a red silk handkerchief about his neck, and a straw hat. His black hair was only slightly grayed. He had very broad cheeks, and his features were decidedly and refreshingly different from those of any of the upstart Native American party whom I have seen. He was no darker than many old white men. He told me that he was eighty-nine; but he was going a-moose-hunting that fall, as he had been the previous one. Probably his companions did the hunting. We saw various squaws dodging about. One sat on the bed by his side and helped him out with his stories. They were remarkably corpulent, with smooth, round faces, apparently full of good humor. Certainly our much-abused climate had not dried up their adipose substance. While we were there, — for we stayed a good while, — one went over to Oldtown, returned and cut out a dress, which she had bought, on another bed in the room. The Governor said that "he could remember when the moose were much larger; that they did not use to be in the woods, but came out of the water, as all deer did. Moose was whale once. Away down Merrimack way, a whale came ashore in a shallow bay. Sea went out and left him, and he came up on land a moose. What made them know he was a whale was, that at first, before he began to run in bushes, he had no bowels inside, but" — and then the squaw who sat on the bed by his side, as the Governor's aid, and had been putting in a word now and then and confirming the story, asked me what we called that soft thing we find along the seashore. "Jelly-fish," I suggested. "Yes," said he, "no bowels, but jelly-fish."

There may be some truth in what he said about the moose growing larger formerly; for the quaint John Josselyn, a physician who spent many years in this very district of Maine in the seventeenth century, says that the tips of their horns "are sometimes found to be two fathoms asunder," — and he is particular to tell us that a fathom is six feet, — "and [they are] in height, from the toe of the fore-foot to the pitch of the shoulder, twelve foot, both which hath been taken by some of my sceptique readers to be monstrous lies;" and he adds, "There are certain transcendentia in every creature, which are the indelible character of God, and which discover God." This is a greater dilemma to be caught in than is presented by the cranium of the young Bechuana ox, apparently another of the *transcendentia*, in the collection of Thomas Steel, Upper Brook Street, London, whose "entire length of horn, from tip to tip, along the curve, is 13 ft. 5 in.; distance (straight) between the tips of the horns, 8 ft. $8\frac{1}{2}$ in." However, the size both of the moose and the cougar, as I have found, is generally rather underrated than overrated, and I should be inclined to add to the popular estimate a part of what I subtracted from Josselyn's.

But we talked mostly with the Governor's son-in-law, a very sensible Indian; and the

Governor, being so old and deaf, permitted himself to be ignored, while we asked questions about him. The former said that there were two political parties among them, — one in favor of schools, and the other opposed to them, or rather they did not wish to resist the priest, who was opposed to them. The first had just prevailed at the election and sent their man to the legislature. Neptune and Aitteon and he himself were in favor of schools. He said, "If Indians got learning, they would keep their money." When we asked where Joe's father, Aitteon, was, he knew that he must be at Lincoln, though he was about going a-moose-hunting, for a messenger had just gone to him there to get his signature to some papers. I asked Neptune if they had any of the old breed of dogs yet. He answered, "Yes." "But that," said I, pointing to one that had just come in, "is a Yankee dog." He assented. I said that he did not look like a good one. "Oh, yes!" he said, and he told, with much gusto, how, the year before, he had caught and held by the throat a wolf. A very small black puppy rushed into the room and made at the Governor's feet, as he sat in his stockings with his legs dangling from the bedside. The Governor rubbed his hands and dared him to come on, entering into the sport with spirit. Nothing more that was significant transpired, to my knowledge, during this interview. This was the first time that I ever called on a governor, but, as I did not ask for an office, I can speak of it with the more freedom.

An Indian who was making canoes behind a house, looking up pleasantly from his work, — for he knew my companion, — said that his name was Old John Pennyweight. I had heard of him long before, and I inquired after one of his contemporaries, Joe Four-pence-ha'penny; but alas! he no longer circulates. I made a faithful study of canoe-building, and I thought that I should like to serve an apprenticeship at that trade for one season, going into the woods for bark with my "boss," making the canoe there, and returning in it at last.

While the batteau was coming over to take us off, I picked up some fragments of arrow-heads on the shore, and one broken stone chisel, which were greater novelties to the Indians than to me. After this, on Old Fort Hill, at the bend of the Penobscot, three miles above Bangor, looking for the site of an Indian town which some think stood thereabouts, I found more arrow-heads, and two little dark and crumbling fragments of Indian earthenware, in the ashes of their fires. The Indians on the island appeared to live quite happily and to be well treated by the inhabitants of Oldtown.

We visited Veazie's mills, just below the island, where were sixteen sets of saws, — some gang saws, sixteen in a gang, not to mention circular saws. On one side, they were hauling the logs up an inclined plane by water-power; on the other, passing out the boards, planks, and sawed timber, and forming them into rafts. The trees were literally drawn and quartered there. In forming the rafts, they use the lower three feet of hard-wood saplings, which have a crooked and knobbed butt-end, for bolts, passing them up through holes bored in the corners and sides of the rafts, and keying them. In another apartment they were making fence-slats, such as stand all over New England, out of odds and ends, — and it may be that I saw where the picket-fence behind which I dwell at home came from. I was surprised to find a boy collecting the long edgings of boards as fast as cut off, and thrusting them down a hopper, where they were *ground up* beneath the mill, that they might be out of the way; otherwise they accumulate in vast piles by the side of the building, increasing the danger from fire, or, floating off, they obstruct the river. This was not only a saw-mill, but a grist-mill, then. The inhabitants of Oldtown, Stillwater, and Bangor cannot suffer for want of kindling stuff, surely. Some get their living exclusively by picking up the drift-wood and selling it by the cord in the winter. In one place I saw where an Irishman, who keeps a team and a man for the purpose, had covered the shore for a long distance with regular piles, and I was told that he had sold twelve hundred dollars' worth in a year. Another, who lived by the shore, told me that he got all the material of his out-buildings and fences from the river; and in that neighborhood I perceived that this refuse wood was frequently used instead of sand to fill hollows with, being apparently cheaper than dirt.

I got my first clear view of Ktaadn, on this excursion, from a hill about two miles northwest of Bangor, whither I went for this purpose. After this I was ready to return to Massachusetts.

Humboldt has written an interesting chapter on the primitive forest, but no one has yet described for me the difference between that wild forest which once occupied our oldest townships, and the tame one which I find there to-day. It is a difference which would be worth attending to. The civilized man not only clears the land permanently to a great extent, and cultivates open fields, but he tames and cultivates to a certain extent the forest itself. By his mere presence, almost, he changes the nature of the trees as no other creature does. The sun and air, and perhaps fire, have been introduced, and grain raised where it stands. It has lost its wild, damp, and shaggy look, the countless fallen and decaying trees are gone, and consequently that thick coat of moss which lived on them is gone too. The earth is comparatively bare and smooth and dry. The most primitive places left with us are the swamps, where the spruce still grows shaggy with usnea. The surface of the ground in the Maine woods is everywhere spongy and saturated with moisture. I noticed that the plants which cover the forest floor there are such as are commonly confined to swamps with us, — the *Clintonia borealis*, orchises, creeping snowberry, and others; and the prevailing aster there is the *Aster acuminatus*, which with us grows in damp and shady woods. The asters *cordifolius* and *macrophyllus* also are common, asters of little or no color, and sometimes without petals. I saw no soft, spreading, second-growth white-pines, with smooth bark, acknowledging the presence of the woodchopper, but even the young white-pines were all tall and slender rough-barked trees.

Those Maine woods differ essentially from ours. There you are never reminded that the wilderness which you are threading is, after all, some villager's familiar wood-lot, some widow's thirds, from which her ancestors have sledded fuel for generations, minutely described in some old deed which is recorded, of which the owner has got a plan, too, and old bound-marks may be found every forty rods, if you will search. 'T is true, the map may inform you that you stand on land granted by the State to some academy, or on Bingham's purchase; but these names do not impose on you, for you see nothing to remind you of the academy or of Bingham. What were the "forests" of England to these? One writer relates of the Isle of Wight, that in Charles the Second's time "there were woods in the island so complete and extensive, that it is said a squirrel might have traveled in several parts many leagues together on the top of the trees." If it were not for the rivers (and he might go round their heads), a squirrel could here travel thus the whole breadth of the country.

We have as yet had no adequate account of a primitive pine forest. I have noticed that in a physical atlas lately published in Massachusetts, and used in our schools, the "wood land" of North America is limited almost solely to the valleys of the Ohio and some of the Great Lakes, and the great pine forests of the globe are not represented. In our vicinity, for in-stance, New Brunswick and Maine are exhibited as bare as Greenland. It may be that the children of Greenville, at the foot of Moosehead Lake, who surely are not likely to be scared by an owl, are referred to the valley of the Ohio to get an idea of a forest; but they would not know what to do with their moose, bear, caribou, beaver, etc., there. Shall we leave it to an Englishman to inform us, that "in North America, both in the United States and Canada, are the most extensive pine forests in the world"? The greater part of New Brunswick, the northern half of Maine, and adjacent parts of Canada, not to mention the northeastern part of New York and other tracts farther off, are still covered with an almost unbroken pine forest.

But Maine, perhaps, will soon be where Massachusetts is. A good part of her territory is already as bare and commonplace as much of our neighborhood, and her villages generally are not so well shaded as ours. We seem to think that the earth must go through the ordeal of sheep-pasturage before it is habitable by man. Consider Nahant, the resort of all the fashion of Boston, — which peninsula I saw but indistinctly in the twilight, when I steamed by it, and thought that it was unchanged since the discovery. John Smith described it in 1614 as "the Mattahunts, two pleasant isles of groves, gardens, and cornfields;" and others tell us that it was once well wooded, and even furnished

timber to build the wharves of Boston. Now it
is difficult to make a tree grow there, and the
visitor comes away with a vision of Mr. Tudor's
ugly fences, a rod high, designed to protect a
few pear-shrubs. And what are we coming
to in our Middlesex towns? — a bald, staring
town-house, or meeting-house, and a bare liberty-
pole, as leafless as it is fruitless, for all I can
see. We shall be obliged to import the timber
for the last, hereafter, or splice such sticks as
we have; — and our ideas of liberty are equally
mean with these. The very willow-rows lopped
every three years for fuel or powder, — and
every sizable pine and oak, or other forest tree,
cut down within the memory of man! As if
individual speculators were to be allowed to ex-
port the clouds out of the sky, or the stars out
of the firmament, one by one. We shall be reduced to gnaw the very crust of the earth for
nutriment.

They have even descended to smaller game.
They have lately, as I hear, invented a machine
for chopping up huckleberry-bushes fine, and so
converting them into fuel! — bushes which, for
fruit alone, are worth all the pear-trees in the
country many times over. (I can give you a list
of the three best kinds, if you want it.) At
this rate, we shall all be obliged to let our
beards grow at least, if only to hide the naked-

ness of the land and make a sylvan appearance. The farmer sometimes talks of "brushing up," simply as if bare ground looked better than clothed ground, than that which wears its natural vesture, — as if the wild hedges, which, perhaps, are more to his children than his whole farm beside, were *dirt*. I know of one who deserves to be called the Tree-hater, and, perhaps, to leave this for a new patronymic to his children. You would think that he had been warned by an oracle that he would be killed by the fall of a tree, and so was resolved to anticipate them. The journalists think that they cannot say too much in favor of such "improvements" in husbandry; it is a safe theme, like piety; but as for the beauty of one of these "model farms," I would as lief see a patent churn and a man turning it. They are, commonly, places merely where somebody is making money, it may be counterfeiting. The virtue of making two blades of grass grow where only one grew before does not begin to be superhuman.

Nevertheless, it was a relief to get back to our smooth, but still varied landscape. For a permanent residence, it seemed to me that there could be no comparison between this and the wilderness, necessary as the latter is for a resource and a background, the raw material of all our civilization. The wilderness is simple, almost to barrenness. The partially cultivated country it is which chiefly has inspired, and will continue to inspire, the strains of poets, such as compose the mass of any literature. Our woods are sylvan, and their inhabitants woodmen and rustics, — that is, *selvaggia*, and the inhabitants are *salvages*. A civilized man, using the word in the ordinary sense, with his ideas and associations, must at length pine there, like a cultivated plant, which clasps its fibres about a crude and undissolved mass of peat. At the extreme North, the voyagers are obliged to dance and act plays for employment. Perhaps our own woods and fields, — in the best wooded towns, where we need not quarrel about the huckleberries, — with the primitive swamps scattered here and there in their midst, but not prevailing over them, are the perfection of parks and groves, gardens, arbors, paths, vistas, and landscapes. They are the natural consequence of what art and refinement we as a people have, — the common which each village possesses, its true paradise, in comparison with which all elaborately and willfully wealth-constructed parks and gardens are paltry imitations. Or, I would rather say, such *were* our groves twenty years ago. The poet's, commonly, is not a logger's path, but a woodman's. The logger and pioneer have preceded him, like John the Baptist; eaten the wild honey, it may be, but the locusts also; banished decaying wood and the spongy mosses which feed on it, and built hearths and humanized Nature for him.

But there are spirits of a yet more liberal culture, to whom no simplicity is barren. There are not only stately pines, but fragile flowers, like the orchises, commonly described as too delicate for cultivation, which derive their nutriment from the crudest mass of peat. These remind us, that, not only for strength, but for beauty, the poet must, from time to time, travel the logger's path and the Indian's trail, to drink at some new and more bracing fountain of the Muses, far in the recesses of the wilderness.

The kings of England formerly had their forests "to hold the king's game," for sport or food, sometimes destroying villages to create or extend them; and I think that they were impelled by a true instinct. Why should not we, who have renounced the king's authority, have our national preserves, where no villages need be destroyed, in which the bear and panther, and some even of the hunter race, may still exist, and not be "civilized off the face of the earth," — our forests, not to hold the king's game merely, but to hold and preserve the king himself also, the lord of creation, — not for idle sport or food, but for inspiration and our own true recreation? or shall we, like the villains, grub them all up, poaching on our own national domains?

THE ALLEGASH AND EAST BRANCH

I STARTED on my third excursion to the
Maine woods Monday, July 20, 1857, with one
companion, arriving at Bangor the next day at
noon. We had hardly left the steamer, when
we passed Molly Molasses in the street. As
long as she lives, the Penobscots may be considered extant as a tribe. The succeeding morning, a relative of mine, who is well acquainted
with the Penobscot Indians, and who had been
my companion in my two previous excursions
into the Maine woods, took me in his wagon to
Oldtown, to assist me in obtaining an Indian
for this expedition. We were ferried across to
the Indian Island in a batteau. The ferryman's
boy had got the key to it, but the father, who
was a blacksmith, after a little hesitation cut
the chain with a cold-chisel on the rock. He
told me that the Indians were nearly all gone to
the seaboard and to Massachusetts, partly on
account of the small-pox, of which they are very
much afraid, having broken out in Oldtown,
and it was doubtful whether we should find a
suitable one at home. The old chief Neptune,

however, was there still. The first man we saw
on the island was an Indian named Joseph
Polis, whom my relative had known from a boy,
and now addressed familiarly as "Joe." He
was dressing a deer-skin in his yard. The skin
was spread over a slanting log, and he was
scraping it with a stick, held by both hands.
He was stoutly built, perhaps a little above the
middle height, with a broad face, and, as others
said, perfect Indian features and complexion.
His house was a two-story white one, with
blinds, the best looking that I noticed there,
and as good as an average one on a New England village street. It was surrounded by a
garden and fruit-trees, single cornstalks standing thinly amid the beans. We asked him if
he knew any good Indian who would like to go
into the woods with us, that is, to the Allegash
Lakes, by way of Moosehead, and return by the
East Branch of the Penobscot, or vary from this
as we pleased. To which he answered, out of
that strange remoteness in which the Indian ever
dwells to the white man, "Me like to go myself;
me want to get some moose;" and kept on
scraping the skin. His brother had been into
the woods with my relative only a year or two
before, and the Indian now inquired what the
latter had done to him, that he did not come
back, for he had not seen nor heard from him
since.

At length we got round to the more interesting topic again. The ferryman had told us that all the best Indians were gone except Polis, who was one of the aristocracy. He to be sure would be the best man we could have, but if he went at all would want a great price; so we did not expect to get him. Polis asked at first two dollars a day, but agreed to go for a dollar and a half, and fifty cents a week for his canoe. He would come to Bangor with his canoe by the seven o'clock train that evening, — we might depend on him. We thought ourselves lucky to secure the services of this man, who was known to be particularly steady and trustworthy.

I spent the afternoon with my companion, who had remained in Bangor, in preparing for our expedition, purchasing provisions, hard bread, pork, coffee, sugar, etc., and some India-rubber clothing.

We had at first thought of exploring the St. John from its source to its mouth, or else to go up the Penobscot by its East Branch to the lakes of the St. John, and return by way of Chesuncook and Moosehead. We had finally inclined to the last route, only reversing the order of it, going by way of Moosehead, and returning by the Penobscot, otherwise it would have been all the way up stream and taken twice as long.

At evening the Indian arrived in the cars, and I led the way while he followed me three quarters of a mile to my friend's house, with the canoe on his head. I did not know the exact route myself, but steered by the lay of the land, as I do in Boston, and I tried to enter into conversation with him, but as he was puffing under the weight of his canoe, not having the usual apparatus for carrying it, but, above all, was an Indian, I might as well have been thumping on the bottom of his birch the while. In answer to the various observations which I made by way of breaking the ice, he only grunted vaguely from beneath his canoe once or twice, so that I knew he was there.

Early the next morning (July 23) the stage called for us, the Indian having breakfasted with us, and already placed the baggage in the canoe to see how it would go. My companion and I had each a large knapsack as full as it would hold, and we had two large India-rubber bags which held our provision and utensils. As for the Indian, all the baggage he had, beside his axe and gun, was a blanket, which he brought loose in his hand. However, he had laid in a store of tobacco and a new pipe for the excursion. The canoe was securely lashed diagonally across the top of the stage, with bits of carpet tucked under the edge to prevent its

chafing. The very accommodating driver appeared as much accustomed to carrying canoes
in this way as bandboxes.

At the Bangor House we took in four men
bound on a hunting excursion, one of the men
going as cook. They had a dog, a middling-
sized brindled cur, which ran by the side of the
stage, his master showing his head and whistling from time to time; but after we had gone
about three miles the dog was suddenly missing,
and two of the party went back for him, while
the stage, which was full of passengers, waited.
I suggested that he had taken the back track
for the Bangor House. At length one man
came back, while the other kept on. This
whole party of hunters declared their intention
to stop till the dog was found; but the very
obliging driver was ready to wait a spell longer.
He was ·evidently unwilling to lose so many
passengers, who would have taken a private
conveyance, or perhaps the other line of stages,
the next day. Such progress did we make with
a journey of over sixty miles, to be accomplished
that day, and a rain-storm just setting in. We
discussed the subject of dogs and their instincts
till it was threadbare, while we waited there, and
the scenery of the suburbs of Bangor is still
distinctly impressed on my memory. After full
half an hour the man returned, leading the dog

by a rope. He had overtaken him just as he was entering the Bangor House. He was then tied on the top of the stage, but being wet and cold, several times in the course of the journey he jumped off, and I saw him dangling by his neck. This dog was depended on to stop bears with. He had already stopped one somewhere in New Hampshire, and I can testify that he stopped a stage in Maine. This party of four probably paid nothing for the dog's ride, nor for his run, while our party of three paid two dollars, and were charged four for the light canoe which lay still on the top.

It soon began to rain, and grew more and more stormy as the day advanced. This was the third time that I had passed over this route, and it rained steadily each time all day. We accordingly saw but little of the country. The stage was crowded all the way, and I attended the more to my fellow-travelers. If you had looked inside this coach you would have thought that we were prepared to run the gauntlet of a band of robbers, for there were four or five guns on the front seat, the Indian's included, and one or two on the back one, each man holding his darling in his arms. One had a gun which carried twelve to a pound. It appeared that this party of hunters was going our way, but much farther down the Allegash and St. John, and thence up some other stream, and across to the Ristigouche and the Bay of Chaleur, to be gone six weeks. They had canoes, axes, and supplies deposited some distance along the route. They carried flour, and were to have new bread made every day. Their leader was a handsome man about thirty years old, of good height, but not apparently robust, of gentlemanly address and faultless toilet; such a one as you might expect to meet on Broadway. In fact, in the popular sense of the word, he was the most "gentlemanly" appearing man in the stage, or that we saw on the road. He had a fair white complexion, as if he had always lived in the shade, and an intellectual face, and with his quiet manners might have passed for a divinity student who had seen something of the world. I was surprised to find, on talking with him in the course of the day's journey, that he was a hunter at all, — for his gun was not much exposed, — and yet more to find that he was probably the chief white hunter of Maine, and was known all along the road. He had also hunted in some of the States farther south and west. I afterwards heard him spoken of as one who could endure a great deal of exposure and fatigue without showing the effect of it; and he could not only use guns, but make them, being himself a gunsmith. In the spring, he had saved a stage-driver and two passengers from drowning in the backwater of the Piscataquis in Foxcroft on this road, having swum ashore in the freezing water and made a raft and got them off, — though the horses were drowned, — at great risk to himself, while the only other man who could swim withdrew to the nearest house to prevent freezing. He could now ride over this road for nothing. He knew our man, and remarked that we had a good Indian there, a good hunter; adding that he was said to be worth $6000. The Indian also knew him, and said to me, "the great hunter."

The former told me that he practiced a kind of still hunting, new or uncommon in those parts; that the caribou, for instance, fed round and round the same meadow, returning on the same path, and he lay in wait for them.

The Indian sat on the front seat, saying nothing to anybody, with a stolid expression of face, as if barely awake to what was going on. Again I was struck by the peculiar vagueness of his replies when addressed in the stage, or at the taverns. He really never said anything on such occasions. He was merely stirred up, like a wild beast, and passively muttered some insignificant response. His answer, in such cases, was never the consequence of a positive mental energy, but vague as a puff of smoke, suggesting no *responsibility*, and if you considered it, you would find that you had got nothing out of him. This was instead of the conventional palaver and smartness of the white man, and equally profitable. Most get no more than this out of the Indian, and pronounce him stolid accordingly. I was surprised to see what a foolish and impertinent style a Maine man, a passenger, used in addressing him, as if he were a child, which only made his eyes glisten a little. A tipsy Canadian asked him at a tavern, in a drawling tone, if he smoked, to which he answered with an indefinite "yes." "Won't you lend me your pipe a little while?" asked the other. He replied, looking straight by the man's head, with a face singularly vacant to all neighboring interests, "Me got no pipe;" yet I had seen him put a new one, with a supply of tobacco, into his pocket that morning.

Our little canoe, so neat and strong, drew a favorable criticism from all the wiseacres among the tavern loungers along the road. By the roadside, close to the wheels, I noticed a splendid great purple-fringed orchis with a spike as big as an epilobium, which I would fain have stopped the stage to pluck, but as this had never been known to stop a bear, like the cur on the stage, the driver would probably have thought it a waste of time.

When we reached the lake, about half past eight in the evening, it was still steadily raining, and harder than before; and, in that fresh, cool atmosphere, the hylodes were peeping and the toads singing about the lake universally, as in the spring with us. It was as if the season had revolved backward two or three months, or I had arrived at the abode of perpetual spring.

We had expected to go upon the lake at once, and, after paddling up two or three miles, to camp on one of its islands; but on account of the steady and increasing rain, we decided to go to one of the taverns for the night, though, for my own part, I should have preferred to camp out.

About four o'clock the next morning (July 24), though it was quite cloudy, accompanied by the landlord to the water's edge, in the twilight, we launched our canoe from a rock on the Moosehead Lake. When I was there four years before, we had a rather small canoe for three persons, and I had thought that this time I would get a larger one, but the present one was even smaller than that. It was $18\frac{1}{4}$ feet long by 2 feet $6\frac{1}{2}$ inches wide in the middle, and one foot deep within, so I found by measurement, and I judged that it would weigh not far from eighty pounds. The Indian had recently made it himself, and its smallness was partly compensated for by its newness, as well as stanchness and solidity, it being made of very thick bark and ribs. Our baggage weighed about 166 pounds, so that the canoe carried about 600 pounds in all, or the weight of four men. The principal part of the baggage was, as usual, placed in the middle of the broadest part, while we stowed ourselves in the chinks and crannies that were left before and behind it, where there was no room to extend our legs, the loose articles being tucked into the ends. The canoe was thus as closely packed as a market-basket, and might possibly have been upset without spilling any of its contents. The Indian sat on a cross-bar in the stern, but we flat on the bottom, with a splint or chip behind our backs, to protect them from the cross-bar, and one of us commonly paddled with the Indian. He foresaw that we should not want a pole till we reached the Umbazookskus River, it being either dead water or down stream so far, and he was prepared to make a sail of his blanket in the bows if the wind should be fair; but we never used it.

It had rained more or less the four previous days, so that we thought we might count on some fair weather. The wind was at first southwesterly.

Paddling along the eastern side of the lake in the still of the morning, we soon saw a few sheldrakes, which the Indian called *Shecorways*, and some peetweets, *Naramekechus*, on the rocky shore; we also saw and heard loons, *Medawisla*, which he said was a sign of wind. It was inspiriting to hear the regular dip of the paddles, as if they were our fins or flippers, and to realize that we were at length fairly embarked. We who had felt strangely as stage-passengers and tavern-lodgers were suddenly naturalized there and presented with the freedom of the lakes and the woods. Having passed the small rocky isles within two or three miles of the foot of the lake, we had a short consultation respecting our course, and inclined to the western shore for the sake of its lee; for otherwise, if the wind should rise, it would be impossible for us to reach Mount Kineo, which is about midway up the lake on the east side, but at its narrowest part, where probably we could recross if we took the western side. The wind is the chief obstacle to crossing the lakes, especially in so small a canoe. The Indian remarked several times that he did not like to cross the lakes "in littlum canoe," but nevertheless, "just as we say, it made no odds to him." He sometimes took a straight course up the middle of the lake between Sugar and Deer islands, when there was no wind.

Measured on the map, Moosehead Lake is

twelve miles wide at the widest place, and thirty miles long in a direct line, but longer as it lies. The captain of the steamer called it thirty-eight miles as he steered. We should probably go about forty. The Indian said that it was called "*Mspame*, because large water." Squaw Mountain rose darkly on our left, near the outlet of the Kennebec, and what the Indian called Spencer Bay Mountain, on the east, and already we saw Mount Kineo before us in the north.

Paddling near the shore, we frequently heard the *pe-pe* of the olive-sided flycatcher, also the wood-pewee, and the kingfisher, thus early in the morning. The Indian reminding us that he could not work without eating, we stopped to breakfast on the main shore, southwest of Deer Island, at a spot where the *Mimulus ringens* grew abundantly. We took out our bags, and the Indian made a fire under a very large bleached log, using white-pine bark from a stump, though he said that hemlock was better, and kindling with canoe-birch bark. Our table was a large piece of freshly peeled birch-bark, laid wrong side up, and our breakfast consisted of hard bread, fried pork, and strong coffee, well sweetened, in which we did not miss the milk.

While we were getting breakfast a brood of twelve black dippers, half grown, came paddling by within three or four rods, not at all alarmed; and they loitered about as long as we stayed, now huddled close together, within a circle of eighteen inches in diameter, now moving off in a long line, very cunningly. Yet they bore a certain proportion to the great Moosehead Lake on whose bosom they floated, and I felt as if they were under its protection.

Looking northward from this place it appeared as if we were entering a large bay, and we did not know whether we should be obliged to diverge from our course and keep outside a point which we saw, or should find a passage between this and the mainland. I consulted my map and used my glass, and the Indian did the same, but we could not find our place exactly on the map, nor could we detect any break in the shore. When I asked the Indian the way, he answered "I don't know," which I thought remarkable, since he had said that he was familiar with the lake; but it appeared that he had never been up this side. It was misty dog-day weather, and we had already penetrated a smaller bay of the same kind, and knocked the bottom out of it, though we had been obliged to pass over a small bar, between an island and the shore, where there was but just breadth and depth enough to float the canoe, and the Indian had observed, "Very easy makum bridge here," but now it seemed that, if we held on, we should be fairly embayed. Presently, however, though we had not stirred, the mist lifted somewhat, and revealed a break in the shore northward, showing that the point was a portion of Deer Island, and that our course lay westward of it. Where it had seemed a continuous shore even through a glass, one portion was now seen by the naked eye to be much more distant than the other which overlapped it, merely by the greater thickness of the mist which still rested on it, while the nearer or island portion was comparatively bare and green. The line of separation was very distinct, and the Indian immediately remarked, "I guess you and I go there, — I guess there's room for my canoe there." This was his common expression instead of saying we. He never addressed us by our names, though curious to know how they were spelled and what they meant, while we called him Polis. He had already guessed very accurately at our ages, and said that he was forty-eight.

After breakfast I emptied the melted pork that was left into the lake, making what sailors call a "slick," and watching to see how much it spread over and smoothed the agitated surface. The Indian looked at it a moment and said, "That make hard paddlum thro'; hold 'em canoe. So say old times."

We hastily reloaded, putting the dishes loose in the bows, that they might be at hand when wanted, and set out again. The western shore, near which we paddled along, rose gently to a considerable height, and was everywhere densely covered with the forest, in which was a large proportion of hard wood to enliven and relieve the fir and spruce.

The Indian said that the usnea lichen which we saw hanging from the trees was called *chor-chorque*. We asked him the names of several small birds which we heard this morning. The wood-thrush, which was quite common, and whose note he imitated, he said was called *Adelungquamooktum ;* but sometimes he could not tell the name of some small bird which I heard and knew, but he said, "I tell all the birds about here, — this country ; can't tell lit-tlum noise, but I see 'em, then I can tell."

I observed that I should like to go to school to him to learn his language, living on the Indian island the while ; could not that be done? "Oh, yer," he replied, "good many do so." I asked how long he thought it would take. He said one week. I told him that in this voyage I would tell him all I knew, and he should tell me all he knew, to which he readily agreed.

The birds sang quite as in our woods, — the red-eye, red-start, veery, wood-pewee, etc., but we saw no bluebirds in all our journey, and several told me in Bangor that they had not the bluebird there. Mount Kineo, which was generally visible, though occasionally concealed by islands or the mainland in front, had a level bar of cloud concealing its summit, and all the mountain-tops about the lake were cut off at the same height. Ducks of various kinds, — sheldrake, summer ducks, etc., — were quite common, and ran over the water before us as fast as a horse trots. Thus they were soon out of sight.

The Indian asked the meaning of *reality*, as near as I could make out the word, which he said one of us had used; also of "*interrent*," that is, intelligent. I observed that he could rarely sound the letter r, but used l, as also r for l sometimes; as *load* for road, *pickelel* for pickerel, *Soogle* Island for Sugar Island, *lock* for rock, etc. Yet he trilled the r pretty well after me.

He generally added the syllable *um* to his words when he could, — as pad*lum*, etc. I have once heard a Chippewa lecture, who made his audience laugh unintentionally by putting *ne* after the word *too*, which word he brought in continually and unnecessarily, accenting and prolonging this sound into *m ar* sonorously as if it were necessary to bring in so much of his

vernacular as a relief to his organs, a compensation for twisting his jaws about, and putting
his tongue into every corner of his mouth, as he
complained that he was obliged to do when he
spoke English.   There was so much of the Indian accent resounding through his English, so
much of the "bow-arrow tang" as my neighbor
calls it, and I have no doubt that word seemed
to him the best pronounced.   It was a wild and
refreshing sound, like that of the wind among
the pines, or the booming of the surf on the
shore.

I asked him the meaning of the word *Musketicook*, the Indian name of Concord River.
He pronounced it *Muskéeticook*, emphasizing
the second syllable with a peculiar guttural
sound, and said that it meant "Dead-water,"
which it is, and in this definition he agreed exactly with the St. Francis Indian with whom I
talked in 1853.

On a point on the mainland some miles southwest of Sand-bar Island, where we landed to
stretch our legs and look at the vegetation, going inland a few steps, I discovered a fire still
glowing beneath its ashes, where somebody had
breakfasted, and a bed of twigs prepared for the
following night.   So I knew not only that they
had just left, but that they designed to return,
and by the breadth of the bed that there was

more than one in the party. You might have
gone within six feet of these signs without seeing them. There grew the beaked hazel, the
only hazel which I saw on this journey, the
Diervilla, rue seven feet high, which was very
abundant on all the lake and river shores, and
Cornus stolonifera, or red osier, whose bark,
the Indian said, was good to smoke, and was
called *maquoxigill*, "tobacco before white people
came to this country, Indian tobacco."

The Indian was always very careful in approaching the shore, lest he should injure his
canoe on the rocks, letting it swing round slowly
sidewise, and was still more particular that we
should not step into it on shore, nor till it
floated free, and then should step gently lest we
should open its seams, or make a hole in the
bottom. He said that he would tell us when to
jump.

Soon after leaving this point we passed the
mouth of the Kennebec, and heard and saw the
falls at the dam there, for even Moosehead Lake
is dammed. After passing Deer Island, we saw
the little steamer from Greenville, far east in
the middle of the lake, she appeared nearly
stationary. Sometimes we could hardly tell her
from an island which had a few trees on it.
Here we were exposed to the wind from over the
whole breadth of the lake, and ran a little risk

of being swamped. While I had my eye fixed on the spot where a large fish had leaped, we took in a gallon or two of water, which filled my lap; but we soon reached the shore and took the canoe over the bar, at Sand-bar Island, a few feet wide only, and so saved a considerable distance. One landed first at a more sheltered place, and walking round caught the canoe by the prow, to prevent it being injured against the shore.

Again we crossed a broad bay opposite the mouth of Moose River, before reaching the narrow strait at Mount Kineo, made what the voyageurs call a *traverse*, and found the water quite rough. A very little wind on these broad lakes raises a sea which will swamp a canoe. Looking off from a lee shore, the surface may appear to be very little agitated, almost smooth, a mile distant, or if you see a few white crests they appear nearly level with the rest of the lake; but when you get out so far, you may find quite a sea running, and erelong, before you think of it, a wave will gently creep up the side of the canoe and fill your lap, like a monster deliberately covering you with its slime before it swallows you, or it will strike the canoe violently, and break into it. The same thing may happen when the wind rises suddenly, though it were perfectly calm and smooth there a few minutes before; so that nothing can save you, unless you can swim ashore, for it is impossible to get into a canoe again when it is upset. Since you sit flat on the bottom, though the danger should not be imminent, a little water is a great inconvenience, not to mention the wetting of your provisions. We rarely crossed even a bay directly, from point to point, when there was wind, but made a slight curve corresponding somewhat to the shore, that we might the sooner reach it if the wind increased.

When the wind is aft, and not too strong, the Indian makes a sprit-sail of his blanket. He thus easily skims over the whole length of this lake in a day.

The Indian paddled on one side, and one of us on the other, to keep the canoe steady, and when he wanted to change hands he would say "t' other side." He asserted, in answer to our questions, that he had never upset a canoe himself, though he may have been upset by others.

Think of our little eggshell of a canoe tossing across that great lake, a mere black speck to the eagle soaring above it.

My companion trailed for trout as we paddled along, but the Indian warning him that a big fish might upset us, for there are some very large ones there, he agreed to pass the line quickly to him in the stern if he had a bite.

Beside trout, I heard of cusk, white-fish, etc., as found in this lake.

While we were crossing this bay, where Mount Kineo rose dark before us, within two or three miles, the Indian repeated the tradition respecting this mountain's having anciently been a cow moose, — how a mighty Indian hunter, whose name I forget, succeeding in killing this queen of the moose tribe with great difficulty, while her calf was killed somewhere among the islands in Penobscot Bay, and, to his eyes, this mountain had still the form of the moose in a reclining posture, its precipitous side presenting the outline of her head. He told this at some length, though it did not amount to much, and with apparent good faith, and asked us how we supposed the hunter could have killed such a mighty moose as that, — how we could do it. Whereupon a man-of-war to fire broadsides into her was suggested, etc. An Indian tells such a story as if he thought it deserved to have a good deal said about it, only he has not got it to say, and so he makes up for the deficiency by a drawling tone, long-windedness, and a dumb wonder which he hopes will be contagious.

We approached the land again through pretty rough water, and then steered directly across the lake, at its narrowest part, to the eastern side, and were soon partly under the lee of the mountain, about a mile north of the Kineo House, having paddled about twenty miles. It was now about noon.

We designed to stop there that afternoon and night, and spent half an hour looking along the shore northward for a suitable place to camp. We took out all our baggage at one place in vain, it being too rocky and uneven, and while engaged in this search we made our first acquaintance with the moose-fly. At length, half a mile farther north, by going half a dozen rods into the dense spruce and fir wood on the side of the mountain, almost as dark as a cellar, we found a place sufficiently clear and level to lie down on, after cutting away a few bushes. We required a space only seven feet by six for our bed, the fire being four or five feet in front, though it made no odds how rough the hearth was; but it was not always easy to find this in those woods. The Indian first cleared a path to it from the shore with his axe, and we then carried up all our baggage, pitched our tent, and made our bed, in order to be ready for foul weather, which then threatened us, and for the night. He gathered a large armful of fir twigs, breaking them off, which he said were the best for our bed, partly, I thought, because they were the largest and could be most rapidly collected. It had been raining more or less for four or five days, and the wood was even damper than usual, but he got dry bark for the fire from the under side of a dead leaning hemlock, which, he said, he could always do.

This noon his mind was occupied with a law question, and I referred him to my companion, who was a lawyer. It appeared that he had been buying land lately (I think it was a hundred acres), but there was probably an incumbrance to it, somebody else claiming to have bought some grass on it for this year. He wished to know to whom the grass belonged, and was told that if the other man could prove that he bought the grass before he, Polis, bought the land, the former could take it, whether the latter knew it or not. To which he only answered, "Strange!" He went over this several times, fairly sat down to it, with his back to a tree, as if he meant to confine us to this topic henceforth; but as he made no headway, only reached the jumping-off place of his wonder at white men's institutions after each explanation, we let the subject die.

He said that he had fifty acres of grass, potatoes, etc., somewhere above Oldtown, beside some about his house; that he hired a good deal of his work, hoeing, etc., and preferred white men to Indians, because "they keep steady, and know how."

After dinner we returned southward along the shore, in the canoe, on account of the difficulty of climbing over the rocks and fallen trees, and began to ascend the mountain along the edge of the precipice.   But a smart shower coming up just then, the Indian crept under his canoe, while we, being protected by our rubber coats, proceeded to botanize.   So we sent him back to the camp for shelter, agreeing that he should come there for us with his canoe toward night. It had rained a little in the forenoon, and we trusted that this would be the clearing-up shower, which it proved; but our feet and legs were thoroughly wet by the bushes.   The clouds breaking away a little, we had a glorious wild view, as we ascended, of the broad lake with its fluctuating surface and numerous forest-clad islands, extending beyond our sight both north and south, and the boundless forest undulating away from its shores on every side, as densely packed as a rye-field, and enveloping nameless mountains in succession; but above all, looking westward over a large island was visible a very distant part of the lake, though we did not then suspect it to be Moosehead, — at first a mere broken white line seen through the tops of the island trees, like hay-caps, but spreading to a lake when we got higher.   Beyond this we saw what appears to be called Bald Mountain on the map, some twenty-five miles distant, near the sources of the Penobscot. It was a perfect lake of the woods. But this was only a transient gleam, for the rain was not quite over.

Looking southward, the heavens were completely overcast, the mountains capped with clouds, and the lake generally wore a dark and stormy appearance, but from its surface just north of Sugar Island, six or eight miles distant, there was reflected upward to us through the misty air a bright blue tinge from the distant unseen sky of another latitude beyond. They probably had a clear sky then at Greenville, the south end of the lake. Standing on a mountain in the midst of a lake, where would you look for the first sign of approaching fair weather? Not into the heavens, it seems, but into the lake.

Again we mistook a little rocky islet seen through the "drisk," with some taller bare trunks or stumps on it, for the steamer with its smoke-pipes, but as it had not changed its position after half an hour, we were undeceived. So much do the works of man resemble the works of nature. A moose might mistake a steamer for a floating isle, and not be scared till he heard its puffing or its whistle.

If I wished to see a mountain or other scenery under the most favorable auspices, I would go to it in foul weather, so as to be there when it cleared up; we are then in the most suitable mood, and nature is most fresh and inspiring. There is no serenity so fair as that which is just established in a tearful eye.

Jackson, in his Report on the Geology of Maine, in 1838, says of this mountain: "Hornstone, which will answer for flints, occurs in various parts of the State, where trap-rocks have acted upon silicious slate. The largest mass of this stone known in the world is Mount Kineo, upon Moosehead Lake, which appears to be entirely composed of it, and rises seven hundred feet above the lake level. This variety of hornstone I have seen in every part of New England in the form of Indian arrow-heads, hatchets, chisels, etc., which were probably obtained from this mountain by the aboriginal inhabitants of the country." I have myself found hundreds of arrow-heads made of the same material. It is generally slate-colored, with white specks, becoming a uniform white where exposed to the light and air, and it breaks with a conchoidal fracture, producing a ragged cutting edge. I noticed some conchoidal hollows more than a foot in diameter. I picked up a small thin piece which had so sharp an edge that I used it as a dull knife, and to see what I could do, fairly cut off an aspen one inch

thick with it, by bending it and making many
cuts; though I cut my fingers badly with the
back of it in the mean while.

From the summit of the precipice which forms
the southern and eastern sides of this mountain
peninsula, and is its most remarkable feature,
being described as five or six hundred feet high,
we looked, and probably might have jumped
down to the water, or to the seemingly dwarfish
trees on the narrow neck of land which connects
it with the main. It is a dangerous place to try
the steadiness of your nerves. Hodge says that
these cliffs descend "perpendicularly ninety
feet" below the surface of the water.

The plants which chiefly attracted our attention on this mountain were the mountain cinquefoil (*Potentilla tridentata*), abundant and in
bloom still at the very base, by the water-side,
though it is usually confined to the summits of
mountains in our latitude; very beautiful harebells overhanging the precipice; bear-berry;
the Canada blueberry (*Vaccinium Canadense*),
similar to (the *V. Pennsylvanicum*) our earliest
one, but entire leaved and with a downy stem
and leaf; I have not seen it in Massachusetts;
Diervilla trifida; Microstylis ophioglossoides,
an orchidaceous plant new to us; wild holly
(*Nemopanthes Canadensis*); the great round-
leaved orchis (*Platanthera orbiculata*), not long

in bloom; *Spiranthes cernua*, at the top; bunch-berry, reddening as we ascended, green at the base of the mountain, red at the top; and the small fern, *Woodsia ilvensis*, growing in tufts, now in fruit. I have also received *Liparis liliifolia*, or tway-blade, from this spot. Having explored the wonders of the mountain, and the weather being now entirely cleared up, we commenced the descent. We met the Indian, puffing and panting, about one third of the way up, but thinking that he must be near the top, and saying that it took his breath away. I thought that superstition had something to do with his fatigue. Perhaps he believed that he was climbing over the back of a tremendous moose. He said that he had never ascended Kineo. On reaching the canoe we found that he had caught a lake trout weighing about three pounds, at the depth of twenty-five or thirty feet, while we were on the mountain.

When we got to the camp, the canoe was taken out and turned over, and a log laid across it to prevent its being blown away. The Indian cut some large logs of damp and rotten hard wood to smoulder and keep fire through the night. The trout was fried for supper. Our tent was of thin cotton cloth and quite small, forming with the ground a triangular prism closed at the rear end, six feet long, seven wide, and four high, so that we could barely sit up in the middle. It required two forked stakes, a smooth ridge-pole, and a dozen or more pins to pitch it. It kept off dew and wind, and an ordinary rain, and answered our purpose well enough. We reclined within it till bedtime, each with his baggage at his head, or else sat about the fire, having hung our wet clothes on a pole before the fire for the night.

As we sat there, just before night, looking out through the dusky wood, the Indian heard a noise which he said was made by a snake. He imitated it at my request, making a low whistling note,— *pheet — pheet,*-- two or three times repeated, somewhat like the peep of the hylodes, but not so loud. In answer to my inquiries, he said that he had never seen them while making it, but going to the spot he finds the snake. This, he said on another occasion, was a sign of rain. When I had selected this place for our camp, he had remarked that there were snakes there, — he saw them. But they won't do any hurt, I said. "Oh, no," he answered, "just as you say, it makes no difference to me."

He lay on the right side of the tent, because, as he said, he was partly deaf in one ear, and he wanted to lie with his good ear up. As we lay there, he inquired if I ever heard "Indian sing." I replied that I had not often, and asked him if he would not favor us with a song. He readily assented, and lying on his back, with his blanket wrapped around him, he commenced a slow, somewhat nasal, yet musical chant, in his own language, which probably was taught his tribe long ago by the Catholic missionaries. He translated it to us, sentence by sentence, afterward, wishing to see if we could remember it. It proved to be a very simple religious exercise or hymn, the burden of which was, that there was only one God who ruled all the world. This was hammered (or sung) out very thin, so that some stanzas wellnigh meant nothing at all, merely keeping up the idea. He then said that he would sing us a Latin song; but we did not detect any Latin, only one or two Greek words in it, — the rest may have been Latin with the Indian pronunciation.

His singing carried me back to the period of the discovery of America, to San Salvador and the Incas, when Europeans first encountered the simple faith of the Indian. There was, indeed, a beautiful simplicity about it; nothing of the dark and savage, only the mild and infantile. The sentiments of humility and reverence chiefly were expressed.

It was a dense and damp spruce and fir wood in which we lay, and, except for our fire, perfectly dark; and when I awoke in the night, I

either heard an owl from deeper in the forest
behind us, or a loon from a distance over the
lake. Getting up some time after midnight to
collect the scattered brands together, while my
companions were sound asleep, I observed,
partly in the fire, which had ceased to blaze, a
perfectly regular elliptical ring of light, about
five inches in its shortest diameter, six or seven
in its longer, and from one eighth to one quarter
of an inch wide. It was fully as bright as the
fire, but not reddish or scarlet, like a coal, but
a white and slumbering light, like the glow-
worm's. I could tell it from the fire only by its
whiteness. I saw at once that it must be phosphorescent wood, which I had so often heard of,
but never chanced to see. Putting my finger
on it, with a little hesitation, I found that it
was a piece of dead moose-wood (*Acer striatum*)
which the Indian had cut off in a slanting direction the evening before. Using my knife, I discovered that the light proceeded from that portion of the sap-wood immediately under the
bark, and thus presented a regular ring at the
end, which, indeed, appeared raised above the
level of the wood, and when I pared off the bark
and cut into the sap, it was all aglow along the
log. I was surprised to find the wood quite
hard and apparently sound, though probably
decay had commenced in the sap, and I cut out

some little triangular chips, and, placing them in the hollow of my hand, carried them into the camp, waked my companion, and showed them to him. They lit up the inside of my hand, revealing the lines and wrinkles, and appearing exactly like coals of fire raised to a white heat, and I saw at once how, probably, the Indian jugglers had imposed on their people and on travelers, pretending to hold coals of fire in their mouths.

I also noticed that part of a decayed stump within four or five feet of the fire, an inch wide and six inches long, soft and shaking wood, shone with equal brightness.

I neglected to ascertain whether our fire had anything to do with this, but the previous day's rain and long-continued wet weather undoubtedly had.

I was exceedingly interested by this phenomenon, and already felt paid for my journey. It could hardly have thrilled me more if it had taken the form of letters, or of the human face. If I had met with this ring of light while groping in this forest alone, away from any fire, I should have been still more surprised. I little thought that there was such a light shining in the darkness of the wilderness for me.

The next day the Indian told me their name for this light, — *Artoosoqu'*, — and on my in-

quiring concerning the will-o'-the-wisp, and the
like phenomena, he said that his "folks" sometimes saw fires passing along at various heights,
even as high as the trees, and making a noise.
I was prepared after this to hear of the most
startling and unimagined phenomena, witnessed
by "his folks;" they are abroad at all hours and
seasons in scenes so unfrequented by white men.
Nature must have made a thousand revelations
to them which are still secrets to us.

I did not regret my not having seen this
before, since I now saw it under circumstances
so favorable. I was in just the frame of mind
to see something wonderful, and this was a phenomenon adequate to my circumstances and expectation, and it put me on the alert to see
more like it. I exulted like "a pagan suckled
in a creed" that had never been worn at all,
but was bran new, and adequate to the occasion. I let science slide, and rejoiced in that
light as if it had been a fellow-creature. I saw
that it was excellent, and was very glad to know
that it was so cheap. A scientific *explanation*,
as it is called, would have been altogether out
of place there. That is for pale daylight. Science with its retorts would have put me to sleep;
it was the opportunity to be ignorant that I improved. It suggested to me that there was
something to be seen if one had eyes. It made

a believer of me more than before. I believed that the woods were not tenantless, but choke-full of honest spirits as good as myself any day, — not an empty chamber, in which chemistry was left to work alone, but an inhabited house, — and for a few moments I enjoyed fellowship with them. Your so-called wise man goes trying to persuade himself that there is no entity there but himself and his traps, but it is a great deal easier to believe the truth. It suggested, too, that the same experience always gives birth to the same sort of belief or religion. One revelation has been made to the Indian, another to the white man. I have much to learn of the Indian, nothing of the missionary. I am not sure but all that would tempt me to teach the Indian my religion would be his promise to teach me *his*. Long enough I had heard of irrelevant things; now at length I was glad to make acquaintance with the light that dwells in rotten wood. Where is all your knowledge gone to? It evaporates completely, for it has no depth.

I kept those little chips and wet them again the next night, but they emitted no light.

SATURDAY, *July* 25.

At breakfast this Saturday morning, the Indian, evidently curious to know what would be expected of him the next day, whether we should go along or not, asked me how I spent the Sunday when at home. I told him that I commonly sat in my chamber reading, etc., in the forenoon, and went to walk in the afternoon. At which he shook his head and said, "Er, that is ver bad." "How do you spend it?" I asked. He said that he did no work, that he went to church at Oldtown when he was at home; in short, he did as he had been taught by the whites. This led to a discussion in which I found myself in the minority. He stated that he was a Protestant, and asked me if I was. I did not at first know what to say, but I thought that I could answer with truth that I was.

When we were washing the dishes in the lake, many fishes, apparently chivin, came close up to us to get the particles of grease.

The weather seemed to be more settled this morning, and we set out early in order to finish our voyage up the lake before the wind arose. Soon after starting, the Indian directed our attention to the northeast carry, which we could plainly see, about thirteen miles distant in that direction as measured on the map, though it is called much farther. This carry is a rude wooden railroad, running north and south about two miles, perfectly straight, from the lake to the Penobscot, through a low tract, with a clearing three or four rods wide; but low as it is, it passes over the height of land there. This opening appeared as a clear bright, or light point in the horizon, resting on the edge of the lake, whose breadth a hair could have covered at a considerable distance from the eye, and of no appreciable height. We should not have suspected it to be visible if the Indian had not drawn our attention to it. It was a remarkable kind of light to steer for, — daylight seen through a vista in the forest, — but visible as far as an ordinary beacon at night.

We crossed a deep and wide bay which makes eastward north of Kineo, leaving an island on our left, and keeping up the eastern side of the lake. This way or that led to some Tomhegan or *Socatarian* stream, up which the Indian had hunted, and whither I longed to go. The last name, however, had a bogus sound, too much like sectarian for me, as if a missionary had tampered with it; but I knew that the Indians were very liberal. I think I should have inclined to the Tomhegan first.

We then crossed another broad bay, which, as we could no longer observe the shore particularly, afforded ample time for conversation. The Indian said that he had got his money by hunting, mostly high up the west branch of the Penobscot, and toward the head of the

St. John; he had hunted there from a boy, and knew all about that region. His game had been, beaver, otter, black cat (or fisher), sable, moose, etc. Loup cervier (or Canada lynx) were plenty yet in burnt grounds. For food in the woods, he uses partridges, ducks, dried moose meat, hedge-hog, etc. Loons, too, were good, only "bile 'em good." He told us at some length how he had suffered from starvation when a mere lad, being overtaken by winter when hunting with two grown Indians in the northern part of Maine, and obliged to leave their canoe on account of ice.

Pointing into the bay, he said that it was the way to various lakes which he knew. Only solemn bear-haunted mountains, with their great wooded slopes, were visible; where, as man is not, we suppose some other power to be. My imagination personified the slopes themselves, as if by their very length they would waylay you, and compel you to camp again on them before night. Some invisible glutton would seem to drop from the trees and gnaw at the heart of the solitary hunter who threaded those woods; and yet I was tempted to walk there. The Indian said that he had been along there several times.

I asked him how he guided himself in the woods. "Oh," said he, "I can tell good many ways." When I pressed him further, he answered, "Sometimes I lookum side-hill," and he glanced toward a high hill or mountain on the eastern shore, "great difference between the north and south, see where the sun has shone most. So trees, — the large limbs bend toward south. Sometimes I lookum locks" (rocks). I asked what he saw on the rocks, but he did not describe anything in particular, answering vaguely, in a mysterious or drawling tone, "Bare locks on lake shore, — great difference between N. S. E. W. side, — can tell what the sun has shone on." "Suppose," said I, "that I should take you in a dark night, right up here into the middle of the woods a hundred miles, set you down, and turn you round quickly twenty times, could you steer straight to Oldtown?" "Oh, yer," said he, "have done pretty much same thing. I will tell you. Some years ago I met an old white hunter at Millinocket; very good hunter. He said he could go anywhere in the woods. He wanted to hunt with me that day, so we start. We chase a moose all the forenoon, round and round, till middle of afternoon, when we kill him. Then I said to him, now you go straight to camp. Don't go round and round where we've been, but go straight. He said, I can't do that, I don't know where I am. Where you think camp? I asked. He pointed so. Then I laugh at him. I take the lead and go right off the other way, cross our tracks many times, straight camp." "How do you do that?" asked I. "Oh, I can't tell *you*," he replied. "Great difference between me and white man."

It appeared as if the sources of information were so various that he did not give a distinct, conscious attention to any one, and so could not readily refer to any when questioned about it, but he found his way very much as an animal does. Perhaps what is commonly called instinct in the animal, in this case is merely a sharpened and educated sense. Often, when an Indian says, "I don't know," in regard to the route he is to take, he does not mean what a white man would by those words, for his Indian instinct may tell him still as much as the most confident white man knows. He does not carry things in his head, nor remember the route exactly like a white man, but relies on himself at the moment. Not having experienced the need of the other sort of knowledge, all labeled and arranged, he has not acquired it.

The white hunter with whom I talked in the stage knew some of the resources of the Indian. He said that he steered by the wind, or by the limbs of the hemlocks, which were largest on the south side; also sometimes, when he knew that there was a lake near, by firing his gun and listening to hear the direction and distance of the echo from over it.

The course we took over this lake, and others afterward, was rarely direct, but a succession of curves from point to point, digressing considerably into each of the bays; and this was not merely on account of the wind, for the Indian, looking toward the middle of the lake, said it was hard to go there, easier to keep near the shore, because he thus got over it by successive reaches and saw by the shore how he got along.

The following will suffice for a common experience in crossing lakes in a canoe. As the forenoon advanced, the wind increased. The last bay which we crossed before reaching the desolate pier at the northeast carry was two.or three miles over, and the wind was southwesterly. After going a third of the way, the waves had increased so as occasionally to wash into the canoe, and we saw that it was worse and worse ahead. At first we might have turned about, but were not willing to. It would have been of no use to follow the course of the shore, for not only the distance would have been much greater, but the waves ran still higher there on account of the greater sweep the wind had. At any rate it would have been dangerous now to alter our course, because the waves would have struck us at an advantage. It will not do to meet them at right angles, for then they will wash in both sides, but you must take them quartering. So the Indian stood up in the canoe, and exerted all his skill and strength for a mile or two, while I paddled right along in order to give him more steerage-way. For more than a mile he did not allow a single wave to strike the canoe as it would, but turned it quickly from this side to that, so that it would always be on or near the crest of a wave when it broke, where all its force was spent, and we merely settled down with it. At length I jumped out on to the end of the pier, against which the waves were dashing violently, in order to lighten the canoe, and catch it at the landing, which was not much sheltered; but just as I jumped we took in two or three gallons of water. I remarked to the Indian, "You managed that well," to which he replied, "Ver few men do that. Great many waves; when I look out for one, another come quick."

While the Indian went to get cedar-bark, etc., to carry his canoe with, we cooked the dinner on the shore, at this end of the carry, in the midst of a sprinkling rain.

He prepared his canoe for carrying in this wise. He took a cedar shingle or splint eighteen inches long and four or five wide, rounded at one end, that the corners might not be in the way, and tied it with cedar-bark by two holes made midway, near the edge on each side, to the middle cross-bar of the canoe. When the canoe was lifted upon his head bottom up, this shingle, with its rounded end uppermost, distributed the weight over his shoulders and head, while a band of cedar-bark, tied to the cross-bar on each side of the shingle, passed round his breast, and another longer one, outside of the last, round his forehead; also a hand on each side-rail served to steer the canoe and keep it from rocking. He thus carried it with his shoulders, head, breast, forehead, and both hands, as if the upper part of his body were all one hand to clasp and hold it. If you know of a better way, I should like to hear of it. A cedar-tree furnished all the gear in this case, as it had the woodwork of the canoe. One of the paddles rested on the cross-bars in the bows. I took the canoe upon my head and found that I could carry it with ease, though the straps were not fitted to my shoulders; but I let him carry it, not caring to establish a different precedent, though he said that if I would carry the canoe, he would take all the rest of the baggage, except my companion's. This shingle remained tied to the cross-bar throughout the voyage, was always ready for the carries, and also served to protect the back of one passenger.

We were obliged to go over this carry twice, our load was so great. But the carries were an agreeable variety, and we improved the opportunity to gather the rare plants which we had seen, when we returned empty handed.

We reached the Penobscot about four o'clock, and found there some St. Francis Indians encamped on the bank, in the same place where I camped with four Indians four years before. They were making a canoe, and, as then, drying moose meat. The meat looked very suitable to make a *black* broth at least. Our Indian said it was not good. Their camp was covered with spruce-bark. They had got a young moose, taken in the river a fortnight before, confined in a sort of cage of logs piled up cobfashion, seven or eight feet high. It was quite tame, about four feet high, and covered with moose-flies. There was a large quantity of cornel (*C. stolonifera*), red maple, and also willow and aspen boughs, stuck through between the logs on all sides, butt-ends out, and on their leaves it was browsing. It looked at first as if it were in a bower rather than a pen.

Our Indian said that *he* used *black* spruce roots to sew canoes with, obtaining it from high lands or mountains. The St. Francis Indian thought that *white* spruce roots might be best. But the former said, "No good, break, can't split 'em; " also that they were hard to get, deep in ground, but the black were near the surface, on higher land, as well as tougher. He said that the white spruce was *subekoondark*, black, *skusk*. I told him I thought that I could make a canoe, but he expressed great doubt of it; at any rate, he thought that my work would not be "neat" the first time. An Indian at Greenville had told me that the winter bark, that is, bark taken off before the sap flows in May, was harder and much better than summer bark.

Having reloaded, he paddled down the Penobscot, which, as the Indian remarked, and even I detected, remembering how it looked before, was uncommonly full. We soon after saw a splendid yellow lily (*Lilium Canadense*) by the shore, which I plucked. It was six feet high, and had twelve flowers, in two whorls, forming a pyramid, such as I have seen in Concord. We afterward saw many more thus tall along this stream, and also still more numerous on the East Branch, and, on the latter, one which I thought approached yet nearer to the *Lilium superbum*. The Indian asked what we called it, and said that the "loots" (roots) were good for soup, that is, to cook with meat, to thicken it, taking the place of flour. They get them in the fall. I dug some, and found a mass of bulbs pretty deep in the earth, two inches in diameter, looking, and even tasting, somewhat like raw green corn on the ear.

When we had gone about three miles down the Penobscot, we saw through the tree-tops a thunder-shower coming up in the west, and we looked out a camping-place in good season, about five o'clock, on the west side, not far below the mouth of what Joe Aitteon, in '53, called Lobster Stream, coming from Lobster Pond. Our present Indian, however, did not admit this name, nor even that of *Matahumkeag*, which is on the map, but called the lake *Besk-abekuk*.

I will describe, once for all, the routine of camping at this season. We generally told the Indian that we would stop at the first suitable place, so that he might be on the lookout for it. Having observed a clear, hard, and flat beach to land on, free from mud, and from stones which would injure the canoe, one would run up the bank to see if there were open and level space enough for the camp between the trees, or if it could be easily cleared, preferring at the same time a cool place, on account of insects. Sometimes we paddled a mile or more before finding one to our minds, for where the shore was suitable, the bank would often be too steep, or else too low and grassy, and therefore mos-quitoey. We then took out the baggage and drew up the canoe, sometimes turning it over on shore for safety. The Indian cut a path to the spot we had selected, which was usually within two or three rods of the water, and we carried up our baggage. One, perhaps, takes canoe-birch bark, always at hand, and dead dry wood or bark, and kindles a fire five or six feet in front of where we intend to lie. It matters not, commonly, on which side this is, because there is little or no wind in so dense a wood at that season; and then he gets a kettle of water from the river, and takes out the pork, bread, coffee, etc., from their several packages.

Another, meanwhile, having the axe, cuts down the nearest dead rock-maple or other dry hard wood, collecting several large logs to last through the night, also a green stake, with a notch or fork to it, which is slanted over the fire, perhaps resting on a rock or forked stake, to hang the kettle on, and two forked stakes and a pole for the tent.

The third man pitches the tent, cuts a dozen or more pins with his knife, usually of moose-wood, the common underwood, to fasten it down with, and then collects an armful or two of fir-twigs [1] arbor-vitæ, spruce, or hemlock, whichever is at hand, and makes the bed, beginning at either end, and laying the twigs wrong side up,

[1] These twigs are called in Rasle's Dictionary, *Sediak*.

in regular rows, covering the stub ends of the last row; first, however, filling the hollows, if there are any, with coarser material. Wrangel says that his guides in Siberia first strewed a quantity of dry brushwood on the ground, and then cedar twigs on that.

Commonly, by the time the bed is made, or within fifteen or twenty minutes, the water boils, the pork is fried, and supper is ready. We eat this sitting on the ground, or a stump, if there is any, around a large piece of birch-bark for a table, each holding a dipper in one hand and a piece of ship-bread or fried pork in the other, frequently making a pass with his hand, or thrusting his head into the smoke, to avoid the mosquitoes.

Next, pipes are lit by those who smoke, and veils are donned by those who have them, and we hastily examine and dry our plants, anoint our faces and hands, and go to bed, — and — the mosquitoes.

Though you have nothing to do but see the country, there 's rarely any time to spare, hardly enough to examine a plant, before the night or drowsiness is upon you.

Such was the ordinary experience, but this evening we had camped earlier on account of the rain, and had more time.

We found that our camp to-night was on an

old, and now more than usually indistinct, supply road, running along the river. What is
called a road there shows no ruts or trace of
wheels, for they are not used; nor, indeed, of
runners, since they are used only in the winter
when the snow is several feet deep. It is only
an indistinct vista through the wood, which it
takes an experienced eye to detect.

We had no sooner pitched our tent than the
thunder-shower burst on us, and we hastily
crept under it, drawing our bags after us, curious to see how much of a shelter our thin cotton roof was going to be in this excursion.
Though the violence of the rain forced a fine
shower through the cloth before it was fairly
wetted and shrunk, with which we were well be-
dewed, we managed to keep pretty dry, only a
box of matches having been left out and spoiled,
and before we were aware of it the shower was
over, and only the dripping trees imprisoned
us.

Wishing to see what fishes there were in the
river there, we cast our lines over the wet
bushes on the shore, but they were repeatedly
swept down the swift stream in vain. So, leaving the Indian, we took the canoe just before
dark, and dropped down the river a few rods
to fish at the mouth of a sluggish brook on the
opposite side. We pushed up this a rod or

two, where, perhaps, only a canoe had been before. But though there were a few small fishes,
mostly chivin, there, we were soon driven off
by the mosquitoes. While there we heard the
Indian fire his gun twice in such rapid succession that we thought it must be double-barreled,
though we observed afterward that it was single. His object was to clean out and dry it
after the rain, and he then loaded it with ball,
being now on ground where he expected to meet
with large game. This sudden, loud, crashing
noise in the still aisles of the forest, affected
me like an insult to nature, or ill manners at
any rate, as if you were to fire a gun in a hall
or temple. It was not heard far, however,
except along the river, the sound being rapidly
hushed up or absorbed by the damp trees and
mossy ground.

The Indian made a little smothered fire of
damp leaves close to the back of the camp, that
the smoke might drive through and keep out the
mosquitoes; but just before we fell asleep this
suddenly blazed up, and came near setting fire
to the tent. We were considerably molested
by mosquitoes at this camp.

SUNDAY, *July* 26.

The note of the white-throated sparrow, a
very inspiriting but almost wiry sound, was the
first heard in the morning, and with this all the

woods rang. This was the prevailing bird in the northern part of Maine. The forest generally was all alive with them at this season, and they were proportionally numerous and musical about Bangor. They evidently breed in that State. Wilson did not know where they bred, and says, "Their only note is a kind of chip." Though commonly unseen, their simple *ah, te-te-te, te-te-te, te-te-te,* so sharp and piercing, was as distinct to the ear as the passage of a spark of fire shot into the darkest of the forest would be to the eye. I thought that they commonly uttered it as they flew. I hear this note for a few days only in the spring, as they go through Concord, and in the fall see them again going southward, but then they are mute. We were commonly aroused by their lively strain very early. What a glorious time they must have in that wilderness, far from mankind and election day!

I told the Indian that we would go to church to Chesuncook this (Sunday) morning, some fifteen miles. It was settled weather at last. A few swallows flitted over the water, we heard the white throats along the shore, the phebe notes of the chickadee, and, I believe, red-starts and moose-flies of large size pursued us in midstream.

The Indian thought that we should lie by on

Sunday. Said he, "We come here lookum things, look all round; but come Sunday, lock up all that, and then Monday look again." He spoke of an Indian of his acquaintance who had been with some ministers to Ktaadn, and had told him how they conducted. This he described in a low and solemn voice. "They make a long prayer every morning and night, and at every meal. Come Sunday," said he, "they stop 'em, no go at all that day, — keep still, — preach all day, — first one, then another, just like church. Oh, ver good men." "One day," said he, "going along a river, they came to the body of a man in the water, drowned good while, all ready fall to pieces. They go right ashore, — stop there, go no farther that day, — they have meeting there, preach and pray just like Sunday. Then they get poles and lift up the body, and they go back and carry the body with them. Oh, they ver good men."

I judged from this account that their every camp was a camp-meeting, and they had mistaken their route, — they should have gone to Eastham; that they wanted an opportunity to preach somewhere more than to see Ktaadn. I read of another similar party that seem to have spent their time there singing the songs of Zion. I was glad that I did not go to that mountain with such slow coaches.

However, the Indian added, plying the paddle all the while, that if we would go along, he must go with us, he our man, and he suppose that if he no takum pay for what he do Sunday, then ther 's no harm, but if he takum pay, then wrong. I told him that he was stricter than white men. Nevertheless, I noticed that he did not forget to reckon in the Sundays at last.

He appeared to be a very religious man, and said his prayers in a loud voice, in Indian, kneeling before the camp, morning and evening, — sometimes scrambling up again in haste when he had forgotten this, and saying them with great rapidity. In the course of the day, he remarked, not very originally, "Poor man rememberum God more than rich."

We soon passed the island where I had camped four years before, and I recognized the very spot. The dead water, a mile or two below it, the Indian called *Beska bekukskishtuk*, from the lake *Beskabekuk*, which empties in above. This dead water, he said, was "a great place for moose always." We saw the grass bent where a moose came out the night before, and the Indian said that he could smell one as far as he could see him; but, he added, that if he should see five or six to-day close by canoe, he no shoot 'em. Accordingly, as he was the only one of the party who had a gun, or had come a-hunting, the moose were safe.

Just below this, a cat-owl flew heavily over the stream, and he, asking if I knew what it was, imitated very well the common *hoo, hoo, hoo, hoorer, hoo,* of our woods; making a hard, guttural sound, "Ugh, ugh, ugh, — ugh, ugh." When we passed the Moose-horn, he said that it had no name. What Joe Aitteon had called Ragmuff, he called *Pay tay te quick,* and said that it meant Burnt Ground Stream. We stopped there, where I had stopped before, and I bathed in this tributary. It was shallow but cold, apparently too cold for the Indian, who stood looking on. As we were pushing away again, a white-beaked eagle sailed over our heads. A reach some miles above Pine Stream, where there were several islands, the Indian said was *Nonglangyis,* dead water. Pine Stream he called Black River, and said that its Indian name was *Karsaootuk.* He could go to Caribou Lake that way.

We carried a part of the baggage about Pine-Stream Falls, while the Indian went down in the canoe. A Bangor merchant had told us that two men in his employ were drowned some time ago while passing these falls in a batteau, and a third clung to a rock all night, and was taken off in the morning. There were magnificent great purple-fringed orchises on this carry and the neighboring shores. I measured the largest canoe-birch which I saw in this journey near the end of the carry. It was $14\frac{1}{2}$ feet in circumference at two feet from the ground, but at five feet divided into three parts. The canoe-birches thereabouts were commonly marked by conspicuous dark spiral ridges, with a groove between, so that I thought at first that they had been struck by lightning, but, as the Indian said, it was evidently caused by the grain of the tree. He cut a small, woody knob, as big as a filbert, from the trunk of a fir, apparently an old balsam vesicle filled with wood, which he said was good medicine.

After we had embarked and gone half a mile, my companion remembered that he had left his knife, and we paddled back to get it, against the strong and swift current. This taught us the difference between going up and down the stream, for while we were working our way back a quarter of a mile, we should have gone down a mile and a half at least. So we landed, and while he and the Indian were gone back for it, I watched the motions of the foam, a kind of white water-fowl near the shore, forty or fifty rods below. It alternately appeared and disappeared behind the rock, being carried round by an eddy. Even this semblance of life was interesting on that lonely river.

Immediately below these falls was the Chesuncook dead-water, caused by the flowing back of the lake. As we paddled slowly over this, the Indian told us a story of his hunting thereabouts, and something more interesting about himself. It appeared that he had represented his tribe at Augusta, and also once at Washington, where he had met some Western chiefs. He had been consulted at Augusta, and gave advice, which he said was followed, respecting the eastern boundary of Maine, as determined by highlands and streams, at the time of the difficulties on that side. He was employed with the surveyors on the line. Also he had called on Daniel Webster in Boston, at the time of his Bunker Hill oration.

I was surprised to hear him say that he liked to go to Boston, New York, Philadelphia, etc., etc.; that he would like to live there. But then, as if relenting a little, when he thought what a poor figure he would make there, he added, "I suppose, I live in New York, I be poorest hunter, I expect." He understood very well both his superiority and his inferiority to the whites. He criticised the people of the United States as compared with other nations, but the only distinct idea with which he labored was, that they were "very strong," but, like some individuals, "too fast." He must have the credit of saying this just before the general breaking down of railroads and banks. He had a great idea of education, and would occasionally break out into such expressions as this, "Kademy — a-cad-e-my — good thing — I suppose they usum Fifth Reader there. . . . You been college?"

From this dead water the outlines of the mountains about Ktaadn were visible. The top of Ktaadn was concealed by a cloud, but the Souneunk Mountains were nearer, and quite visible. We steered across the northwest end of the lake, from which we looked down south-southeast, the whole length to Joe Merry Mountain, seen over its extremity. It is an agreeable change to cross a lake, after you have been shut up in the woods, not only on account of the greater expanse of water, but also of sky. It is one of the surprises which Nature has in store for the traveler in the forest. To look down, in this case, over eighteen miles of water, was liberating and civilizing even. No doubt, the short distance to which you can see in the woods, and the general twilight, would at length react on the inhabitants, and make them *salvages*. The lakes also reveal the mountains, and give ample scope and range to our thought. The very gulls which we saw sitting on the rocks, like white specks, or circling about, reminded me of custom-house officers. Already

there were half a dozen log-huts about this end
of the lake, though so far from a road. I perceive that in these woods the earliest settlements
are, for various reasons, clustering about the
lakes, but partly, I think, for the sake of the
neighborhood as the oldest clearings. They are
forest schools already established, — great cen-
tres of light. Water is a pioneer which the
settler follows, taking advantage of its improvements.

Thus far only I had been before. About
noon we turned northward, up a broad kind of
estuary, and at its northeast corner found the
Caucomgomoc River, and after going about a
mile from the lake, reached the Umbazookskus,
which comes in on the right at a point where the
former river, coming from the west, turns short
to the south. Our course was up the Umbazookskus, but as the Indian knew of a good
camping-place, that is, a cool place where there
were few mosquitoes about half a mile farther
up the Caucomgomoc, we went thither. The
latter river, judging from the map, is the longer
and principal stream, and, therefore, its name
must prevail below the junction. So quickly
we changed the civilizing sky of Chesuncook
for the dark wood of the Caucomgomoc. On
reaching the Indian's camping-ground, on the
south side, where the bank was about a dozen

feet high, I read on the trunk of a fir-tree, blazed by an axe, an inscription in charcoal which had been left by him. It was surmounted by a drawing of a bear paddling a canoe, which he said was the sign which had been used by his family always. The drawing, though rude, could not be mistaken for anything but a bear, and he doubted my ability to copy it. The inscription ran thus, *verbatim et literatim.* I interline the English of his Indian as he gave it to me.

[The figure of a bear in a boat.]

July 26,
1853.

Niasoseb.

We alone Joseph.
Polis	*clioi*
Polis	start
sia	*olta*
for	Oldtown
ouke	*ni*
right	away.
quambi	

July 15,
1855.
Niasoseb.

He added now below: —

1857,
July 26.
Io.   Polis.

This was one of his homes. I saw where he had sometimes stretched. his moose-hides on the opposite or sunny north side of the river, where there was a narrow meadow.

After we had selected a place for our camp, and kindled our fire, almost exactly on the site of the Indian's last camp here, he, looking up, observed, "That tree danger." It was a dead part, more than a foot in diameter, of a large canoe-birch, which branched at the ground. This branch, rising thirty feet or more, slanted directly over the spot which we had chosen for our bed. I told him to try it with his axe; but he could not shake it perceptibly, and therefore seemed inclined to disregard it, and my companion expressed his willingness to run the risk. But it seemed to me that we should be fools to lie under it, for though the lower part was firm, the top, for aught we knew, might be just ready to fall, and we should at any rate be very uneasy if the wind arose in the night. It is a common accident for men camping in the woods to be killed by a falling tree. So the camp was moved to the other side of the fire.

It was, as usual, a damp and shaggy forest, that Caucomgomoc one, and the most you knew about it was, that on this side it stretched toward the settlements, and on that to still more unfrequented regions. You carried so much

topography in your mind always, — and sometimes it seemed to make a considerable difference whether you sat or lay nearer the settlements, or farther off, than your companions, —
were the rear or frontier man of the camp.
But there is really the same difference between
our positions wherever we may be camped, and
some are nearer the frontiers on feather-beds in
the towns than others on fir-twigs in the backwoods.

The Indian said that the Umbazookskus, being a dead stream with broad meadows, was a
good place for Moose, and he frequently came
a-hunting here, being out alone three weeks or
more from Oldtown. He sometimes, also, went
a-hunting to the Seboois Lakes, taking the
stage, with his gun and ammunition, axe and
blankets, hard bread and pork, perhaps for a
hundred miles of the way, and jumped off at
the wildest place on the road, where he was at
once at home, and every rod was a tavern-site
for him. Then, after a short journey through
the woods, he would build a spruce-bark canoe
in one day, putting but few ribs into it, that it
might be light, and, after doing his hunting with
it on the lakes, would return with his furs the
same way he had come. Thus you have an Indian availing himself cunningly of the advantages of civilization, without losing any of his

woodcraft, but proving himself the more successful hunter for it.

This man was very clever and quick to learn
anything in his line. Our tent was of a kind
new to him; but when he had once seen it
pitched, it was surprising how quickly he would
find and prepare the pole and forked stakes to
pitch it with, cutting and placing them right
the first time, though I am sure that the majority of white men would have blundered several
times.

This river came from Caucomgomoc Lake,
about ten miles farther up. Though it was
sluggish here, there were falls not far above us,
and we saw the foam from them go by from
time to time. The Indian said that *Caucomgomoc* meant Big-gull Lake (*i. e.*, Herring-gull,
I suppose), *gomoc* meaning lake. Hence this
was *Caucomgomoctook*, or the river from that
lake. This was the Penobscot *Caucomgomoc-
took!* there was another St. John, one not far
north. He finds the eggs of this gull, sometimes twenty together, as big as hen's eggs, on
rocky ledges on the west side of Millinocket
River, for instance, and eats them.

Now I thought I would observe how he spent
his Sunday. While I and my companion were
looking about at the trees and river, he went to
sleep. Indeed, he improved every opportunity
to get a nap, whatever the day.

Rambling about the woods at this camp, I noticed that they consisted chiefly of firs, black spruce, and some white, red maple, canoe-birch, and, along the river, the hoary alder, *Alnus incana*. I name them in the order of their abundance. The *Viburnum nudum* was a common shrub, and of smaller plants, there were the dwarf-cornel, great round-leaved orchis, abundant and in bloom (a greenish-white flower growing in little communities), *Uvularia grandiflora*, whose stem tasted like a cucumber, *Pyrola secunda*, apparently the commonest Pyrola in those woods, now out of bloom, *Pyrola elliptica*, and *Chiogenes hispidula*. The *Clintonia borealis*, with ripe berries, was very abundant, and perfectly at home there. Its leaves, disposed commonly in triangles about its stem, were just as handsomely formed and green, and its berries as blue and glossy, as if it grew by some botanist's favorite path.

I could trace the outlines of large birches that had fallen long ago, collapsed and rotted and turned to soil, by faint yellowish-green lines of feather-like moss, eighteen inches wide and twenty or thirty feet long, crossed by other similar lines.

I heard a Maryland yellow-throat's midnight strain, wood-thrush, kingfisher (tweezer bird), or parti-colored warbler, and a night-hawk. I also heard and saw red squirrels, and heard a bullfrog. The Indian said that he heard a snake.

Wild as it was, it was hard for me to get rid of the associations of the settlements. Any steady and monotonous sound, to which I did not distinctly attend, passed for a sound of human industry. The waterfalls which I heard were not without their dams and mills to my imagination, — and several times I found that I had been regarding the steady rushing sound of the wind from over the woods beyond the rivers as that of a train of cars, — the cars at Quebec. Our minds anywhere, when left to themselves, are always thus busily drawing conclusions from false premises.

I asked the Indian to make us a sugar-bowl of birch-bark, which he did, using the great knife which dangled in a sheath from his belt; but the bark broke at the corners when he bent it up, and he said it was not good; that there was a great difference in this respect between the bark of one canoe-birch and that of another, *i.e.*, one cracked more easily than another. I used some thin and delicate sheets of this bark which he split and cut, in my flower-book; thinking it would be good to separate the dried specimens from the green.

My companion, wishing to distinguish between the black and white spruce, asked Polis to show him a twig of the latter, which he did at once, together with the black; indeed, he could distinguish them about as far as he could see them; but as the two twigs appeared very much alike, my companion asked the Indian to point out the difference; whereupon the latter, taking the twigs, instantly remarked, as he passed his hand over them successively in a stroking manner, that the white was rough (*i. e.*, the needles stood up nearly perpendicular), but the black smooth (*i. e.*, as if bent or combed down). This was an obvious difference, both to sight and touch. However, if I remember rightly, this would not serve to distinguish the white spruce from the light-colored variety of the black.

I asked him to let me see him get some black spruce root, and make some thread. Whereupon, without looking up at the trees overhead, he began to grub in the ground, instantly distinguishing the black spruce roots, and cutting off a slender one, three or four feet long, and as big as a pipe-stem, he split the end with his knife, and, taking a half between the thumb and forefinger of each hand, rapidly separated its whole length into two equal semi-cylindrical halves; then giving me another root, he said, "You try." But in my hands it immediately ran off one side, and I got only a very short piece. In short, though it looked very easy, I found that there was a great art in splitting these roots. The split is skillfully humored by bending short with this hand or that, and so kept in the middle. He then took off the bark from each half, pressing a short piece of cedar bark against the convex side with both hands, while he drew the root upward with his teeth. An Indian's teeth are strong, and I noticed that he used his often where we should have used a hand. They amounted to a third hand. He thus obtained, in a moment, a very neat, tough, and flexible string, which he could tie into a knot, or make into a fish-line even. It is said that in Norway and Sweden the roots of the Norway spruce (*Abies excelsa*) are used in the same way for the same purpose. He said that you would be obliged to give half a dollar for spruce root enough for a canoe, thus prepared. He had hired the sewing of his own canoe, though he made all the rest. The root in his canoe was of a pale slate color, probably acquired by exposure to the weather, or perhaps from being boiled in water first.

He had discovered the day before that his canoe leaked a little, and said that it was owing to stepping into it violently, which forced the water under the edge of the horizontal seams on

the side. I asked him where he would get pitch
to mend it with, for they commonly use hard
pitch, obtained of the whites at Oldtown.   He
said that he could make something very similar,
and equally good, not of spruce gum, or the
like, but of material which we had with us; and
he wished me to guess what.   But I could not,
and he would not tell me, though he showed me
a ball of it when made, as big as a pea, and like
black pitch, saying, at last, that there were
some things which a man did not tell even his
wife.   It may have been his own discovery.   In
Arnold's expedition the pioneers used for their
canoe "the turpentine of the pine, and the
scrapings of the pork-bag."

Being curious to see what kind of fishes there
were in this dark, deep, sluggish river, I cast in
my line just before night, and caught several
small somewhat yellowish sucker-like fishes,
which the Indian at once rejected, saying that
they were *Michigan* fish (*i. e.*, *soft* and *stinking*
fish) and good for nothing.   Also, he would not
touch a pout, which I caught, and said that
neither Indians nor whites thereabouts ever ate
them, which I thought was singular, since they
are esteemed in Massachusetts, and he had told
me that he ate hedgehogs, loons, etc.   But he
said that some small silvery fishes, which I
called white chivin, which were similar in size

and form to the first, were the best fish in the
Penobscot waters, and if I would toss them up
the bank to him, he would cook them for me.
After cleaning them, not very carefully, leaving
the heads on, he laid them on the coals and so
broiled them.

Returning from a short walk, he brought a
vine in his hand, and asked me if I knew what
it was, saying that it made the best tea of anything in the woods. It was the Creeping Snowberry (*Chiogenes hispidula*), which was quite
common there, its berries just grown. He
called it *cowosnebagosar*, which name implies
that it grows where old prostrate trunks have
collapsed and rotted. So we determined to
have some tea made of this to-night. It had a
slight checkerberry flavor, and we both agreed
that it was really better than the black tea
which we had brought. We thought it quite a
discovery, and that it might well be dried, and
sold in the shops. I, for one, however, am not
an old tea-drinker, and cannot speak with authority to others. It would have been particularly good to carry along for a cold drink during
the day, the water thereabouts being invariably
warm. The Indian said that they also used for
tea a certain herb which grew in low ground,
which he did not find there, and *Ledum*, or
Labrador tea, which I have since found and

tried in Concord; also hemlock leaves, the last especially in the winter, when the other plants were covered with snow; and various other things; but he did not approve of *arbor vitæ*, which I said I had drunk in those woods. We could have had a new kind of tea every night.

Just before night we saw a *musquash* (he did not say muskrat), the only one we saw in this voyage, swimming downward on the opposite side of the stream. The Indian, wishing to get one to eat, hushed us, saying, "Stop, me call 'em;" and, sitting flat on the bank, he began to make a curious squeaking, wiry sound with his lips, exerting himself considerably. I was greatly surprised, — thought that I had at last got into the wilderness, and that he was a wild man indeed, to be talking to a musquash! I did not know which of the two was the strangest to me. He seemed suddenly to have quite forsaken humanity, and gone over to the musquash side. The musquash, however, as near as I could see, did not turn aside, though he may have hesitated a little, and the Indian said that he saw our fire; but it was evident that he was in the habit of calling the musquash to him, as he said. An acquaintance of mine who was hunting moose in those woods a month after this, tells me that his Indian in this way repeatedly called the musquash within reach of his paddle in the moonlight, and struck at them.

The Indian said a particularly long prayer this Sunday evening, as if to atone for working in the morning.

MONDAY, *July* 27.

Having rapidly loaded the canoe, which the Indian always carefully attended to, that it might be well trimmed, and each having taken a look, as usual, to see that nothing was left, we set out again, descending the Caucomgomoc, and turning northeasterly up the *Umbazook-skus*. This name, the Indian said, meant *Much Meadow River*. We found it a very meadowy stream, and dead water, and now very wide on account of the rains, though, he said, it was sometimes quite narrow. The space between the woods, chiefly bare meadow, was from fifty to two hundred rods in breadth, and is a rare place for moose. It reminded me of the Concord; and what increased the resemblance was one old musquash house almost afloat.

In the water on the meadows grew sedges, wool-grass, the common blue-flag abundantly, its flower just showing itself above the high water, as if it were a blue water-lily, and higher in the meadows a great many clumps of a peculiar narrow-leaved willow (*Salix petiolaris*),

which is common in our river meadows. It was
the prevailing one here, and the Indian said
that the musquash ate much of it; and here
also grew the red osier (*Cornus stolonifera*), its
large fruit·now whitish.

Though it was still early in the·morning, we
saw night-hawks circling over the meadow, and
as usual heard the *Pepe* (*Muscicapa Cooperi*),
which is one of the prevailing birds in these
woods, and the robin.

It was unusual for the woods to be so distant
from the shore, and there was quite an echo
from them, but when I was shouting in order
to awake it, the Indian reminded me that I
should scare the moose, which he was looking
out for, and which we all wanted to see.   The
word for echo was *Pockadunkquaywayle*.

A broad belt of dead larch-trees along the
distant edge of the meadow, against the forest
on each side, increased the usual wildness of the
scenery.   The Indian called these juniper, and
said that they had been killed by the back-water
caused by the dam at the outlet of Chesuncook
Lake, some twenty miles distant.   I plucked
at the water's edge the *Asclepias incarnata*,
with quite handsome flowers, a brighter red
than our variety (the *pulchra*).   It was the only
form of it which I saw there.

Having paddled several miles up the Umba-

zookskus, it suddenly contracted to a mere
brook, narrow and swift, the larches and other
trees approaching the bank and leaving no open
meadow, and we landed to get a black-spruce
pole for pushing against the stream. This was
the first occasion for one. The one selected
was quite slender, cut about ten feet long,
merely whittled to a point, and the bark shaved
off. The stream, though narrow and swift,
was still deep, with a muddy bottom, as I
proved by diving to it. Beside the plants
which I have mentioned, I observed on the
bank here the *Salix cordata* and *rostrata*,
Ranunculus recurvatus, and *Rubus triflorus*
with ripe fruit.

While we were thus employed, two Indians
in a canoe hove in sight round the bushes, coming down stream. Our Indian knew one of
them, an old man, and fell into conversation.
with him in Indian. He belonged at the foot
of Moosehead. The other was of another tribe.
They were returning from hunting. I asked
the younger if they had seen any moose, to
which he said no; but I, seeing the moose-hides
sticking out from a great bundle made with
their blankets in the middle of the canoe,
added, "Only their hides." As he was a foreigner, he may have wished to deceive me, for
it is against the law for white men and foreign-

ers to kill moose in Maine at this season. But, perhaps, he need not have been alarmed, for the moose-wardens are not very particular. I heard quite directly of one who being asked by a white man going into the woods what he would say if he killed a moose, answered, "If you bring me a quarter of it, I guess you won't be troubled." His duty being, as he said, only to prevent the "indiscriminate" slaughter of them for their hides. I suppose that he would consider it an *indiscriminate* slaughter when a quarter was not reserved for himself. Such are the perquisites of this office.

We continued along through the most extensive larch wood which I had seen, — tall and slender trees with fantastic branches. But though this was the prevailing tree here, I do not remember that we saw any afterward. You do not find straggling trees of this species here and there throughout the wood, but rather a little forest of them. The same is the case with the white and red pines, and some other trees, greatly to the convenience of the lumberer. They are of a social habit, growing in "veins," "clumps," "groups," or "communities," as the explorers call them, distinguishing them far away, from the top of a hill or a tree, the white-pines towering above the surrounding forest, or else they form extensive forests by themselves. I would have liked to come across a large community of pines, which had never been invaded by the lumbering army.

We saw some fresh moose tracks along the shore, but the Indian said that the moose were not driven out of the woods by the flies, as usual at this season, on account of the abundance of water everywhere. The stream was only from one and one half to three rods wide, quite winding, with occasional small islands, meadows, and some very swift and shallow places. When we came to an island, the Indian never hesitated which side to take, as if the current told him which was the shortest and deepest. It was lucky for us that the water was so high. We had to walk but once.on this stream, carrying a part of the load, at a swift and shallow reach, while he got up with the canoe, not being obliged to take out, though he said it was very strong water. Once or twice we passed the red wreck of a batteau which had been stove some spring.

While making this portage I saw many splendid specimens of the great purple-fringed orchis, three feet high. It is remarkable that such delicate flowers should here adorn these wilderness paths.

Having resumed our seats in the canoe, I felt the Indian wiping my back, which he had

accidentally spat upon.   He said it was a sign
that I was going to be married.

The Umbazookskus River is called ten miles
long.   Having polled up the narrowest point
some three or four miles, the next opening in
the sky was over Umbazookskus Lake, which
we suddenly entered about eleven o'clock in
the forenoon.   It stretches northwesterly four
or five miles, with what the Indian called the
Caucomgomoc Mountain seen far beyond it.   It
was an agreeable change.

This lake was very shallow a long distance
from the shore, and I saw stone heaps on the
bottom, like those in the Assabet at home.   The
canoe ran into one.   The Indian thought that
they were made by an eel.   Joe Aitteon in
1853 thought that they were made by chub.
We crossed the southeast end of the lake to the
carry into Mud Pond.

Umbazookskus Lake is the head of the Penobscot in this direction, and Mud Pond is the
nearest bend of the Allegash, one of the chief
sources of the St. John.   Hodge, who went
through this way to the St. Lawrence in the
service of the State, calls the portage here a
mile and three quarters long, and states that
Mud Pond has been found to be fourteen feet
higher than Umbazookskus Lake.   As the west
branch of the Penobscot at the Moosehead carry

is considered about twenty-five feet lower than
Moosehead Lake, it appears that the Penobscot in the upper part of its course runs in a
broad and shallow valley, between the Kennebec
and St. John, and lower than either of them,
though, judging from the map, you might expect it to be the highest.

Mud Pond is about halfway from Umbazookskus to Chamberlain Lake, into which it
empties, and to which we were bound. The
Indian said that this was the wettest carry in
the State, and as the season was a very wet one,
we anticipated an unpleasant walk. As usual
he made one large bundle of the pork-keg, cooking utensils, and other loose traps, by tying
them up in his blanket. We should be obliged
to go over the carry twice, and our method was
to carry one half part way, and then go back
for the rest.

Our path ran close by the door of a log-hut
in a clearing at this end of the carry, which the
Indian, who alone entered it, found to be occupied by a Canadian and his family, and that the
man had been blind for a year. He seemed
peculiarly unfortunate to be taken blind there,
where there were so few eyes to see for him.
He could not even be led out of that country by
a dog, but must be taken down the rapids as
passively as a barrel of flour. This was the

first house above Chesuncook, and the last on the Penobscot waters, and was built here, no doubt, because it was the route of the lumberers in the winter and spring.

After a slight ascent from the lake through the springy soil of the Canadian's clearing, we entered on a level and very wet and rocky path through the universal dense evergreen forest, a loosely paved gutter merely, where we went leaping from rock to rock and from side to side, in the vain attempt to keep out of the water and mud. We concluded that it was yet Penobscot water, though there was no flow to it. It was on this carry that the white hunter whom I met in the stage, as he told me, had shot two bears a few months before. They stood directly in the path, and did not turn out for him. They might be excused for not turning out there, or only taking the right as the law directs. He said that at this season bears were found on the mountains and hillsides, in search of berries, and were apt to be saucy, — that we might come across them up Trout Stream; and he added, what I hardly credited, that many Indians slept in their canoes, not daring to sleep on land, on account of them.

Here commences what was called, twenty years ago, the best timber land in the State. This very spot was described as "covered with the greatest abundance of pine," but now this appeared to me, comparatively, an uncommon tree there, — and yet you did not see where any more could have stood, amid the dense growth of cedar, fir, etc. It was then proposed to cut a canal from lake to lake here, but the outlet was finally made farther east, at Telos Lake, as we shall see.

The Indian with his canoe soon disappeared before us; but erelong he came back and told us to take a path which turned off westward, it being better walking, and, at my suggestion, he agreed to leave a bough in the regular carry at that place, that we might not pass it by mistake. Thereafter, he said, we were to keep the main path, and he added, "You see 'em my tracks." But I had not much faith that we could distinguish his tracks, since others had passed over the carry within a few days.

We turned off at the right place, but were soon confused by numerous logging-paths, coming into the one we were on, by which lumberers had been to pick out those pines which I have mentioned. However, we kept what we considered the main path, though it was a winding one, and in this, at long intervals, we distinguished a faint trace of a footstep. This, though comparatively unworn, was at first a better, or, at least, a drier road than the regular

carry which we had left. It led through an
arbor-vitæ wilderness of the grimmest character.
The great fallen and rotting trees had been cut
through and rolled aside, and their huge trunks
abutted on the path on each side, while others
still lay across it two or three feet high. It was
impossible for us to discern the Indian's trail
in the elastic moss, which, like a thick carpet,
covered every rock and fallen tree, as well as
the earth. Nevertheless, I did occasionally detect the track of a man, and I gave myself some
credit for it. I carried my whole load at once,
a heavy knapsack, and a large India-rubber
bag, containing our bread and a blanket, swung
on a paddle; in all, about sixty pounds; but my
companion preferred to make two journeys, by
short stages, while I waited for him. We
could not be sure that we were not depositing
our loads each time farther off from the true
path.

As I sat waiting for my companion, he would
seem to be gone a long time, and I had ample
opportunity to make observations on the forest.
I now first began to be seriously molested by the
black-fly, a very small but perfectly formed fly
of that color, about one tenth of an inch long,
which I first felt, and then saw, in swarms about
me, as I sat by a wider and more than usually
doubtful fork in this dark forest path. The

hunters tell bloody stories about them, — how they settle in a ring about your neck, before you know it, and are wiped off in great numbers with your blood. But remembering that I had a wash in my knapsack, prepared by a thoughtful hand in Bangor, I made haste to apply it to my face and hands, and was glad to find it effectual, as long as it was fresh, or for twenty minutes, not only against black-flies, but all the insects that molested us. They would not alight on the part thus defended. It was composed of sweet-oil and oil of turpentine, with a little oil of spearmint, and camphor. However, I finally concluded that the remedy was worse than the disease. It was so disagreeable and inconvenient to have your face and hands covered with such a mixture.

Three large slate-colored birds of the jay genus (*Garrulus Canadensis*), the Canada jay, moose-bird, meat-bird, or what not, came flitting silently and by degrees toward me, and hopped down the limbs inquisitively to within seven or eight feet. They were more clumsy and not nearly so handsome as the blue-jay. Fish-hawks, from the lake, uttered their sharp whistling notes low over the top of the forest near me, as if they were anxious about a nest there.

After I had sat there some time, I noticed at this fork in the path a tree which had been blazed, and the letters "Chamb. L." written on it with red chalk. This I knew to mean Chamberlain Lake. So I concluded that on the whole we were on the right course, though as we had come nearly two miles, and saw no signs of Mud Pond, I did harbor the suspicion that we might be on a direct course to Chamberlain Lake, leaving out Mud Pond. This I found by my map would be about five miles northeasterly, and I then took the bearing by my compass.

My companion having returned with his bag, and also defended his face and hands with the insect wash, we set forward again. The walking rapidly grew worse, and the path more indistinct, and at length, after passing through a patch of *calla palustris*, still abundantly in bloom, we found ourselves in a more open and regular swamp, made less passable than ordinary by the unusual wetness of the season. We sank a foot deep in water and mud at every step, and sometimes up to our knees, and the trail was almost obliterated, being no more than that a musquash leaves in similar places, when he parts the floating sedge. In fact, it probably was a musquash trail in some places. We concluded that if Mud Pond was as muddy as the approach to it was wet, it certainly deserved its name. It would have been amusing to behold the dogged and deliberate pace at which we entered that swamp, without interchanging a word, as if determined to go through it, though it should come up to our necks. Having pene-trated a considerable distance into this, and found a tussock on which we could deposit our loads, though there was no place to sit, my com-panion went back for the rest of his pack. I had thought to observe on this carry when we crossed the dividing line between the Penobscot and St. John, but as my feet had hardly been out of water the whole distance, and it was all level and stagnant, I began to despair of finding it. I remembered hearing a good deal about the "highlands" dividing the waters of the Penob-scot from those of the St. John, as well as the St. Lawrence, at the time of the northeast boundary dispute, and I observed by my map, that the line claimed by Great Britain as the boundary prior to 1842 passed between Umba-zookskus Lake and Mud Pond, so that we had either crossed or were then on it. These, then, according to *her* interpretation of the treaty of '83, were the "highlands which divide those rivers that empty themselves into the St. Law-rence from those which fall into the Atlantic Ocean." Truly an interesting spot to stand on, — if that were it, — though you could not sit down there. I thought that if the commissioners themselves, and the king of Holland with them, had spent a few days here, with their packs upon their backs, looking for that "highland," they would have had an interesting time, and perhaps it would have modified their views of the question somewhat. The king of Holland would have been in his element. Such were my meditations while my companion was gone back for his bag.

It was a cedar swamp, through which the peculiar note of the white-throated sparrow rang loud and clear. There grew the side-saddle flower, Labrador tea, *Kalmia glauca*, and, what was new to me, the Low Birch (*Betula pumila*), a little round-leafed shrub, two or three feet high only. We thought to name this swamp after the latter.

After a long while my companion came back, and the Indian with him. We had taken the wrong road, and the Indian had lost us. He had very wisely gone back to the Canadian's camp, and asked him which way we had probably gone, since he could better understand the ways of white men, and he told him correctly that we had undoubtedly taken the supply road to Chamberlain Lake (slender supplies they would get over such a road at this season). The Indian was greatly surprised that we should have taken what he called a "tow" (*i. e.*, tote or

toting or supply) road, instead of a carry path,
— that we had not followed his tracks, — said it
was "strange," and evidently thought little of
our woodcraft.

Having held a consultation, and eaten a
mouthful of bread, we concluded that it would
perhaps be nearer for us two now to keep on to
Chamberlain Lake, omitting Mud Pond, than
to go back and start anew for the last place,
though the Indian had never been through this
way, and knew nothing about it. In the mean
while he would go back and finish carrying over
his canoe and bundle to Mud Pond, cross that,
and go down its outlet and up Chamberlain
Lake, and trust to meet us there before night.
It was now a little after noon. He supposed
that the water in which we stood had flowed
back from Mud Pond, which could not be far
off eastward, but was unapproachable through
the dense cedar swamp.

Keeping on, we were erelong agreeably dis-
appointed by reaching firmer ground, and we
crossed a ridge where the path was more distinct, but there was never any outlook over the
forest. While descending the last, I saw many
specimens of the great round-leaved orchis, of
large size; one which I measured had leaves, as
usual, flat on the ground, nine and a half inches
long, and nine wide, and was two feet high.

The dark, damp wilderness is favorable to some of these orchidaceous plants, though they are too delicate for cultivation. I also saw the swamp gooseberry (*Ribes lacustre*), with green fruit, and in all the low ground, where it was not too wet, the *Rubus triflorus* in fruit. At one place I heard a very clear and piercing note from a small hawk, like a single note from a white-throated sparrow, only very much louder, as he dashed through the tree-tops over my head. I wondered that he allowed himself to be disturbed by our presence, since it seemed as if he could not easily find his nest again himself in that wilderness. We also saw and heard several times the red squirrel, and often, as before observed, the bluish scales of the fir cones which it had left on a rock or fallen tree. This, according to the Indian, is the only squirrel found in those woods, except a very few striped ones. It must have a solitary time in that dark evergreen forest, where there is so little life, seventy-five miles from a road as we had come. I wondered how he could call any particular tree there his home; and yet he would run up the stem of one out of the myriads, as if it were an old road to him. How can a hawk ever find him there? I fancied that he must be glad to see us, though he did seem to chide us. One of those sombre fir and spruce woods is not complete unless you hear from out its cavernous mossy and twiggy recesses his fine alarum, — his spruce voice, like the working of the sap through some crack in a tree, — the working of the spruce-beer. Such an impertinent fellow would occasionally try to alarm the wood about me. "Oh," said I, "I am well acquainted with your family, I know your cousins in Concord very well. Guess the mail's irregular in these parts, and you 'd like to hear from 'em." But my overtures were vain, for he would withdraw by his aerial turnpikes into a more distant cedar-top, and spring his rattle again.

We then entered another swamp, at a necessarily slow pace, where the walking was worse than ever, not only on account of the water, but the fallen timber, which often obliterated the indistinct trail entirely. The fallen trees were so numerous, that for long distances the route was through a succession of small yards, where we climbed over fences as high as our heads, down into water often up to our knees, and then over another fence into a second yard, and so on; and going back for his bag my companion once lost his way and came back without it. In many places the canoe would have run if it had not been for the fallen timber. Again it would be more open, but equally wet, too wet for trees to grow, and no place to sit down. It was a mossy swamp, which it required the long legs of a moose to traverse, and it is very likely that we scared some of them in our transit, though we saw none. It was ready to echo the growl of a bear, the howl of a wolf, or the scream of a panther; but when you get fairly into the middle of one of these grim forests, you are surprised to find that the larger inhabitants are not at home commonly, but have left only a puny red squirrel to bark at you. Generally speaking, a howling wilderness does not howl: it is the imagination of the traveler that does the howling. I did, however, see one dead porcupine; perhaps he had succumbed to the difficulties of the way. These bristly fellows are a very suitable small fruit of such unkempt wildernesses.

Making a logging-road in the Maine woods is called "swamping it," and they who do the work are called "swampers." I now perceived the fitness of the term. This was the most perfectly swamped of all the roads I ever saw. Nature must have coöperated with art here. However, I suppose they would tell you that this name took its origin from the fact that the chief work of road-makers in those woods is to make the swamps passable. We came to a stream where the bridge, which had been made of logs tied together with cedar bark, had been broken up, and we got over as we could. This probably emptied into Mud Pond, and perhaps the Indian might have come up it and taken us in there if he had known it. Such as it was, this ruined bridge was the chief evidence that we were on a path of any kind.

We then crossed another low rising ground, and I, who wore shoes, had an opportunity to wring out my stockings, but my companion, who used boots, had found that this was not a safe experiment for him, for he might not be able to get his wet boots on again. He went over the whole ground, or water, three times, for which reason our progress was very slow; beside that the water softened our feet, and to some extent unfitted them for walking. As I sat waiting for him, it would naturally seem an unaccountable time that he was gone. Therefore, as I could see through the woods that the sun was getting low, and it was uncertain how far the lake might be, even if we were on the right course, and in what part of the world we should find ourselves at nightfall, I proposed that I should push through with what speed I could, leaving boughs to mark my path, and find the lake and the Indian, if possible, before night, and send the latter back to carry my companion's bag.

Having gone about a mile, and got into low ground again, I heard a noise like the note of an owl, which I soon discovered to be made by the Indian, and, answering him, we soon came together. He had reached the lake, after crossing Mud Pond, and running some rapids below it, and had come up about a mile and a half on our path. If he had not come back to meet us, we probably should not have found him that night, for the path branched once or twice before reaching this particular part of the lake. So he went back for my companion and his bag, while I kept on. Having waded through another stream, where the bridge of logs had been broken up and half floated away, — and this was not altogether worse than our ordinary walking, since it was less muddy, — we continued on, through alternate mud and water, to the shore of Apmoojenegamook Lake, which we reached in season for a late supper, instead of dining there, as we had expected, having gone without our dinner. It was at least five miles by the way we had come, and as my companion had gone over most of it three times, he had walked full a dozen miles, bad as it was. In the winter, when the water is frozen, and the snow is four feet deep, it is no doubt a tolerable path to a footman. As it was, I would not have missed that walk for a good deal. If you want an exact recipe for making such a road, take one part Mud Pond, and dilute it with equal parts of Umbazookskus and Apmoojenegamook; then send a family of musquash through to locate it, look after the grades and culverts, and finish it to their minds, and let a hurricane follow to do the fencing.

We had come out on a point extending into Apmoojenegamook, or Chamberlain Lake, west of the outlet of Mud Pond, where there was a broad, gravelly, and rocky shore, encumbered with bleached logs and trees. We were rejoiced to see such dry things in that part of the world. But at first we did not attend to dryness so much as to mud and wetness. We all three walked into the lake up to our middle to wash our clothes.

This was another noble lake, called twelve miles long, east and west; if you add Telos Lake, which, since the dam was built, has been connected with it by dead water, it will be twenty; and it is apparently from a mile and a half to two miles wide. We were about midway its length, on the south side. We could see the only clearing in these parts, called the "Chamberlain Farm," with two or three log buildings close together, on the opposite shore, some two and a half miles distant. The smoke of our fire on the shore brought over two men in a canoe from the farm, that being a common signal agreed on when one wishes to cross. It took them about half an hour to come over, and they had their labor for their pains this time. Even the English name of the lake had a wild, woodland sound, reminding me of that Chamberlain who killed Paugus at Lovewell's fight.

After putting on such dry clothes as we had, and hanging the others to dry on the pole which the Indian arranged over the fire, we ate our supper, and lay down on the pebbly shore with our feet to the fire, without pitching our tent, making a thin bed of grass to cover the stones.

Here first I was molested by the little midge called the No-see-em (*Simulium nocivum*, the latter word is not the Latin for no-see-em), especially over the sand at the water's edge, for it is a kind of sand-fly. You would not observe them but for their light-colored wings. They are said to get under your clothes, and produce a feverish heat, which I suppose was what I felt that night.

Our insect foes in this excursion, to sum them up, were, first, mosquitoes, the chief ones, but only troublesome at night, or when we sat still on shore by day; second, black flies (*Simulium molestum*), which molested us more or less on the carries by day, as I have before described, and sometimes in narrower parts of the stream.

Harris mistakes when he says that they are not seen after June. Third, moose-flies. The big ones, Polis said, were called *Bososquasis*. It is a stout, brown fly, much like a horse-fly, about eleven sixteenths of an inch long, commonly rusty colored beneath, with unspotted wings. They can bite smartly, according to Polis, but are easily avoided or killed. Fourth, the No-see-ems above mentioned. Of all these, the mosquitoes are the only ones that troubled me seriously; but, as I was provided with a wash and a veil, they have not made any deep impression.

The Indian would not use our wash to protect his face and hands, for fear that it would hurt his skin, nor had he any veil; he, therefore, suffered from insects now, and throughout this journey, more than either of us. I think that he suffered more than I did, when neither of us was protected. He regularly tied up his face in his handkerchief, and buried it in his blanket, and he now finally lay down on the sand between us and the fire for the sake of the smoke, which he tried to make enter his blanket about his face, and for the same purpose he lit his pipe and breathed the smoke into his blanket.

As we lay thus on the shore, with nothing between us and the stars, I inquired what stars he was acquainted with, or had names for. They

were the Great Bear, which he called by this
name, the Seven Stars, which he had no English name for, "the morning star," and "the
north star."

In the middle of the night, as indeed each
time that we lay on the shore of a lake, we
heard the voice of the loon, loud and distinct,
from far over the lake. It is a very wild sound,
quite in keeping with the place and the circumstances of the traveler, and very unlike the
voice of a bird. I could lie awake for hours
listening to it, it is so thrilling. When camping
in such a wilderness as this, you are prepared
to hear sounds from some of its inhabitants
which will give voice to its wildness. Some
idea of bears, wolves, or panthers runs in your
head naturally, and when this note is first heard
very far off at midnight, as you lie with your
ear to the ground, — the forest being perfectly
still about you, you take it for granted that it
is the voice of a wolf or some other wild beast,
for only the last part is heard when at a distance, — you conclude that it is a pack of
wolves baying the moon, or, perchance, canter-
ing after a moose. Strange as it may seem,
the "mooing" of a cow on a mountain-side
comes nearest to my idea of the voice of a bear;
and this bird's note resembled that. It was the
unfailing and characteristic sound of those

lakes. We were not so lucky as to hear wolves howl, though that is an occasional serenade. Some friends of mine, who two years ago went up the Caucomgomoc River, were serenaded by wolves while moose-hunting by moonlight. It was a sudden burst, as if a hundred demons had broke loose, — a startling sound enough, which, if any, would make your hair stand on end, and all was still again. It lasted but a moment, and you'd have thought there were twenty of them, when probably there were only two or three. They heard it twice only, and they said that it gave expression to the wilderness which it lacked before. I heard of some men who, while skinning a moose lately in those woods, were driven off from the carcass by a pack of wolves, which ate it up.

This of the loon — I do not mean its laugh, but its looning, — is a long-drawn call, as it were, sometimes singularly human to my ear, — *hoo-hoo-ooooo*, like the hallooing of a man on a very high key, having thrown his voice into his head. I have heard a sound exactly like it when breathing heavily through my own nostrils, half awake at ten at night, suggesting my affinity to the loon; as if its language were but a dialect of my own, after all. Formerly, when lying awake at midnight in those woods, I had listened to hear some words or syllables of their language, but it chanced that I listened in vain until I heard the cry of the loon. I have heard it occasionally on the ponds of my native town, but there its wildness is not enhanced by the surrounding scenery.

I was awakened at midnight by some heavy, low-flying bird, probably a loon, flapping by close over my head, along the shore. So, turning the other side of my half-clad body to the fire, I sought slumber again.

TUESDAY, *July* 28.

When we awoke, we found a heavy dew on our blankets. I lay awake very early, and listened to the clear, shrill *ah-tette-tette-te*, of the white-throated sparrow, repeated at short intervals, without the least variation, for half an hour, as if it could not enough express its happiness. Whether my companions heard it or not, I know not, but it was a kind of matins to me, and the event of that forenoon.

It was a pleasant sunrise, and we had a view of the mountains in the southeast. Ktaadn appeared about southeast by south. A double-topped mountain, about southeast by east, and another portion of the same, east-southeast. The last the Indian called Nerlumskeechticook, and said that it was at the head of the East Branch, and we should pass near it on our return that way.

We did some more washing in the lake this morning, and with our clothes hung about on the dead trees and rocks, the shore looked like washing-day at home. The Indian, taking the hint, borrowed the soap, and, walking into the lake, washed his only cotton shirt on his person, then put on his pants and let it dry on him.

I observed that he wore a cotton shirt, originally white, a greenish flannel one over it, but no waistcoat, flannel drawers, and strong linen or duck pants, which also had been white, blue woolen stockings, cowhide boots, and a Kossuth hat. He carried no change of clothing, but putting on a stout, thick jacket, which he laid aside in the canoe, and seizing a full-sized axe, his gun and ammunition, and a blanket, which would do for a sail or knapsack, if wanted, and strapping on his belt, which contained a large sheath-knife, he walked off at once, ready to be gone all summer. This looked very independent; a few simple and effective tools, and no India-rubber clothing. He was always the first ready to start in the morning, and if it had not held some of our property, would not have been obliged to roll up his blanket. Instead of carrying a large bundle of his own extra clothing, etc., he brought back the great-coats of moose tied up in his blanket. I found that his outfit was the result of a long experience, and in the main hardly to be improved on, unless by washing and an extra shirt. Wanting a button here, he walked off to a place where some Indians had recently encamped, and searched for one, but I believe in vain.

Having softened our stiffened boots and shoes with the pork fat, the usual disposition of what was left at breakfast, we crossed the lake early, steering in a diagonal direction, northeasterly about four miles, to the outlet, which was not to be discovered till we were close to it. The Indian name, Apmoojenegamook, means lake that is crossed, because the usual course lies across, and not along it. This is the largest of the Allegash lakes, and was the first St. John's water that we floated on. It is shaped in the main like Chesuncook. There are no mountains or high hills very near it. At Bangor we had been told of a township many miles farther northwest; it was indicated to us as containing the highest land thereabouts, where, by climbing a particular tree in the forest, we could get a general idea of the country. I have no doubt that the last was good advice, but we did not go there. We did not intend to go far down the Allegash, but merely to get a view of the great lakes which are its source, and then return this way to the East Branch of the Penobscot. The water now, by good rights, flowed northward, if it could be said to flow at all.

After reaching the middle of the lake, we found the waves as usual pretty high, and the Indian warned my companion, who was nodding, that he must not allow himself to fall asleep in the canoe lest he should upset us; adding, that when Indians want to sleep in a canoe, they lie down straight on the bottom. But in this crowded one that was impossible. However, he said that he would nudge him if he saw him nodding.

A belt of dead trees stood all around the lake, some far out in the water, with others prostrate behind them, and they made the shore, for the most part, almost inaccessible. This is the effect of the dam at the outlet. Thus the natural sandy or rocky shore, with its green fringe, was concealed and destroyed. We coasted westward along the north side, searching for the outlet, about one quarter of a mile distant from this savage-looking shore, on which the waves were breaking violently, knowing that it might easily be concealed amid this rubbish, or by the over-lapping of the shore. It is remarkable how little these important gates to a lake are blazoned. There is no triumphal arch over the modest inlet or outlet, but at some undistinguished point it trickles in or out through the uninterrupted forest, almost as through a sponge.

We reached the outlet in about an hour, and

carried over the dam there, which is quite a
solid structure, and about one quarter of a mile
farther there was a second dam. The reader
will perceive that the result of this particular
damming about Chamberlain Lake is, that the
head-waters of the St. John are made to flow
by Bangor. They have thus dammed all the
larger lakes, raising their broad surfaces many
feet; Moosehead, for instance, some forty miles
long, with its steamer on it; thus turning the
forces of nature against herself, that they might
float their spoils out of the country. They rapidly run out of these immense forests all the
finer, and more accessible pine timber, and
then leave the bears to watch the decaying dams,
not clearing nor cultivating the land, nor making roads, nor building houses, but leaving it
a wilderness as they found it. In many parts,
only these dams remain, like deserted beaver-
dams. Think how much land they have flowed,
without asking Nature's leave! When the
State wishes to endow an academy or university, it grants it a tract of forest land: one saw
represents an academy; a gang, a university.

The wilderness experiences a sudden rise of
all her streams and lakes, she feels ten thousand vermin gnawing at the base of her noblest
trees, many combining, drag them off, jarring
over the roots of the survivors, and tumble

them into the nearest stream, till, the fairest
having fallen, they scamper off to ransack some
new wilderness, and all is still again. It is as
when a migrating army of mice girdles a forest
of pines. The chopper fells trees from the
same motive that the mouse gnaws them, — to
get his living. You tell me that he has a more
interesting family than the mouse. That is as
it happens. He speaks of a "berth" of timber,
a good place for him to get into, just as a worm
might. When the chopper would praise a
pine, he will commonly tell you that the one
he cut was so big that a yoke of oxen stood on
its stump; as if that were what the pine had
grown for, to become the footstool of oxen. In
my mind's eye, I can see these unwieldy tame
deer, with a yoke binding them together, and
brazen-tipped horns betraying their servitude,
taking their stand on the stump of each giant
pine in succession throughout this whole forest,
and chewing their cud there, until it is nothing
but an ox-pasture, and run out at that. As if
it were good for the oxen, and some terebin-
thine or other medicinal quality ascended into
their nostrils. Or is their elevated position intended merely as a symbol of the fact that the
pastoral comes next in order to the sylvan or
hunter life?

The character of the logger's admiration is

betrayed by his very mode of expressing it. If he told all that was in his mind, he would say, it was so big that I cut it down and then a yoke of oxen could stand on its stump. He admires the log, the carcass or corpse, more than the tree. Why, my dear sir, the tree might have stood on its own stump, and a great deal more comfortably and firmly than a yoke of oxen can, if you had not cut it down. What right have you to celebrate the virtues of the man you murdered?

The Anglo-American can indeed cut down, and grub up all this waving forest, and make a stump speech, and vote for Buchanan on its ruins, but he cannot converse with the spirit of the tree he fells, he cannot read the poetry and mythology which retire as he advances. He ignorantly erases mythological tablets in order to print his handbills and town-meeting warrants on them. Before he has learned his a b c in the beautiful but mystic lore of the wilderness which Spenser and Dante had just begun to read, he cuts it down, coins a *pine-tree* shilling (as if to signify the pine's value to him), puts up a *dee*strict school-house, and introduces Wesbter's spelling-book.

Below the last dam, the river being swift and shallow, though broad enough, we two walked about half a mile to lighten the canoe. I made it a rule to carry my knapsack when I walked, and also to keep it tied to a cross-bar when in the canoe, that it might be found with the canoe if we should upset.

I heard the dog-day locust here, and afterward on the carries, a sound which I had associated only with more open, if not settled countries. The area for locusts must be small in the Maine woods.

We were now fairly on the Allegash River, which name our Indian said meant hemlock bark. These waters flow northward about one hundred miles, at first very feebly, then southeasterly two hundred and fifty more to the Bay of Fundy. After perhaps two miles of river, we entered Heron Lake, called on the map *Pongokwahem*, scaring up forty or fifty young *shecorways*, sheldrakes, at the entrance, which ran over the water with great rapidity, as usual in a long line.

This was the fourth great lake, lying northwest and southeast, like Chesuncook, and most of the long lakes in that neighborhood, and, judging from the map, it is about ten miles long. We had entered it on the southwest side, and saw a dark mountain northeast over the lake, not very far off nor high, which the Indian said was called *Peaked Mountain*, and used by explorers to look for timber from. There was also some other high land more easterly. The shores were in the same ragged and unsightly condition, encumbered with dead timber, both fallen and standing, as in the last lake, owing to the dam on the Allegash below. Some low points or islands were almost drowned.

I saw something white a mile off on the water, which turned out to be a great gull on a rock in the middle, which the Indian would have been glad to kill and eat, but it flew away long before we were near; and also a flock of summer ducks that were about the rock with it. I asking him about herons, since this was Heron Lake, he said that he found the blue heron's nests in the hard-wood trees. I thought that I saw a light-colored object move along the opposite or northern shore, four or five miles distant. He did not know what it could be, unless it were a moose, though he had never seen a white one; but he said that he could distinguish a moose "anywhere on shore, clear across the lake."

Rounding a point, we stood across a bay for a mile and a half or two miles, toward a large island, three or four miles down the lake. We met with ephemeræ (shad-fly) midway, about a mile from the shore, and they evidently fly over the whole lake. On Moosehead I had seen a large devil's-needle half a mile from the shore, coming from the middle of the lake, where it was three or four miles wide at least. It had probably crossed. But at last, of course, you come to lakes so large that an insect cannot fly across them; and this, perhaps, will serve to distinguish a large lake from a small one.

We landed on the southeast side of the island, which was rather elevated and densely wooded, with a rocky shore, in season for an early dinner. Somebody had camped there not long before, and left the frame on which they stretched a moose-hide, which our Indian criticised severely, thinking it showed but little woodcraft. Here were plenty of the shells of crayfish, or fresh-water lobsters, which had been washed ashore, such as have given a name to some ponds and streams. They are commonly four or five inches long. The Indian proceeded at once to cut a canoe-birch, slanted it up against another tree on the shore, tying it with a withe, and lay down to sleep in its shade.

When we were on the Caucomgomoc, he recommended to us a new way home, the very one which we had first thought of, by the St. John. He even said that it was easier, and would take but little more time than the other, by the East Branch of the Penobscot, though very much farther round; and, taking the map, he showed where we should be each night, for he was

familiar with the route. According to his calculation, we should reach the French settlements
the next night after this, by keeping northward
down the Allegash, and when we got into the
main St. John the banks would be more or less
settled all the way; as if that were a recommen-
dation. There would be but one or two falls,
with short carrying-places, and we should go
down the stream very fast, even a hundred miles
a day, if the wind allowed; and he indicated
where we should carry over into Eel River to
save a bend below Woodstock in New Brunswick, and so into the Schoodic Lake, and
thence to the Mattawamkeag. It would be
about three hundred and sixty miles to Bangor
this way, though only about one hundred and
sixty by the other; but in the former case we
should explore the St. John from its source
through two thirds of its course, as well as the
Schoodic Lake and Mattawamkeag, — and we
were again tempted to go that way. I feared,
however, that the banks of the St. John were
too much settled. When I asked him which
course would take us through the wildest country, he said the route by the East Branch.
Partly from this consideration, as also from its
shortness, we resolved to adhere to the latter
route, and perhaps ascend Ktaadn on the way.
We made this island the limit of our excursion
in this direction.

We had now seen the largest of the Allegash lakes. The next dam "was about fifteen miles" farther north, down the Allegash, and it was dead water so far. We had been told in Bangor of a man who lived alone, a sort of hermit, at that dam, to take care of it, who spent his time tossing a bullet from one hand to the other, for want of employment, — as if we might want to call on him. This sort of tit-for-tat intercourse between his two hands, bandying to and fro a leaden subject, seems to have been his symbol for society.

This island, according to the map, was about a hundred and ten miles in a straight line north-northwest from Bangor, and about ninety-nine miles east-southeast from Quebec. There was another island visible toward the north end of the lake, with an elevated clearing on it; but we learned afterward that it was not inhabited, had only been used as a pasture for cattle which summered in these woods, though our informant said that there was a hut on the mainland near the outlet of the lake. This unnaturally smooth-shaven, squarish spot, in the midst of the otherwise uninterrupted forest, only reminded us how uninhabited the country was. You would sooner expect to meet with a bear than an ox in such a clearing. At any rate, it must have been a surprise to the bears when they came across it.

Such, seen far or near, you know at once to be man's work, for Nature never does it. In order to let in the light to the earth as on a lake, he clears off the forest on the hillsides and plains, and sprinkles fine grass-seed, like an enchanter, and so carpets the earth with a firm sward.

Polis had evidently more curiosity respecting the few settlers in those woods than we. If nothing was said, he took it for granted that we wanted to go straight to the next log-hut. Having observed that we came by the log-huts at Chesuncook, and the blind Canadian's at the Mud Pond carry, without stopping to communicate with the inhabitants, he took occasion now to suggest that the usual way was, when you came near a house, to go to it, and tell the inhabitants what you had seen or heard, and then they tell you what they had seen; but we laughed, and said that we had had enough of houses for the present, and had come here partly to avoid them.

In the mean while, the wind, increasing, blew down the Indian's birch, and created such a sea that we found ourselves prisoners on the island, the nearest shore, which was the western, being perhaps a mile distant, and we took the canoe out to prevent its drifting away. We did not know but we should be compelled to spend the rest of the day and the night there. At any rate, the Indian went to sleep again in the shade of his birch, my companion busied himself drying his plants, and I rambled along the shore westward, which was quite stony, and obstructed with fallen, bleached, or drifted trees for four or five rods in width. I found growing on this broad, rocky, and gravelly shore the *Salix rostrata*, *discolor*, and *lucida*, *Ranunculus recurvatus*, *Potentilla Norvegica*, *Scutellaria lateriflora*, *Eupatorium purpureum*, *Aster Tradescanti*, *Mentha Canadensis*, *Epilobium angustifolium*, abundant. *Lycopus minatus*, *Solidago lanceolata*, *Spiræa salicifolia*, *Antennaria margaraticea*, *Prunella*, *Rumex acetosella*, Raspberries, Wool-grass, *Onoclea*, etc. The nearest trees were *Betula papyracea* and *excelsa*, and *Populus tremuloides*. I give these names because it was my farthest northern point.

Our Indian said that he was a doctor, and could tell me some medicinal use for every plant I could show him. I immediately tried him. He said that the inner bark of the aspen (*Populus tremuloides*) was good for sore eyes; and so with various other plants, proving himself as good as his word. According to his account, he had acquired such knowledge in his youth from a wise old Indian with whom he associated, and he lamented that the present generation of Indians "had lost a great deal."

He said that the caribou was a "very great runner," that there was none about this lake now, though there used to be many, and pointing to the belt of dead trees caused by the dams, he added, "No likum stump, — when he sees that he scared."

Pointing southeasterly over the lake and distant forest, he observed, "Me go Oldtown in three days." I asked how he would get over the swamps and fallen trees. "Oh," said he, "in winter all covered, go anywhere on snow-shoes, right across lakes." When I asked how he went, he said, "First I go Ktaadn, west side, then I go Millinocket, then Pamadumcook, then Nicketow, then Lincoln, then Oldtown," or else he went a shorter way by the Piscataquis. What a wilderness walk for a man to take alone! None of your half-mile swamps, none of your mile-wide woods merely, as on the skirts of our towns, without hotels, only a dark mountain or a lake for guide-board and station, over ground much of it impassable in summer!

It reminded me of Prometheus Bound. Here was traveling of the old heroic kind over the unaltered face of nature. From the Allegash, or Hemlock River, and Pongoquahem Lake, across great Apmoojenegamook, and leaving the Nerlumskeechticook Mountain on his left, he takes his way under the bear-haunted slopes of

Souneunk and Ktaadn Mountains to Pamadumcook and Millinocket's inland seas (where often
gulls'-eggs may increase his store), and so on to
the forks of the Nicketow (*nia soseb* "we alone
Joseph" seeing what our folks see), ever pushing the boughs of the fir and spruce aside, with
his load of furs, contending day and night, night
and day, with the shaggy demon vegetation,
traveling through the mossy graveyard of trees.
Or he could go by "that rough tooth of the
sea," Kineo, great source of arrows and of
spears to the ancients, when weapons of stone
were used. Seeing and hearing moose, caribou,
bears, porcupines, lynxes, wolves, and panthers.
Places where he might live and die and never
hear of the United States, which make such a
noise in the world, — never hear of America, so
called from the name of a European gentleman.

There is a lumberer's road called the Eagle
Lake road, from the Seboois to the east side of
this lake. It may seem strange that any road
through such a wilderness should be passable,
even in winter, when the snow is three or four
feet deep, but at that season, wherever lumbering operations are actively carried on, teams are
continually passing on the single track, and it
becomes as smooth almost as a railway. I am
told that in the Aroostook country the sleds are
required by law to be of one width (four feet),

and sleighs must be altered to fit the track, so that one runner may go in one rut and the other follow the horse. Yet it is very bad turning out.

We had for some time seen a thunder-shower coming up from the west over the woods of the island, and heard the muttering of the thunder, though we were in doubt whether it would reach us; but now the darkness rapidly increasing, and a fresh breeze rustling the forest, we hastily put up the plants which we had been drying, and with one consent made a rush for the tent material and set about pitching it. A place was selected and stakes and pins cut in the shortest possible time, and we were pinning it down lest it should be blown away, when the storm suddenly burst over us.

As we lay huddled together under the tent, which leaked considerably about the sides, with our baggage at our feet, we listened to some of the grandest thunder which I ever heard, — rapid peals, round and plump, bang, bang, bang, in succession, like artillery from some fortress in the sky; and the lightning was proportionally brilliant. The Indian said, "It must be good powder." All for the benefit of the moose and us, echoing far over the concealed lakes. I thought it must be a place which the thunder loved, where the lightning practised to keep its hand in, and it would do no harm to shatter a few pines. What had become of the ephemeræ and devil's-needles then? Were they prudent enough to seek harbor before the storm? Perhaps their motions might guide the voyageur.

Looking out I perceived that the violent shower falling on the lake had almost instantaneously flattened the waves, — the commander of that fortress had smoothed it for us so, — and, it clearing off, we resolved to start immediately, before the wind raised them again.

Going outside, I said that I saw clouds still in the southwest, and heard thunder there. The Indian asked if the thunder went "lound" (round), saying that if it did we should have more rain. I thought that it did. We embarked, nevertheless, and paddled rapidly back toward the dams. The white-throated sparrows on the shore were about, singing, *Ah te, e, e, te, e, e, te,* or else *ah te, e, e, te, e, e, te, e, e, te, e, e.*

At the outlet of Chamberlain Lake we were overtaken by another gusty rain-storm, which compelled us to take shelter, the Indian under his canoe on the bank, and we ran under the edge of the dam. However, we were more scared than wet. From my covert I could see the Indian peeping out from beneath his canoe to see what had become of the rain. When we had taken our respective places thus once or twice, the rain not coming down in earnest, we commenced rambling about the neighborhood, for the wind had by this time raised such waves on the lake that we could not stir, and we feared that we should be obliged to camp there. We got an early supper on the dam and tried for fish there, while waiting for the tumult to subside. The fishes were not only few, but small and worthless, and the Indian declared that there were no good fishes in the St. John's waters; that we must wait till we got to the Penobscot waters.

At length, just before sunset, we set out again. It was a wild evening when we coasted up the north side of this Apmoojenegamook Lake. One thunder-storm was just over, and the waves which it had raised still running with violence, and another storm was now seen coming up in the southwest, far over the lake; but it might be worse in the morning, and we wished to get as far as possible on our way up the lake while we might. It blowed hard against the northern shore about an eighth of a mile distant on our left, and there was just as much sea as our shallow canoe would bear, without our taking unusual care. That which we kept off, and toward which the waves were driving, was as dreary and harborless a shore as you can con-

ceive. For half a dozen rods in width it was a
perfect maze of submerged trees, all dead and
bare and bleaching, some standing half their
original height, others prostrate, and criss-
across, above or beneath the surface, and mingled with them were loose trees and limbs and
stumps, beating about. Imagine the wharves
of the largest city in the world, decayed, and
the earth and planking washed away, leaving
the spiles standing in loose order, but often of
twice the ordinary height, and mingled with and
beating against them the wreck of ten thousand
navies, all their spars and timbers, while there
rises from the water's edge the densest and
grimmest wilderness, ready to supply more material when the former fails, and you may get a
faint idea of that coast. We could not have
landed if we would, without the greatest danger
of being swamped; so blow as it might, we must
depend on coasting by it. It was twilight, too,
and that stormy cloud was advancing rapidly in
our rear. It was a pleasant excitement, yet we
were glad to reach, at length, in the dusk, the
cleared shore of the Chamberlain Farm.

We landed on a low and thinly wooded point
there, and while my companions were pitching
the tent, I ran up to the house to get some
sugar, our six pounds being gone; — it was no
wonder they were, for Polis had a sweet tooth.

He would first fill his dipper nearly a third full of sugar, and then add the coffee to it. Here was a clearing extending back from the lake to a hill-top, with some dark-colored log buildings and a storehouse in it, and half a dozen men standing in front of the principal hut, greedy for news. Among them was the man who tended the dam on the Allegash and tossed the bullet. He having charge of the dams, and learning that we were going to Webster Stream the next day, told me that some of their men, who were haying at Telos Lake, had shut the dam at the canal there in order to catch trout, and if we wanted more water to take us through the canal, we might raise the gate, for he would like to have it raised. The Chamberlain Farm is no doubt a cheerful opening in the woods, but such was the lateness of the hour that it has left but a dusky impression on my mind. As I have said, the influx of light merely is civilizing, yet I fancied that they walked about on Sundays in their clearing somewhat as in a prison-yard.

They were unwilling to spare more than four pounds of brown sugar, — unlocking the store-house to get it, — since they only kept a little for such cases as this, and they charged twenty cents a pound for it, which certainly it was worth to get it up there.

When I returned to the shore it was quite dark, but we had a rousing fire to warm and dry us by, and a snug apartment behind it. The Indian went up to the house to inquire after a brother who had been absent hunting a year or two, and while another shower was beginning, I groped about cutting spruce and arbor-vitæ twigs for a bed. I preferred the arbor-vitæ on account of its fragrance, and spread it particularly thick about the shoulders. It is remarkable with what pure satisfaction the traveler in these woods will reach his camping-ground on the eve of a tempestuous night like this, as if he had got to his inn, and, rolling himself in his blanket, stretch himself on his six feet by two bed of dripping fir-twigs, with a thin sheet of cotton for roof, snug as a meadow-mouse in its nest. Invariably our best nights were those when it rained, for then we were not troubled with mosquitoes.

You soon come to disregard rain on such excursions, at least in the summer, it is so easy to dry yourself, supposing a dry change of clothing is not to be had. You can much sooner dry you by such a fire as you can make in the woods than in anybody's kitchen, the fireplace is so much larger, and wood so much more abundant. A shed-shaped tent will catch and reflect the heat like a Yankee-baker, and you may be drying while you are sleeping.

Some who have leaky roofs in the towns may have been kept awake, but we were soon lulled asleep by a steady, soaking rain, which lasted all night. To-night, the rain not coming at once with violence, the twigs were soon dried by the reflected heat.

Wednesday, *July* 29.

When we awoke it had done raining, though it was still cloudy. The fire was put out, and the Indian's boots, which stood under the eaves of the tent, were half full of water. He was much more improvident in such respects than either of us, and he had to thank us for keeping his powder dry. We decided to cross the lake at once, before breakfast, or while we could; and before starting I took the bearing of the shore which we wished to strike, S. S. E. about three miles distant, lest a sudden misty rain should conceal it when we were midway. Though the bay in which we were was perfectly quiet and smooth, we found the lake already wide awake outside, but not dangerously or unpleasantly so; nevertheless, when you get out on one of those lakes in a canoe like this, you do not forget that you are completely at the mercy of the wind, and a fickle power it is. The playful waves may at any time become too rude for you in their sport, and play right on over you. We saw a few *she-cor-ways* and a *fish-hawk* thus early, and after much steady paddling and dancing over the dark waves of Apmoojenegamook, we found ourselves in the neighborhood of the southern land, heard the waves breaking on it, and turned our thoughts wholly to that side. After coasting eastward along this shore a mile or two, we breakfasted on a rocky point, the first convenient place that offered.

It was well enough that we crossed thus early, for the waves now ran quite high, and we should have been obliged to go round somewhat, but beyond this point we had comparatively smooth water. You can commonly go along one side or the other of a lake, when you cannot cross it.

The Indian was looking at the hard-wood ridges from time to time, and said that he would like to buy a few hundred acres somewhere about this lake, asking our advice. It was to buy as near the crossing-place as possible.

My companion and I, having a minute's discussion on some point of ancient history, were amused by the attitude which the Indian, who could not tell what we were talking about, assumed. He constituted himself umpire, and, judging by our air and gesture, he very seriously remarked from time to time, "you beat," or "he beat."

Leaving a spacious bay, a northeasterly prolongation of Chamberlain Lake, on our left, we entered through a short strait into a small lake a couple of miles over, called on the map *Telasinis*, but the Indian had no distinct name for it, and thence into *Telos* Lake, which he called *Paytaywecomgomoc*, or Burnt-Ground Lake. This curved round toward the northeast, and may have been three or four miles long as we paddled. He had not been here since 1825. He did not know what Telos meant; thought it was not Indian. He used the word "*Spoke-logan*" (for an inlet in the shore which led nowhere), and when I asked its meaning said that there was "no Indian in 'em." There was a clearing, with a house and barn, on the southwest shore, temporarily occupied by some men who were getting the hay, as we had been told; also a clearing for a pasture on a hill on the west side of the lake.

We landed on a rocky point on the northeast side, to look at some Red Pines (*Pinus resinosa*), the first we had noticed, and get some cones, for our few which grow in Concord do not bear any.

The outlet from the lake into the East Branch of the Penobscot is an artificial one, and it was not very apparent where it was exactly, but the lake ran curving far up northeasterly into two

narrow valleys or ravines, as if it had for a long
time been groping its way toward the Penobscot waters, or remembered when it anciently
flowed there; by observing where the horizon
was lowest, and following the longest of these,
we at length reached the dam, having come
about a dozen miles from the last camp. Somebody had left a line set for trout, and the jackknife with which the bait had been cut on the
dam beside it, an evidence that man was near,
and on a deserted log close by a loaf of bread
baked in a Yankee-baker. These proved the
property of a solitary hunter, whom we soon
met, and canoe and gun and traps were not far
off. He told us that it was twenty miles farther on our route to the foot of Grand Lake,
where you could catch as many trout as you
wanted, and that the first house below the foot
of the lake, on the East Branch, was Hunt's,
about forty-five miles farther; though there
was one about a mile and a half up Trout
Stream, some fifteen miles ahead, but it was
rather a blind route to it. It turned out that,
though the stream was in our favor, we did not
reach the next house till the morning of the
third day after this. The nearest permanently
inhabited house behind us was now a dozen
miles distant, so that the interval between the
two nearest houses on our route was about sixty
miles.

This hunter, who was a quite small, sunburnt man, having already carried his canoe over, and baked his loaf, had nothing so interesting and pressing to do as to observe our transit. He had been out a month or more alone. How much more wild and adventurous his life than that of the hunter in Concord woods, who gets back to his house and the mill-dam every night! Yet they in the towns who have wild oats to sow commonly sow them on cultivated and comparatively exhausted ground. And as for the rowdy world in the large cities, so little enterprise has it that it never adventures in this direction, but like vermin clubs together in alleys and drinking-saloons, its highest accomplishment, perchance, to run beside a fire-engine and throw brickbats. But the former is comparatively an independent and successful man, getting his living in a way that he likes, without disturbing his human neighbors. How much more respectable also is the life of the solitary pioneer or settler in these, or any woods, — having real difficulties, not of his own creation, drawing his subsistence directly from nature, — than that of the helpless multitudes in the towns who depend on gratifying the extremely artificial wants of society and are thrown out of employment by hard times!

Here for the first time we found the raspberries really plenty, — that is, on passing the height of land between the Allegash and the East Branch of the Penobscot; the same was true of the blueberries.

Telos Lake, the head of the St. John on this side, and Webster Pond, the head of the East Branch of the Penobscot, are only about a mile apart, and they are connected by a ravine, in which but little digging was required to make the water of the former, which is the highest, flow into the latter. This canal, which is something less than a mile long and about four rods wide, was made a few years before my first visit to Maine. Since then the lumber of the upper Allegash and its lakes has been run down the Penobscot, that is, up the Allegash, which here consists principally of a chain of large and stagnant lakes, whose thoroughfares, or river-links, have been made nearly equally stagnant by damming, and then down the Penobscot. The rush of the water has produced such changes in the canal that it has now the appearance of a very rapid mountain stream flowing through a ravine, and you would not suspect that any digging had been required to persuade the waters of the St. John to flow into the Penobscot here. It was so winding that one could see but little way down.

It is stated by Springer, in his "Forest Life,"

that the cause of this canal being dug was this: according to the treaty of 1842 with Great Britain, it was agreed that all the timber run down the St. John, which rises in Maine, "when within the Province of New Brunswick . . . shall be dealt with as if it were the produce of the said Province," which was thought by our side to mean that it should be free from taxation. Immediately, the Province, wishing to get something out of the Yankees, levied a duty on all the timber that passed down the St. John; but to satisfy its own subjects "made a corresponding discount on the stumpage charged those hauling timber from the crown lands." The result was that the Yankees made the St. John run the other way, or down the Penobscot, so that the Province lost both its duty and its water, while the Yankees, being greatly enriched, had reason to thank it for the suggestion.

It is wonderful how well watered this country is. As you paddle across a lake, bays will be pointed out to you, by following up which, and perhaps the tributary stream which empties in, you may, after a short portage, or possibly, at some seasons, none at all, get into another river, which empties far away from the one you are on. Generally, you may go in any direction in a canoe, by making frequent but not

very long portages. You are only realizing once
more what all nature distinctly remembers here,
for no doubt the waters flowed thus in a former
geological period, and, instead of being a lake
country, it was an archipelago. It seems as if
the more youthful and impressible streams can
hardly resist the numerous invitations and temp-
tations to leave their native beds and run down
their neighbors' channels. Your carries are
often over half-submerged ground, on the dry
channels of a former period. In carrying from
one river to another, I did not go over such
high and rocky ground as in going about the
falls of the same river. For in the former case
I was once lost in a swamp, as I have related,
and, again, found an artificial canal which appeared to be natural.

I remember once dreaming of pushing a canoe
up the rivers of Maine, and that, when I had
got so high that the channels were dry, I kept
on through the ravines and gorges, nearly as
well as before, by pushing a little harder, and
now it seemed to me that my dream was partially realized.

Wherever there is a channel for water, there
is a road for the canoe. The pilot of the
steamer which ran from Oldtown up the Penobscot in 1854 told me that she drew only fourteen inches, and would run easily in two feet of

water, though they did not like to. It is said
that some Western steamers can run on a heavy
dew, whence we can imagine what a canoe may
do. Montresor, who was sent from Quebec by
the English about 1760 to explore the route to
the Kennebec, over which Arnold afterward
passed, supplied the Penobscot near its source
with water by opening the beaver-dams, and he
says, "This is often done." He afterward
states that the Governor of Canada had forbid-
den to molest the beaver about the outlet of the
Kennebec from Moosehead Lake, on account of
the service which their dams did by raising the
water for navigation.

This canal, so called, was a considerable and
extremely rapid and rocky river. The Indian
decided that there was water enough in it without raising the dam, which would only make it
more violent, and that he would run down it
alone, while we carried the greater part of the
baggage. Our provision being about half con-
sumed, there was the less left in the canoe. We
had thrown away the pork-keg, and wrapt its
contents in birch bark, which is the unequaled
wrapping-paper of the woods.

Following a moist trail through the forest,
we reached the head of Webster Pond about the
same time with the Indian, notwithstanding the
velocity with which he moved, our route being

the most direct. The Indian name of Webster Stream, of which this pond is the source, is, according to him, *Madunkchunk*, i. e., Height of Land, and of the pond, *Madunkchunk-gamooc*, or Height of Land Pond. The latter was two or three miles long. We passed near a pine on its shore which had been splintered by lightning, perhaps the day before. This was the first proper East Branch Penobscot water that we came to.

At the outlet of Webster Lake was another dam, at which we stopped and picked raspberries, while the Indian went down the stream a half-mile through the forest, to see what he had got to contend with. There was a deserted log camp here, apparently used the previous winter, with its "hovel" or barn for cattle. In the hut was a large fir-twig bed, raised two feet from the floor occupying a large part of the single apartment, a long narrow table against the wall, with a stout log bench before it, and above the table a small window, the only one there was, which admitted a feeble light. It was a simple and strong fort erected against the cold, and suggested what valiant trencher work had been done there. I discovered one or two curious wooden traps, which had not been used for a long time, in the woods near by. The principal part consisted of a long and slender pole.

We got our dinner on the shore, on the upper side of the dam. As we were sitting by our fire, concealed by the earth bank of the dam, a long line of sheldrake, half-grown, came waddling over it from the water below, passing within about a rod of us, so that we could almost have caught them in our hands. They were very abundant on all the streams and lakes which we visited, and every two or three hours they would rush away in a long string over the water before us, twenty to fifty of them at once, rarely ever flying, but running with great rapidity up or down the stream, even in the midst of the most violent rapids, and apparently as fast up as down, or else crossing diagonally, the old, as it appeared, behind, and driving them, and flying to the front from time to time, as if to direct them. We also saw many small black dippers, which behaved in a similar manner, and, once or twice, a few black ducks.

An Indian at Oldtown had told us that we should be obliged to carry ten miles between Telos Lake on the St. John and Second Lake on the East Branch of the Penobscot; but the lumberers whom we met assured us that there would not be more than a mile of carry. It turned out that the Indian, who had lately been over this route, was nearest right, as far as we were concerned. However, if one of us could have assisted the Indian in managing the canoe in the rapids, we might have run the greater part of the way; but as he was alone in the management of the canoe in such places, we were obliged to walk the greater part. I did not feel quite ready to try such an experiment on Webster Stream, which has so bad a reputation. According to my observation, a batteau, properly manned, shoots rapids as a matter of course, which a single Indian with a canoe carries round.

My companion and I carried a good part of the baggage on our shoulders, while the Indian took that which would be least injured by wet in the canoe. We did not know when we should see him again, for he had not been this way since the canal was cut, nor for more than thirty years. He agreed to stop when he got to smooth water, come up and find our path if he could, and halloo for us, and after waiting a reasonable time go on and try again, — and we were to look out in like manner for him.

He commenced by running through the sluiceway and over the dam, as usual, standing up in his tossing canoe, and was soon out of sight behind a point in a wild gorge. This Webster Stream is well known to lumbermen as a difficult one. It is exceedingly rapid and rocky, and also shallow, and can hardly be considered navigable, unless that may mean that what is launched in it is sure to be carried swiftly down it, though it may be dashed to pieces by the way. It is somewhat like navigating a thunderspout. With commonly an irresistible force urging you on, you have got to choose your own course each moment, between the rocks and shallows, and to get into it, moving forward always with the utmost possible moderation, and often holding on, if you can, that you may inspect the rapids before you.

By the Indian's direction we took an old path on the south side, which appeared to keep down the stream, though at a considerable distance from it, cutting off bends, perhaps to Second Lake, having first taken the course from the map with a compass, which was northeasterly, for safety. It was a wild wood-path, with a few tracks of oxen which had been driven over it, probably to some old camp clearing, for pasturage, mingled with the tracks of moose which had lately used it. We kept on steadily for about an hour without putting down our packs, occasionally winding around or climbing over a fallen tree, for the most part far out of sight and hearing of the river; till, after walking about three miles, we were glad to find that the path came to the river again at an old camp ground, where there was a small opening in the

forest, at which we paused. Swiftly as the
shallow and rocky river ran here, a continuous
rapid with dancing waves, I saw, as I sat on the
shore, a long string of sheldrakes, which something scared, run up the opposite side of the
stream by me, with the same ease that they
commonly did down it, just touching the surface
of the waves, and getting an impulse from them
as they flowed from under them; but they soon
came back, driven by the Indian, who had
fallen a little behind us on account of the windings. He shot round a point just above, and
came to land by us with considerable water in
his canoe. He had found it, as he said, "very
strong water," and had been obliged to land
once before to empty out what he had taken in.
He complained that it strained him to paddle so
hard in order to keep his canoe straight in its
course, having no one in the bows to aid him,
and, shallow as it was, said that it would be no
joke to upset there, for the force of the water
was such that he had as lief I would strike him
over the head with a paddle as have that water
strike him. Seeing him come out of that gap
was as if you should pour water down an inclined
and zigzag trough, then drop a nutshell into it,
and, taking a short cut to the bottom, get there
in time to see it come out, notwithstanding the
rush and tumult, right side up, and only partly
full of water.

After a moment's breathing-space, while I held his canoe, he was soon out of sight again around another bend, and we, shouldering our packs, resumed our course.

We did not at once fall into our paths again, but made our way with difficulty along the edge of the river, till at length, striking inland through the forest, we recovered it. Before going a mile we heard the Indian calling to us. He had come up through the woods and along the path to find us, having reached sufficiently smooth water to warrant his taking us in. The shore was about one fourth of a mile distant, through a dense, dark forest, and as he led us back to it, winding rapidly about to the right and left, I had the curiosity to look down carefully, and found that he was following his steps backward. I could only occasionally perceive his trail in the moss, and yet he did not appear to look down nor hesitate an instant, but led us out exactly to his canoe. This surprised me, for without a compass, or the sight or noise of the river to guide us, we could not have kept our course many minutes, and could have retraced our steps but a short distance, with a great deal of pains and very slowly, using a laborious circumspection. But it was evident that he could go back through the forest wherever he had been during the day.

After this rough walking in the dark woods it was an agreeable change to glide down the rapid river in the canoe once more. This river, which was about the size of our Assabet (in Concord), though still very swift, was almost perfectly smooth here, and showed a very visible declivity, a regularly inclined plane, for several miles, like a mirror set a little aslant, on which we coasted down. This very obvious regular descent, particularly plain when I regarded the water-line against the shores, made a singular impression on me, which the swiftness of our motion probably enhanced, so that we seemed to be gliding down a much steeper declivity than we were, and that we could not save ourselves from rapids and falls if we should suddenly come to them. My companion did not perceive this slope, but I have a surveyor's eyes, and I satisfied myself that it was no ocular illusion. You could tell at a glance on approaching such a river, which way the water flowed, though you might perceive no motion. I observed the angle at which a level line would strike the surface, and calculated the amount of fall in a rod, which did not need to be remarkably great to produce this effect.

It was very exhilarating, and the perfection of traveling, quite unlike floating on our dead Concord River, the coasting down this inclined mirror, which was now and then gently winding, down a mountain, indeed, between two evergreen forests, edged with lofty dead white-pines, sometimes slanted halfway over the stream, and destined soon to bridge it. I saw some monsters there, nearly destitute of branches, and scarcely diminishing in diameter for eighty or ninety feet.

As we thus swept along, our Indian repeated in a deliberate and drawling tone the words "Daniel Webster, great lawyer," apparently reminded of him by the name of the stream, and he described his calling on him once in Boston, at what he supposed was his boarding-house. He had no business with him, but merely went to pay his respects, as we should say. In answer to our questions, he described his person well enough. It was on the day after Webster delivered his Bunker Hill oration, which I believe Polis heard. The first time he called he waited till he was tired without seeing him, and then went away. The next time, he saw him go by the door of the room in which he was waiting several times, in his shirt-sleeves, without noticing him. He thought that if he had come to see Indians, they would not have treated him so. At length, after very long delay, he came in, walked toward him, and asked in a loud voice, gruffly, "What do you want?" and he, thinking at first, by the motion of his hand, that he was going to strike him, said to himself, "You'd better take care, if you try that I shall know what to do." He did not like him, and declared that all he said "was not worth talk about a musquash." We suggested that probably Mr. Webster was very busy, and had a great many visitors just then.

Coming to falls and rapids, our easy progress was suddenly terminated. The Indian went along shore to inspect the water, while we climbed over the rocks, picking berries. The peculiar growth of blueberries on the tops of large rocks here made the impression of high land, and indeed this was the Height-of-land Stream. When the Indian came back, he remarked, "You got to walk; ver strong water." So, taking out his canoe, he launched it again below the falls, and was soon out of sight. At such times, he would step into the canoe, take up his paddle, and, with an air of mystery, start off, looking far down stream, and keeping his own counsel, as if absorbing all the intelligence of forest and stream into himself; but I sometimes detected a little fun in his face, which could yield to my sympathetic smile, for he was thoroughly good-humored. We meanwhile scrambled along the shore with our packs, without any path. This was the last of *our* boating for the day.

The prevailing rock here was a kind of slate, standing on its edges, and my companion, who was recently from California, thought it exactly like that in which the gold is found, and said that if he had had a pan he would have liked to wash a little of the sand here.

The Indian now got along much faster than we, and waited for us from time to time. I found here the only cool spring that I drank at anywhere on this excursion, a little water filling a hollow in the sandy bank. It was a quite memorable event, and due to the elevation of the country, for wherever else we had been the water in the rivers and the streams emptying in was dead and warm, compared with that of a mountainous region. It was very bad walking along the shore over fallen and drifted trees and bushes, and rocks, from time to time swinging ourselves round over the water, or else taking to a gravel bar or going inland. At one place, the Indian being ahead, I was obliged to take off all my clothes in order to ford a small but deep stream emptying in, while my companion, who was inland, found a rude bridge, high up in the woods, and I saw no more of him for some time. I saw there very fresh moose tracks, found a new goldenrod to me (perhaps *Solidago thyrsoidea*), and I passed one white-pine log, which had lodged, in the forest near the edge of the stream, which was quite five feet in diameter at the butt. Probably its size detained it.

Shortly after this I overtook the Indian at the edge of some burnt land, which extended three or four miles at least, beginning about three miles above Second Lake, which we were expecting to reach that night, and which is about ten miles from Telos Lake. This burnt region was still more rocky than before, but, though comparatively open, we could not yet see the lake. Not having seen my companion for some time, I climbed, with the Indian, a singular high rock on the edge of the river, forming a narrow ridge only a foot or two wide at top, in order to look for him; and, after calling many times, I at length heard him answer from a considerable distance inland, he having taken a trail which led off from the river, perhaps directly to the lake, and was now in search of the river again. Seeing a much higher rock, of the same character, about one third of a mile farther east, or down stream, I proceeded toward it, through the burnt land, in order to look for the lake from its summit, supposing that the Indian would keep down the stream in his canoe, and hallooing all the while that my companion might join me on the way. Before we came together I noticed where a moose,

which possibly I had scared by my shouting,
had apparently just run along a large rotten
trunk of a pine, which made a bridge, thirty or
forty feet long, over a hollow, as convenient for
him as for me. The tracks were as large as
those of an ox, but an ox could not have crossed
there. This burnt land was an exceedingly
wild and desolate region. Judging by the weeds
and sprouts, it appeared to have been burnt
about two years before. It was covered with
charred trunks, either prostrate or standing,
which crocked our clothes and hands, and we
could not easily have distinguished a bear there
by his color. Great shells of trees, sometimes
unburnt without, or burnt on one side only, but
black within, stood twenty or forty feet high.
The fire had run up inside, as in a chimney,
leaving the sap-wood. Sometimes we crossed a
rocky ravine fifty feet wide, on a fallen trunk;
and there were great fields of fire-weed (*Epilobium angustifolium*) on all sides, the most extensive that I ever saw, which presented great
masses of pink. Intermixed with these were
blueberry and raspberry bushes.

Having crossed a second rocky ridge like the
first, when I was beginning to ascend the third,
the Indian, whom I had left on the shore some
fifty rods behind, beckoned to me to come to
him, but I made sign that I would first ascend

the highest rock before me, whence I expected
to see the lake. My companion accompanied
me to the top. This was formed just like the
others. Being struck with the perfect parallel-
ism of these singular rock hills, however much
one might be in advance of another, I took out
my compass and found that they lay northwest
and southeast, the rock being on its edge, and
sharp edges they were. This one, to speak from
memory, was perhaps a third of a mile in
length, but quite narrow, rising gradually from
the northwest to the height of about eighty feet,
but steep on the southeast end. The southwest
side was as steep as an ordinary roof, or as we
could safely climb; the northeast was an abrupt
precipice from which you could jump clean to
the bottom, near which the river flowed; while
the level top of the ridge, on which you walked
along, was only from one to three or four feet
in width. For a rude illustration, take the half
of a pear cut in two lengthwise, lay it on its flat
side, the stem to the northwest, and then halve
it vertically in the direction of its length, keeping the southwest half. Such was the general
form.

There was a remarkable series of these great
rock-waves revealed by the burning; breakers,
as it were. No wonder that the river that
found its way through them was rapid and ob-

structed by falls.   No doubt the absence of soil
on these rocks, or its dryness where there was
any, caused this to be a very thorough burning.
We could see the lake over the woods, two or
three miles ahead, and that the river made an
abrupt turn southward around the northwest
end of the cliff on which we stood, or a little
above us, so that we had cut off a bend, and
that there was an important fall in it a short
distance below us.   I could see the canoe a hundred rods behind, but now on the opposite
shore, and supposed that the Indian had concluded to take out and carry round some bad
rapids on that side, and that that might be what
he had beckoned to me for; but after waiting a
while I could still see nothing of him, and I observed to my companion that I wondered where
he was, though I began to suspect that he had
gone inland to look for the lake from some hill-
top on that side, as we had done.   This proved
to be the case; for after I had started to return
to the canoe, I heard a faint halloo, and descried
him on the top of a distant rocky hill on that
side.   But as, after a long time had elapsed, I
still saw his canoe in the same place, and he had
not returned to it, and appeared in no hurry to
do so, and, moreover, as I remembered that he
had previously beckoned to me, I thought that
there might be something more to delay him

than I knew, and began to return northwest, along the ridge, toward the angle in the river. My companion, who had just been separated from us, and had even contemplated the necessity of camping alone, wishing to husband his steps, and yet to keep with us, inquired where I was going; to which I answered that I was going far enough back to communicate with the Indian, and that then I thought we had better go along the shore together, and keep him in sight.

When we reached the shore, the Indian appeared from out the woods on the opposite side, but on account of the roar of the water it was difficult to communicate with him. He kept along the shore westward to his canoe, while we stopped at the angle where the stream turned southward around the precipice. I again said to my companion, that we would keep along the shore and keep the Indian in sight. We started to do so, being close together, the Indian behind us having launched his canoe again, but just then I saw the latter, who had crossed to our side, forty or fifty rods behind, beckoning to me, and I called to my companion, who had just disappeared behind large rocks at the point of the precipice, three or four rods before me, on his way down the stream, that I was going to help the Indian a moment. I did so, — helped get the canoe over a fall, lying with my breast

over a rock, and holding one end while he received it below, — and within ten or fifteen
minutes at most I was back again at the point
where the river turned southward, in order to
catch up with my companion, while Polis glided
down the river alone, parallel with me. But to
my surprise, when I rounded the precipice,
though the shore was bare of trees, without
rocks, for a quarter of a mile at least, my companion was not to be seen. It was as if he had
sunk into the earth. This was the more unaccountable to me, because I knew that his feet
were, since our swamp walk, very sore, and that
he wished to keep with the party; and besides
this was very bad walking, climbing over or
about the rocks. I hastened along, hallooing
and searching for him, thinking he might be
concealed behind a rock, yet doubting if he had
not taken the other side of the precipice, but
the Indian had got along still faster in his canoe,
till he was arrested by the falls, about a quarter
of a mile below. He then landed, and said that
we could go no farther that night. The sun
was setting, and on account of falls and rapids
we should be obliged to leave this river and
carry a good way into another farther east.
The first thing then was to find my companion,
for I was now very much alarmed about him,
and I sent the Indian along the shore down

stream, which began to be covered with unburnt wood again just below the falls, while I searched backward about the precipice which we had passed. The Indian showed some unwillingness to exert himself, complaining that he was very tired, in consequence of his day's work, that it had strained him very much getting down so many rapids alone; but he went off calling somewhat like an owl. I remembered that my companion was near-sighted, and I feared that he had either fallen from the precipice, or fainted and sunk down amid the rocks beneath it. I shouted and searched above and below this precipice in the twilight till I could not see, expecting nothing less than to find his body beneath it. For half an hour I anticipated and believed only the worst. I thought what I should do the next day, if I did not find him, what I *could* do in such a wilderness, and how his relatives would feel, if I should return without him. I felt that if he were really lost away from the river there, it would be a desperate undertaking to find him; and where were they who could help you? What would it be to raise the country, where there were only two or three camps, twenty or thirty miles apart, and no road, and perhaps nobody at home? Yet we must try the harder, the less the prospect of success.

I rushed down from this precipice to the canoe in order to fire the Indian's gun, but found that my companion had the caps. I was still thinking of getting it off when the Indian returned. He had not found him, but he said that he had seen his tracks once or twice along the shore. This encouraged me very much. He objected to firing the gun, saying that if my companion heard it, which was not likely, on account of the roar of the stream, it would tempt him to come toward us, and he might break his neck in the dark. For the same reason we refrained from lighting a fire on the highest rock. I proposed that we should both keep down the stream to the lake, or that I should go at any rate, but the Indian said, "No use, can't do anything in the dark; come morning, then we find 'em. No harm, — he make 'em camp. No bad animals here, no gristly bears, such as in California, where he 's been, — warm night, — he well off as you and I." I considered that if he was well he could do without us. He had just lived eight years in California, and had plenty of experience with wild beasts and wilder men, was peculiarly accustomed to make journeys of great length, but if he were sick or dead, he was near where we were. The darkness in the woods was by this so thick that it alone decided the question. We must camp where we were. I knew that he had his knapsack, with blankets and matches, and, if well, would fare no worse than we, except that he would have no supper nor society.

This side of the river being so encumbered with rocks, we crossed to the eastern or smoother shore, and proceeded to camp there, within two or three rods of the falls. We pitched no tent, but lay on the sand, putting a few handfuls of grass and twigs under us, there being no evergreen at hand. For fuel we had some of the charred stumps. Our various bags of provisions had got quite wet in the rapids, and I arranged them about the fire to dry. The fall close by was the principal one on this stream, and it shook the earth under us. It was a cool, because dewy, night; the more so, probably, owing to the nearness of the falls. The Indian complained a good deal, and thought afterward that he got a cold there which occasioned a more serious illness. We were not much troubled by mosquitoes at any rate. I lay awake a good deal from anxiety, but, unaccountably to myself, was at length comparatively at ease respecting him. At first I had apprehended the worst, but now I had little doubt but that I should find him in the morning. From time to time I fancied that I heard his voice calling through the roar of the falls from the opposite side of the river; but it is doubtful if we could have heard him across the stream there. Sometimes I doubted whether the Indian had really seen his tracks, since he manifested an unwillingness to make much of a search, and then my anxiety returned.

It was the most wild and desolate region we • had camped in, where, if anywhere, one might expect to meet with befitting inhabitants, but I heard only the squeak of a night-hawk flitting over. The moon in her first quarter, in the fore part of the night, setting over the bare rocky hills garnished with tall, charred, and hollow stumps or shells of trees, served to reveal the desolation.

THURSDAY, *July* 30.

I aroused the Indian early this morning to go in search of our companion, expecting to find him within a mile or two, farther down the stream. The Indian wanted his breakfast first, but I reminded him that my companion had had neither breakfast nor supper. We were obliged first to carry our canoe and baggage over into another stream, the main East Branch, about three fourths of a mile distant, for Webster Stream was no farther navigable. We went twice over this carry, and the dewy bushes wet us through like water up to the middle; I hallooed in a high key from time to time, though I had little expectation that I could be heard over the roar of the rapids, and, moreover, we were necessarily on the opposite side of the stream to him. In going over this portage the last time, the Indian, who was before me with the canoe on his head, stumbled and fell heavily once, and lay for a moment silent, as if in pain. I hastily stepped forward to help him, asking if he was much hurt, but after a moment's pause, without replying, he sprang up and went forward. He was all the way subject to taciturn fits, but they were harmless ones.

We had launched our canoe and gone but little way down the East Branch, when I heard an answering shout from my companion, and soon after saw him standing on a point where there was a clearing a quarter of a mile below, and the smoke of his fire was rising near by. Before I saw him I naturally shouted again and again, but the Indian curtly remarked, "He hears you," as if once was enough. It was just below the mouth of Webster Stream. When we arrived, he was smoking his pipe, and said that he had passed a pretty comfortable night, though it was rather cold, on account of the dew.

It appeared that when we stood together the previous evening, and I was shouting to the Indian across the river, he, being near-sighted, had not seen the Indian nor his canoe, and when I went back to the Indian's assistance, did not see which way I went, and supposed that we were below and not above him, and so, making haste to catch up, he ran away from us.   Having reached this clearing, a mile or more below our camp, the night overtook him, and he made a fire in a little hollow, and lay down by it in his blanket, still thinking that we were ahead of him.   He thought it likely that he had heard the Indian call once the evening before, but mistook it for an owl.   He had seen one botanical rarity before it was dark, — pure white *Epilobium angustifolium* amidst the fields of pink ones, in the burnt lands.   He had already stuck up the remnant of a lumberer's shirt, found on the point, on a pole by the water-side, for a signal, and attached a note to it, to inform us that he had gone on to the lake, and that if he did not find us there, he would be back in a couple of hours.   If he had not found us soon, he had some thoughts of going back in search of the solitary hunter whom we had met at Telos Lake, ten miles behind, and, if successful, hire him to take him to Bangor.   But if this hunter had moved as fast as we, he would have been twenty miles off by this time, and who could guess in what direction?   It would have been like looking for a needle in a hay-

mow, to search for him in these woods. He
had been considering how long he could live on
berries alone.

We substituted for his note a card containing
our names and destination, and the date of our
visit, which Polis neatly inclosed in a piece of
birch-bark to keep it dry. This has probably
been read by some hunter or explorer ere this.

We all had good appetites for the breakfast
which we made haste to cook here, and then,
having partially dried our clothes, we glided
swiftly down the winding stream toward Second
Lake.

As the shores became flatter with frequent
gravel and sand-bars, and the stream more
winding in the lower land near the lake, elms
and ash-trees made their appearance; also the
wild yellow lily (*Lilium Canadense*), some of
whose bulbs I collected for a soup. On some
ridges the burnt land extended as far as the
lake. This was a very beautiful lake, two or
three miles long, with high mountains on the
southwest side, the (as our Indian said) *Nerlumskeechticook*, *i. e.*, Dead-Water Mountain.
It appears to be the same called Carbuncle
Mountain on the map. According to Polis, it
extends in separate elevations all along this and
the next lake, which is much larger. The lake,
too, I think, is called by the same name, or

perhaps with the addition of *gamoc* or *mooc*.
The morning was a bright one, and perfectly
still and serene, the lake as smooth as glass, we
making the only ripple as we paddled into it.
The dark mountains about it were seen through
a glaucous mist, and the brilliant white stems
of canoe-birches mingled with the other woods
around it.   The wood-thrush sang on the distant shore, and the laugh of some loons, sport-
ing in a concealed western bay, as if inspired
by the morning, came distinct over the lake to
us, and, what was remarkable, the echo which
ran round the lake was much louder than the
original note; probably because, the loon being
in a regularly curving bay under the mountain,
we were exactly in the focus of many echoes,
the sound being reflected like light from a concave mirror.   The beauty of the scene may
have been enhanced to our eyes by the fact that
we had just come together again after a night
of some anxiety.   This reminded me of the
Ambejijis Lake on the West Branch, which I
crossed in my first coming to Maine.   Having
paddled down three quarters of the lake, we
came to a standstill, while my companion let
down for fish.   A white (or whitish) gull sat
on a rock which rose above the surface in mid-
lake not far off, quite in harmony with the
scene; and as we rested there in the warm sun,

we heard one loud crushing or crackling sound from the forest, forty or fifty rods distant, as of a stick broken by the foot of some large animal. Even this was an interesting incident there. In the midst of our dreams of giant lake-trout, even then supposed to be nibbling, our fishermen drew up a diminutive red perch, and we took up our paddles again in haste.

It was not apparent where the outlet of this lake was, and while the Indian thought it was in one direction, I thought it was in another. He said, "I bet you fourpence it is there," but he still held on in my direction, which proved to be the right one. As we were approaching the outlet, it being still early in the forenoon, he suddenly exclaimed, "Moose! moose!" and told us to be still. He put a cap on his gun, and, standing up in the stern, rapidly pushed the canoe straight toward the shore and the moose. It was a cow-moose, about thirty rods off, standing in the water by the side of the outlet, partly behind some fallen timber and bushes, and at that distance she did not look very large. She was flapping her large ears, and from time to time poking off the flies with her nose from some part of her body. She did not appear much alarmed by our neighborhood, only occasionally turned her head and looked straight at us, and then gave her attention to the flies again. As we approached nearer, she got out of the water, stood higher and regarded us more suspiciously. Polis pushed the canoe steadily forward in the shallow water, and I for a moment forgot the moose in attending to some pretty rose-colored Polygonums just rising above the surface, but the canoe soon grounded in the mud eight or ten rods distant from the moose, and the Indian seized his gun and prepared to fire. After standing still a moment, she turned slowly, as usual, so as to expose her side, and he improved this moment to fire, over our heads. She thereupon moved off eight or ten rods at a moderate pace, across a shallow bay, to an old standing-place of hers, behind some fallen red maples, on the opposite shore, and there she stood still again a dozen or fourteen rods from us, while the Indian hastily loaded and fired twice at her, without her moving. My companion, who passed him his caps and bullets, said that Polis was as excited as a boy of fifteen, that his hand trembled, and he once put his ramrod back upside down. This was remarkable for so experienced a hunter. Perhaps he was anxious to make a good shot before us. The white hunter had told me that the Indians were not good shots, because they were excited, though he said that we had got a good hunter with us.

The Indian now pushed quickly and quietly back, and a long distance round, in order to get into the outlet, — for he had fired over the neck of a peninsula between it and the lake, — till we approached the place where the moose had stood, when he exclaimed, "She is a goner!" and was surprised that we did not see her as soon as he did. There, to be sure, she lay perfectly dead, with her tongue hanging out, just where she had stood to receive the last shots, looking unexpectedly large and horse-like, and we saw where the bullets had scarred the trees.

Using a tape, I found that the moose measured just six feet from the shoulder to the tip of the hoof, and was eight feet long as she lay. Some portions of the body, for a foot in diameter, were almost covered with flies, apparently the common fly of our woods, with a dark spot on the wing, and not the very large ones which occasionally pursued us in mid-stream, though both are called moose-flies.

Polis, preparing to skin the moose, asked me to help him find a stone on which to sharpen his large knife. It being all a flat alluvial ground where the moose had fallen, covered with red maples, etc., this was no easy matter; we searched far and wide, a long time, till at length I found a flat kind of slate-stone, and soon after he returned with a similar one, on which he soon made his knife very sharp.

While he was skinning the moose, I proceeded to ascertain what kind of fishes were to be found in the sluggish and muddy outlet. The greatest difficulty was to find a pole. It was almost impossible to find a slender, straight pole ten or twelve feet long in those woods. You might search half an hour in vain. They are commonly spruce, arbor-vitæ, fir, etc., short, stout, and branchy, and do not make good fish-poles, even after you have patiently cut off all their tough and scraggy branches. The fishes were red perch and chivin.

The Indian having cut off a large piece of sirloin, the upper lip, and the tongue, wrapped them in the hide, and placed them in the bottom of the canoe, observing that there was "one man," meaning the weight of one. Our load had previously been reduced some thirty pounds, but a hundred pounds were now added, a serious addition, which made our quarters still more narrow, and considerably increased the danger on the lakes and rapids, as well as the labor of the carries. The skin was ours according to custom, since the Indian was in our employ, but we did not think of claiming it. He being a skillful dresser of moose-hides, would make it worth seven or eight dollars to him, as I was told. He said that he sometimes earned fifty or sixty dollars in a day at them; he had killed ten moose in one day, though the skinning and all took two days. This was the way he had got his property. There were the tracks of a calf thereabouts, which he said would come "by, by," and he could get it if we cared to wait, but I cast cold water on the project.

We continued along the outlet toward Grand Lake, through a swampy region, by a long, winding, and narrow dead water, very much choked up by wood, where we were obliged to land sometimes in order to get the canoe over a log. It was hard to find any channel, and we did not know but we should be lost in the swamp. It abounded in ducks, as usual. At length we reached Grand Lake, which the Indian called *Matungamook*.

At the head of this we saw, coming in from the southwest, with a sweep apparently from a gorge in the mountains, Trout Stream, or *Uncardnerheese*, which name, the Indian said, had something to do with mountains.

We stopped to dine on an interesting high rocky island, soon after entering Matungamook Lake, securing our canoe to the cliffy shore. It is always pleasant to step from a boat on to a large rock or cliff. Here was a good opportunity to dry our dewy blankets on the open sunny rock. Indians had recently camped here, and accidentally burned over the western end of the island, and Polis picked up a gun-case of blue broadcloth, and said that he knew the Indian it belonged to, and would carry it to him. His tribe is not so large but he may know all its effects. We proceeded to make a fire and cook our dinner amid some pines, where our prede- cessors had done the same, while the Indian busied himself about his moose-hide on the shore, for he said that he thought it a good plan for one to do all the cooking, *i. e.*, I suppose, if that one were not himself. A peculiar evergreen overhung our fire, which at first glance looked like a pitch pine (*P. rigida*), with leaves lit- tle more than an inch long, spruce-like, but we found it to be the *Pinus Banksiana*, — "Banks's, or the Labrador Pine," also called Scrub Pine, Gray Pine, etc., a new tree to us. These must have been good specimens, for sev- eral were thirty or thirty-five feet high. Rich- ardson found it forty feet high and upward, and states that the porcupine feeds on its bark. Here also grew the Red Pine (*Pinus resinosa*).

I saw where the Indians had made canoes in a little secluded hollow in the woods, on the top of the rock, where they were out of the wind, and large piles of whittlings remained. This must have been a favorite resort for their ances- tors, and, indeed, we found here the point of an arrow-head, such as they have not used for two centuries and now know not how to make. The Indian, picking up a stone, remarked to me, "That very strange lock (rock)." It was a piece of hornstone, which I told him his tribe had probably brought here centuries before to make arrow-heads of. He also picked up a yellowish curved bone by the side of our fireplace and asked me to guess what it was. It was one of the upper incisors of a beaver, on which some party had feasted within a year or two. I found also most of the teeth, and the skull, etc. We here dined on fried moose-meat.

One who was my companion in my two previous excursions to these woods, tells me that when hunting up the Caucomgomoc, about two years ago, he found himself dining one day on moose-meat, mud-turtle, trout, and beaver, and he thought that there were few places in the world where these dishes could easily be brought together on one table.

After the almost incessant rapids and falls of the Madunkchunk (Height-of-Land, or Webster Stream), we had just passed through the dead-water of Second Lake, and were now in the much larger dead-water of Grand Lake, and I thought the Indian was entitled to take an extra nap here. Ktaadn, near which we were to pass the next day, is said to mean "Highest Land." So much geography is there in their names.

The Indian navigator naturally distinguishes by a name those parts of a stream where he has encountered quick water and forks, and again, the lakes and smooth water where he can rest his weary arms, since those are the most interesting and more arable parts to him. The very sight of the *Nerlumskeechticook*, or Dead-Water Mountains, a day's journey off over the forest, as we first saw them, must awaken in him pleasing memories. And not less interesting is it to the white traveler, when he is crossing a placid lake in these out-of-the-way woods, perhaps thinking that he is in some sense one of the earlier discoverers of it, to be reminded that it was thus well known and suitably named by Indian hunters perhaps a thousand years ago.

Ascending the precipitous rock which formed this long narrow island, I was surprised to find that its summit was a narrow ridge, with a precipice on one side, and that its axis of elevation extended from northwest to southeast exactly like that of the great rocky ridge at the commencement of the Burnt Ground, ten miles northwesterly. The same arrangement prevailed here, and we could plainly see that the mountain ridges on the west of the lake trended the same way. Splendid large harebells nodded over the edge and in the clefts of the cliff, and the blueberries (*Vaccinium Canadense*) were for

the first time really abundant in the thin soil on
its top. There was no lack of them hencefor-
ward on the East Branch. There was a fine
view hence over the sparkling lake, which looked
pure and deep, and had two or three, in all,
rocky islands in it. Our blankets being dry,
we set out again, the Indian as usual having left
his gazette on a tree. This time it was we three
in a canoe, my companion smoking. We paddled southward down this handsome lake, which
appeared to extend nearly as far east as south,
keeping near the western shore, just outside a
small island, under the dark *Nerlumskeechticook*
mountain. For I had observed on my map that
this was the course. It was three or four miles
across it. It struck me that the outline of this
mountain on the southwest of the lake, and of
another beyond it, was not only like that of the
huge rock waves of Webster Stream, but in the
main like Kineo, on Moosehead Lake, having a
similar but less abrupt precipice at the southeast
end; in short, that all the prominent hills and
ridges hereabouts were larger or smaller Kineos,
and that possibly there was such a relation between Kineo and the rocks of Webster Stream.

The Indian did not know exactly where the
outlet was, whether at the extreme southwest
angle or more easterly, and had asked to see my
plan at the last stopping-place, but I had for-

gotten to show it to him. As usual, he went feeling his way by a middle course between two probable points, from which he could diverge either way at last without losing much distance. In approaching the south shore, as the clouds looked gusty and the waves ran pretty high, we so steered as to get partly under the lee of an island, though at a great distance from it.

I could not distinguish the outlet till we were almost in it, and heard the water falling over the dam there.

Here was a considerable fall, and a very substantial dam, but no sign of a cabin or camp. The hunter whom we met at Telos Lake had told us that there were plenty of trout here, but at this hour they did not rise to the bait, only cousin trout, from the very midst of the rushing waters. There are not so many fishes in these rivers as in the Concord.

While we loitered here, Polis took occasion to cut with his big knife some of the hair from his moose-hide, and so lightened and prepared it for drying. I noticed at several old Indian camps in the woods the pile of hair which they had cut from their hides.

Having carried over the dam, he darted down the rapids, leaving us to walk for a mile or more, where for the most part there was no path, but very thick and difficult traveling near the stream. At length he would call to let us know where he was waiting for us with his canoe, when, on account of the windings of the stream, we did not know where the shore was, but he did not call often enough, forgetting that we were not Indians. He seemed to be very saving of his breath,—yet he would be surprised if we went by, or did not strike the right spot. This was not because he was unaccommodating, but a proof of superior manners. Indians like to get along with the least possible communication and ado. He was really paying us a great compliment all the while, thinking that we preferred a hint to a kick.

At length, climbing over the willows and fallen trees, when this was easier than to go round or under them, we overtook the canoe, and glided down the stream in smooth but swift water for several miles. I here observed again, as at Webster Stream, and on a still larger scale the next day, that the river was a smooth and regularly inclined plane down which we coasted. As we thus glided along we started the first black ducks which we had distinguished.

We decided to camp early to-night, that we might have ample time before dark; so we stopped at the first favorable shore, where there was a narrow gravelly beach on the western side, some five miles below the outlet of the

lake. It was an interesting spot, where the
river began to make a great bend to the east,
and the last of the peculiar moose-faced *Nerlumskeechticook* mountains not far southwest of
Grand Lake rose dark in the northwest a short
distance behind, displaying its gray precipitous
southeast side, but we could not see this without
coming out upon the shore.

Two steps from the water on either side, and
you come to the abrupt bushy and rooty if not
turfy edge of the bank, four or five feet high,
where the interminable forest begins, as if the
stream had but just cut its way through it.

It is surprising on stepping ashore anywhere
into this unbroken wilderness to see so often, at
least within a few rods of the river, the marks
of the axe, made by lumberers who have either
camped here or driven logs past in previous
springs. You will see perchance where, going
on the same errand that you do, they have cut
large chips from a tall white-pine stump for
their fire. While we were pitching the camp
and getting supper, the Indian cut the rest of
the hair from his moose-hide, and proceeded to
extend it vertically on a temporary frame between two small trees, half a dozen feet from
the opposite side of the fire, lashing and stretching it with arbor-vitæ bark which was always
at hand, and in this case was stripped from one

of the trees it was tied to. Asking for a new kind of tea, he made us some, pretty good, of the checkerberry (*Gaultheria procumbens*), which covered the ground, dropping a little bunch of it tied up with cedar bark into the kettle; but it was not quite equal to the *Chiogenes*. We called this therefore Checkerberry-tea Camp.

I was struck with the abundance of the *Linnæa borealis*, checkerberry, and *Chiogenes hispidula*, almost everywhere in the Maine woods. The wintergreen (*Chimaphila umbellata*) was still in bloom here, and *Clintonia* berries were abundant and ripe. This handsome plant is one of the most common in that forest. We here first noticed the moose-wood in fruit on the banks. The prevailing trees were spruce (commonly black), arbor-vitæ, canoe-birch (black ash and elms beginning to appear), yellow birch, red maple, and a little hemlock skulking in the forest. The Indian said that the white-maple punk was the best for tinder, that yellow birch punk was pretty good, but hard. After supper he put on the moose tongue and lips to boil, cutting out the *septum*. He showed me how to write on the under side of birch bark, with a black spruce twig, which is hard and tough and can be brought to a point.

The Indian wandered off into the woods a

short distance just before night, and, coming back, said, "Me found great treasure, — fifty, sixty dollars worth." "What's that?" we asked. "Steel traps, under a log, thirty or forty, I did n't count 'em. I guess Indian work, — worth three dollars apiece." It was a singular coincidence that he should have chanced to walk to and look under that particular log, in that trackless forest.

I saw chivin and chub in the stream when washing my hands, but my companion tried in vain to catch them. I also heard the sound of bull-frogs from a swamp on the opposite side, thinking at first that they were moose; a duck paddled swiftly by; and sitting in that dusky wilderness, under that dark mountain, by the bright river which was full of reflected light, still I heard the wood-thrush sing, as if no higher civilization could be attained. By this time the night was upon us.

You commonly make your camp just at sundown, and are collecting wood, getting your supper, or pitching your tent while the shades of night are gathering around and adding to the already dense gloom of the forest. You have no time to explore or look around you before it is dark. You may penetrate half a dozen rods farther into that twilight wilderness, after some dry bark to kindle your fire with, and wonder

what mysteries lie hidden still deeper in it, say
at the end of a long day's walk; or you may run
down to the shore for a dipper of water, and get
a clearer view for a short distance up or down
the stream, and while you stand there, see a fish
leap, or duck alight in the river, or hear a
wood-thrush or robin sing in the woods. That
is as if you had been to town or civilized parts.
But there is no sauntering off to see the country, and ten or fifteen rods seems a great way
from your companions, and you come back with
the air of a much traveled man, as from a long
journey, with adventures to relate, though you
may have heard the crackling of the fire all the
while, — and at a hundred rods you might be lost
past recovery, and have to camp out. It is all
mossy and *moosey*. In some of those dense fir
and spruce woods there is hardly room for the
smoke to go up. The trees are a *standing*
night, and every fir and spruce which you fell
is a plume plucked from night's raven wing.
Then at night the general stillness is more impressive than any sound, but occasionally you
hear the note of an owl farther or nearer in the
woods, and if near a lake, the semi-human cry
of the loons at their unearthly revels.

To-night the Indian lay between the fire and
his stretched moose-hide, to avoid the mosquitoes. Indeed, he also made a small smoky fire

of damp leaves at his head and his feet, and then as usual rolled up his head in his blanket. We with our veils and our wash were tolerably comfortable, but it would be difficult to pursue any sedentary occupation in the woods at this season; you cannot see to read much by the light of a fire through a veil in the evening, nor handle pencil and paper well with gloves or anointed fingers.

FRIDAY, *July* 31.

The Indian said, "You and I kill moose last night, therefore use 'em best wood. Always use hard wood to cook moose-meat." His "best wood" was rock-maple. He cast the moose's lip into the fire, to burn the hair off, and then rolled it up with the meat to carry along. Observing that we were sitting down to breakfast without any pork, he said, with a very grave look, "Me want some fat," so he was told that he might have as much as he would fry.

We had smooth but swift water for a considerable distance, where we glided rapidly along, scaring up ducks and kingfishers. But as usual, our smooth progress erelong came to an end, and we were obliged to carry canoe and all about half a mile down the right bank, around some rapids or falls. It required sharp eyes sometimes to tell which side was the carry, before you went over the falls, but Polis never failed to land us rightly. The raspberries were particularly abundant and large here, and all hands went to eating them, the Indian remarking on their size.

Often on bare rocky carries the trail was so indistinct that I repeatedly lost it, but when I walked behind him I observed that he could keep it almost like a hound, and rarely hesitated, or, if he paused a moment on a bare rock, his eye immediately detected some sign which would have escaped me. Frequently *we* found no path at all at these places, and were to him unaccountably delayed. He would only say it was "ver strange."

We had heard of a Grand Fall on this stream, and thought that each fall we came to must be it, but after christening several in succession with this name, we gave up the search. There were more Grand or Petty Falls than I can remember.

I cannot tell how many times we had to walk on account of falls or rapids. We were expecting all the while that the river would take a final leap and get to smooth water, but there was no improvement this forenoon. However, the carries were an agreeable variety. So surely as we stepped out of the canoe and stretched our legs we found ourselves in a blueberry and raspberry garden, each side of our

rocky trail around the falls being lined with one
or both.   There was not a carry on the main
East Branch where we did not find an abundance of both these berries, for these were the
rockiest places, and partially cleared, such as
these plants prefer, and there had been none to
gather the finest before us.

In our three journeys over the carries, for we
were obliged to go over the ground three times
whenever the canoe was taken out, we did full
justice to the berries, and they were just what
we wanted to correct the effect of our hard
bread and pork diet.   Another name for making
a portage would have been going a-berrying.
We also found a few *Amelanchier*, or *service*
berries, though most were abortive, but they
held on rather more generally than they do in
Concord.   The Indian called them *Pemoymenuk*, and said that they bore much fruit in
some places.   He sometimes also ate the northern wild red cherries, saying that they were
good medicine, but they were scarcely edible.
We bathed and dined at the foot of one of these
carries.   It was the Indian who commonly reminded us that it was dinner-time, sometimes
even by turning the prow to the shore.   He
once made an indirect, but lengthy apology, by
saying that we might think it strange, but that
one who worked hard all day was very particular

to have his dinner in good season. At the most considerable fall on this stream, when I was walking over the carry, close behind the Indian, he observed a track on the rock, which was but slightly covered with soil, and, stooping, muttered "caribou." When we returned, he observed a much larger track near the same place, where some animal's foot had sunk into a small hollow in the rock, partly filled with grass and earth, and he exclaimed with surprise, "What that?" "Well, what is it?" I asked. Stooping and laying his hand in it, he answered with a mysterious air, and in a half whisper, "Devil [that is, Indian Devil, or cougar] lodges about here — very bad animal — pull 'em *locks* all to pieces." "How long since it was made?" I asked. "To-day or yesterday," said he. But when I asked him afterward if he was sure it was the devil's track, he said he did not know. I had been told that the scream of a cougar was heard about Ktaadn recently, and we were not far from that mountain.

We spent at least half the time in walking to-day, and the walking was as bad as usual, for the Indian being alone, commonly ran down far below the foot of the carries before he waited for us. The carry-paths themselves were more than usually indistinct, often the route being revealed only by the countless small holes in the fallen

timber made by the tacks in the drivers' boots, or
where there *was* a slight trail we did not find it.
It was a tangled and perplexing thicket, through
which we stumbled and threaded our way, and
when we had finished a mile of it, our starting-
point seemed far away.   We were glad that we
had not got to walk to Bangor along the banks
of this river, which would be a journey of more
than a hundred miles.   Think of the denseness
of the forest, the fallen trees and rocks, the
windings of the river, the streams emptying in,
and the frequent swamps to be crossed.   It
made you shudder.   Yet the Indian from time
to time pointed out to us where he had thus
crept along day after day when he was a boy of
ten, and in a starving condition.   He had been
hunting far north of this with two grown Indians.   The winter came on unexpectedly early,
and the ice compelled them to leave their canoe
at Grand Lake, and walk down the bank.
They shouldered their furs and started for Oldtown.   The snow was not deep enough for snow-
shoes, or to cover the inequalities of the ground.
Polis was soon too weak to carry any burden;
but he managed to catch one otter.   This was
the most they all had to eat on this journey,
and he remembered how good the yellow-lily
roots were, made into a soup with the otter oil.
He shared this food equally with the other two,

but being so small he suffered much more than they. He waded through the Mattawamkeag at its mouth, when it was freezing cold and came up to his chin, and he, being very weak and emaciated, expected to be swept away. The first house which they reached was at Lincoln, and thereabouts they met a white teamster with supplies, who, seeing their condition, gave them as much of his load as they could eat. For six months after getting home, he was very low, and did not expect to live, and was perhaps always the worse for it.

We could not find much more than half of this day's journey on our maps (the "Map of the Public Lands of Maine and Massachusetts," and "Colton's Railroad and Township Map of Maine," which copies the former). By the maps there was not more than fifteen miles between camps at the outside, and yet we had been busily progressing all day, and much of the time very rapidly.

For seven or eight miles below that succession of "Grand" falls, the aspect of the banks as well as the character of the stream was changed. After passing a tributary from the northeast, perhaps Bowlin Stream, we had good swift smooth water, with a regular slope, such as I have described. Low, grassy banks and muddy shores began. Many elms, as well as maples, and more ash-trees, overhung the stream, and supplanted the spruce.

My lily-roots having been lost when the canoe was taken out at a carry, I landed late in the afternoon, at a low and grassy place amid maples, to gather more. It was slow work, grubbing them up amid the sand, and the mosquitoes were all the while feasting on me. Mosquitoes, black flies, etc., pursued us in mid-channel, and we were glad sometimes to get into violent rapids, for then we escaped them.

A red-headed woodpecker flew across the river, and the Indian remarked that it was good to eat. As we glided swiftly down the inclined plane of the river, a great cat-owl launched itself away from a stump on the bank, and flew heavily across the stream, and the Indian, as usual, imitated its note. Soon the same bird flew back in front of us, and we afterwards passed it perched on a tree. Soon afterward a white-headed eagle sailed down the stream before us. We drove him several miles, while we were looking for a good place to camp, for we expected to be overtaken by a shower, — and still we could distinguish him by his white tail, sailing away from time to time from some tree by the shore still farther down the stream. Some shecorways, being surprised by us, a part of them dived, and we passed directly over them, and could trace their course here and there by a bubble on the surface, but we did not see them come up. Polis detected once or twice what he called a "tow" road, an indistinct path leading into the forest. In the meanwhile we passed the mouth of the Seboois on our left. This did not look so large as our stream, which was indeed the main one. It was some time before we found a camping-place, for the shore was either too grassy and muddy, where mosquitoes abounded, or too steep a hillside. The Indian said that there were but few mosquitoes on a steep hillside. We examined a good place, where somebody had camped a long time; but it seemed pitiful to occupy an old site, where there was so much room to choose, so we continued on. We at length found a place to our minds, on the west bank, about a mile below the mouth of the Seboois, where, in a very dense spruce wood above a gravelly shore, there seemed to be but few insects. The trees were so thick that we were obliged to clear a space to build our fire and lie down in, and the young spruce trees that were left were like the wall of an apartment rising around us. We were obliged to pull ourselves up a steep bank to get there. But the place which you have selected for your camp, though never so rough and grim, begins at once to have its attractions, and becomes a very centre of civilization to you: "Home is home, be it never so homely."

It turned out that the mosquitoes were more numerous here than we had found them before, and the Indian complained a good deal, though he lay, as the night before, between three fires and his stretched hide. As I sat on a stump by the fire, with a veil and gloves on, trying to read, he observed, "I make you candle" and in a minute he took a piece of birch bark about two inches wide and rolled it hard, like an allumette fifteen inches long, lit it, and fixed it by the other end horizontally in a split stick three feet high, stuck it in the ground, turning the blazing end to the wind, and telling me to snuff it from time to time. It answered the purpose of a candle pretty well.

I noticed, as I had done before, that there was a lull among the mosquitoes about midnight, and that they began again in the morning. Nature is thus merciful. But apparently they need rest as well as we. Few if any creatures are equally active all night. As soon as it was light I saw, through my veil, that the inside of the tent about our heads was quite blackened with myriads, each one of their wings when flying, as has been calculated, vibrating some three thousand times in a minute, and their combined hum was almost as bad to endure as their stings. I had an uncomfortable night on this account, though I am not sure that one succeeded in his attempt to sting me. We did not suffer so much from insects on this excursion as the statements of some who have explored these woods in midsummer led us to anticipate. Yet I have no doubt that at some seasons and in some places they are a much more serious pest. The Jesuit Hierome Lalemant, of Quebec, reporting the death of Father Reni Menard, who was abandoned, lost his way, and died in the woods, among the Ontarios near Lake Superior, in 1661, dwells chiefly on his probable sufferings from the attacks of mosquitoes when too weak to defend himself, adding that there was a frightful number of them in those parts, "and so insupportable," says he, "that the three Frenchmen who have made that voyage affirm that there was no other means of defending one's self but to run always without stopping, and it was even necessary for two of them to be employed in driving off these creatures while the third wanted to drink, otherwise he could not have done it." I have no doubt that this was said in good faith.

August 1.

I caught two or three large red chivin (*Leuciscus pulchellus*) early this morning, within twenty feet of the camp, which, added to the

moose-tongue, that had been left in the kettle
boiling over-night, and to our other stores,
made a sumptuous breakfast. The Indian made
us some hemlock tea instead of coffee, and we
were not obliged to go as far as China for it;
indeed, not quite so far as for the fish. This
was tolerable, though he said it was not strong
enough. It was interesting to see so simple a
dish as a kettle of water with a handful of green
hemlock sprigs in it, boiling over the huge fire
in the open air, the leaves fast losing their lively
green color, and know that it was for our breakfast.

We were glad to embark once more, and
leave some of the mosquitoes behind. We had
passed the *Wassataquoik* without perceiving it.
This, according to the Indian, is the name of
the main East Branch itself, and not properly
applied to this small tributary alone, as on the
maps.

We found that we had camped about a mile
above Hunt's, which is on the east bank, and is
the last house for those who ascend Ktaadn on
this side.

We also had expected to ascend it from this
point, but omitted it on account of the chafed
feet of one of my companions. The Indian,
however, suggested that perhaps he might get a
pair of moccasins at this place, and that he

could walk very easily in them without hurting
his feet, wearing several pairs of stockings, and
he said beside that they were so porous that
when you had taken in water it all drained out
again in a little while. We stopped to get
some sugar, but found that the family had
moved away, and the house was unoccupied, except temporarily by some men who were getting
the hay. They told me that the road to Ktaadn
left the river eight miles above; also that perhaps we could get some sugar at Fisk's, fourteen miles below. I do not remember that we
saw the mountain at all from the river. I noticed a seine here stretched on the bank, which
probably had been used to catch salmon. Just
below this, on the west bank, we saw a moose-
hide stretched, and with it a bear-skin, which
was comparatively very small. I was the more
interested in this sight, because it was near here
that a townsman of ours, then quite a lad, and
alone, killed a large bear some years ago. The
Indian said that they belonged to Joe Aitteon,
my last guide, but how he told I do not know.
He was probably hunting near, and had left
them for the day. Finding that we were going
directly to Oldtown, he regretted that he had
not taken more of the moose-meat to his family,
saying that in a short time, by drying it, he
could have made it so light as to have brought

away the greater part, leaving the bones.   We
once or twice inquired after the lip, which is a
famous tid-bit, but he said, "That go Oldtown
for my old woman; don't get it every day."

Maples grew more and more numerous.   It
was lowering, and rained a little during the
forenoon, and, as we expected a wetting, we
stopped early and dined on the east side of a
small expansion of the river, just above what
are probably called Whetstone Falls, about a
dozen miles below Hunt's.   There were pretty
fresh moose-tracks by the water-side.   There
were singular long ridges hereabouts, called
"horsebacks," covered with ferns.   My companion having lost his pipe asked the Indian if he
could not make him one.   "Oh, yer," said he,
and in a minute rolled up one of birch bark, telling him to wet the bowl from time to time.   Here
also he left his gazette on a tree.

We carried round the falls just below, on the
west side.   The rocks were on their edges, and
very sharp.   The distance was about three
fourths of a mile.   When we had carried over
one load, the Indian returned by the shore, and
I by the path, and though I made no particular haste, I was nevertheless surprised to find
him at the other end as soon as I.   It was remarkable how easily he got along over the worst
ground.   He said to me, "I take canoe and you

take the rest, suppose you can keep along with
me?" I thought that he meant, that while he
ran down the rapids I should keep along the
shore, and be ready to assist him from time to
time, as I had done before; but as the walking
would be very bad, I answered, "I suppose you
will go too fast for me, but I will try." But I
was to go by the path, he said. This I thought
would not help the matter, I should have so far
to go to get to the river-side when he wanted
me. But neither was this what he meant. He
was proposing a race over the carry, and asked
me if I thought I could keep along with him by
the same path, adding that I must be pretty
smart to do it. As his load, the canoe, would
be much the heaviest and bulkiest, though the
simplest, I thought that I ought to be able to do
it, and said that I would try. So I proceeded
to gather up the gun, axe, paddle, kettle, frying-pan, plates, dippers, carpets, etc., etc., and
while I was thus engaged he threw me his cowhide boots. "What, are these in the bargain?"
I asked. "Oh, yer," said he; but before I
could make a bundle of my load I saw him dis-
appearing over a hill with the canoe on his
head; so, hastily scraping the various articles
together, I started on the run, and immediately
went by him in the bushes, but I had no sooner
left him out of sight in a rocky hollow, than the

greasy plates, dippers, etc., took to themselves
wings, and while I was employed in gathering
them up again, he went by me; but hastily
pressing the sooty kettle to my side, I started
once more, and soon passing him again, I saw
him no more on the carry. I do not mention
this as anything of a feat, for it was but poor
running on my part, and he was obliged to move
with great caution for fear of breaking his canoe
as well as his neck. When he made his appearance, puffing and panting like myself, in answer
to my inquiries where he had been, he said,
"Rocks (locks) cut 'em feet," and laughing
added, "Oh, me love to play sometimes." He
said that he and his companions when they came
to carries several miles long used to try who
would get over first; each perhaps with a canoe
on his head. I bore the sign of the kettle on
my brown linen sack for the rest of the voyage.

We made a second carry on the west side,
around some falls about a mile below this. On
the mainland were Norway pines, indicating a
new geological formation, and it was such a dry
and sandy soil as we had not noticed before.

As we approached the mouth of the East
Branch, we passed two or three huts, the first
sign of civilization after Hunt's, though we saw
no road as yet; we heard a cow-bell, and even
saw an infant held up to a small square window

to see us pass, but apparently the infant and the mother that held it were the only inhabitants then at home for several miles. This took the wind out of our sails, reminding us that we were travelers surely, while it was a native of the soil, and had the advantage of us. Conversation flagged. I would only hear the Indian, perhaps, ask my companion, "You load my pipe?" He said that he smoked alder bark, for medicine. On entering the West Branch at Nicketow it appeared much larger than the East. Polis remarked that the former was all gone and lost now, that it was all smooth water hence to Oldtown, and he threw away his pole which was cut on the Umbazookskus. Thinking of the rapids, he said once or twice, that you would n't catch him to go East Branch again; but he did not by any means mean all that he said.

Things are quite changed since I was here eleven years ago. Where there were but one or two houses, I now found quite a village, with saw-mills and a store (the latter was locked, but its contents were so much the more safely stored), and there was a stage-road to Mattawamkeag, and the rumor of a stage. Indeed, a steamer had ascended thus far once, when the water was very high. But we were not able to get any sugar, only a better shingle to lean our backs against.

We camped about two miles below Nicketow, on the south side of the West Branch, covering with fresh twigs the withered bed of a
former traveler, and feeling that we were now
in a settled country, especially when in the evening we heard an ox sneeze in its wild pasture
across the river. Wherever you land along
the frequented part of the river, you have not
far to go to find these sites of temporary inns,
the withered bed of flattened twigs, the charred
sticks, and perhaps the tent-poles. And not
long since, similar beds were spread along the
Connecticut, the Hudson, and the Delaware,
and longer still ago, by the Thames and Seine,
and they now help to make the soil where private and public gardens, mansions and palaces
are. We could not get fir-twigs for our bed
here, and the spruce was harsh in comparison,
having more twig in proportion to its leaf, but
we improved it somewhat with hemlock. The
Indian remarked as before, "Must have hard
wood to cook moose-meat," as if that were a
maxim, and proceeded to get it. My companion cooked some in California fashion, winding
a long string of the meat round a stick and
slowly turning it in his hand before the fire. It
was very good. But the Indian not approving
of the mode, or because he was not allowed to
cook it his own way, would not taste it. After

the regular supper we attempted to make a lily
soup of the bulbs which I had brought along,
for I wished to learn all I could before I got
out of the woods. Following the Indian's directions, for he began to be sick, I washed the
bulbs carefully, minced some moose-meat and
some pork, salted and boiled all together, but
we had not patience to try the experiment
fairly, for he said it must be boiled till the roots
were completely softened so as to thicken the
soup like flour; but though we left it on all
night, we found it dried to the kettle in the
morning, and not yet boiled to a flour. Perhaps
the roots were not ripe enough, for they commonly
gather them in the fall. As it was, it was palata-
ble enough, but it reminded me of the Irishman's limestone broth. The other ingredients
were enough alone. The Indian's name for
these bulbs was *Sheepnoc*. I stirred the soup
by accident with a striped maple or moose-
wood stick, which I had peeled, and he remarked
that its bark was an emetic.

He prepared to camp as usual between his
moose-hide and the fire, but it beginning to rain
suddenly, he took refuge under the tent with us,
and gave us a song before falling asleep. It
rained hard in the night, and spoiled another
box of matches for us, which the Indian had left
out, for he was very careless; but, as usual, we

had so much the better night for the rain, since
it kept the mosquitoes down.

SUNDAY, *August* 2.

Was a cloudy and unpromising morning. One
of us observed to the Indian, "You did not
stretch your moose-hide last night, did you, Mr.
Polis?" Whereat he replied, in a tone of surprise, though perhaps not of ill humor: "What
you ask me that question for? Suppose I stretch
'em, you see 'em. May be your way talking,
may be all right, no Indian way." I had observed that he did not wish to answer the same
question more than once, and was often silent
when it was put again for the sake of certainty,
as if he were moody. Not that he was incom-
municative, for he frequently commenced a long-
winded narrative of his own accord,— repeated
at length the tradition of some old battle, or
some passage in the recent history of his tribe
in which he had acted a prominent part, from
time to time drawing a long breath, and resum-
ing the thread of his tale, with the true story-
teller's leisureliness, perhaps after shooting a
rapid,— prefacing with "we-ll-by-by," etc., as
he paddled along. Especially after the day's
work was over, and he had put himself in posture for the night, he would be unexpectedly
sociable, exhibit even the *bonhommie* of a
Frenchman, and we would fall asleep before he
got through his periods.

Nicketow is called eleven miles from Mattawamkeag by the river. Our camp was, therefore, about nine miles from the latter place.

The Indian was quite sick this morning with the colic. I thought that he was the worse for the moose-meat he had eaten.

We reached the Mattawamkeag at half past eight in the morning, in the midst of a drizzling rain, and after buying some sugar set out again.

The Indian growing much worse, we stopped in the north part of Lincoln to get some brandy for him, but failing in this, an apothecary recommended Brandreth's pills, which he refused to take, because he was not acquainted with them. He said to me, "Me doctor, — first study my case, find out what ail 'em, — then I know what to take." We dropped down a little farther, and stopped at mid-forenoon on an island and made him a dipper of tea. Here, too, we dined and did some washing and botanizing, while he lay on the bank. In the afternoon we went on a little farther, though the Indian was no better. "Burntibus," as he called it, was a long, smooth, lake-like reach below the Five Islands. He said that he owned a hundred acres somewhere up this way. As a thunder-shower appeared to be coming up, we stopped opposite a barn on the west bank, in Chester, about a mile above Lincoln. Here at last we were obliged to spend the rest of the day and night, on account of our patient, whose sickness did not abate. He lay groaning under his canoe on the bank, looking very woe-begone, yet it was only a common case of colic. You would not have thought, if you had seen him lying about thus, that he was the proprietor of so many acres in that neighborhood, was worth $6,000, and had been to Washington. It seemed to me that, like the Irish, he made a greater ado about his sickness than a Yankee does, and was more alarmed about himself. We talked somewhat of leaving him with his people in Lincoln, — for that is one of their homes, — and taking the stage the next day, but he objected on account of the expense, saying, "Suppose me well in morning, you and I go Oldtown by noon."

As we were taking our tea at twilight, while he lay groaning still under his canoe, having at length found out "what ail him," he asked me to get him a dipper of water. Taking the dipper in one hand he seized his powder-horn with the other, and pouring into it a charge or two of powder, stirred it up with his finger, and drank it off. This was all he took to-day after breakfast beside his tea.

To save the trouble of pitching our tent, when we had secured our stores from wandering dogs,

we camped in the solitary half-open barn near
the bank, with the permission of the owner,
lying on new-mown hay four feet deep. The
fragrance of the hay, in which many ferns, etc.,
were mingled, was agreeable, though it was
quite alive with grasshoppers which you could
hear crawling through it. This served to graduate our approach to houses and feather-beds.
In the night some large bird, probably an owl,
flitted through over our heads, and very early
in the morning we were awakened by the twittering of swallows which had their nests there.

MONDAY, *August* 3.

We started early before breakfast, the Indian
being considerably better, and soon glided by
Lincoln, and after another long and handsome
lake-like reach, we stopped to breakfast on the
west shore, two or three miles below this town.

We frequently passed Indian islands with
their small houses on them. The Governor,
Aitteon, lives in one of them, in Lincoln.

The Penobscot Indians seem to be more social, even, than the whites. Ever and anon in
the deepest wilderness of Maine, you come to
the log-hut of a Yankee or Canada settler, but
a Penobscot never takes up his residence in such
a solitude. They are not even scattered about
on their islands in the Penobscot, which are all

within the settlements, but gathered together on two or three. — though not always on the best soil, — evidently for the sake of society. I saw one or two houses not now used by them, because, as our Indian Polis said, they were too solitary.

The small river emptying in at Lincoln is the Matanancook, which also, we noticed, was the name of a steamer moored there. So we paddled and floated along, looking into the mouths of rivers. When passing the Mohawk Rips, or, as the Indian called them, "Mohog lips," four or five miles below Lincoln, he told us at length the story of a fight between his tribe and the Mohawks there, anciently, — how the latter were overcome by stratagem, the Penobscots using concealed knives, — but they could not for a long time kill the Mohawk chief, who was a very large and strong man, though he was attacked by several canoes at once, when swimming alone in the river.

From time to time we met Indians in their canoes, going up river. Our man did not commonly approach them, but exchanged a few words with them at a distance in his tongue. These were the first Indians we had met since leaving the *Umbazookskus.*

At Piscataquis Falls, just above the river of that name, we walked over the wooden railroad on the eastern shore, about one and a half miles long, while the Indian glided down the rapids. The steamer from Oldtown stops here, and passengers take a new boat above. Piscataquis, whose mouth we here passed, means "branch." It is obstructed by falls at its mouth, but can be navigated with batteaux or canoes above through a settled country, even to the neighborhood of Moosehead Lake, and we had thought at first of going that way. We were not obliged to get out of the canoe after this on account of falls or rapids, nor, indeed, was it quite necessary here. We took less notice of the scenery to-day, because we were in quite a settled country. The river became broad and sluggish, and we saw a blue heron winging its way slowly down the stream before us.

We passed the Passadumkeag River on our left and saw the blue Olamon mountains at a distance in the southeast. Hereabouts our Indian told us at length the story of their contention with the priest respecting schools. He thought a great deal of education and had recommended it to his tribe. His argument in its favor was, that if you had been to college and learnt to calculate, you could "keep 'em property, — no other way." He said that his boy was the best scholar in the school at Oldtown, to which he went with whites. He himself is a

Protestant, and goes to church regularly at Old-town. According to his account, a good many of his tribe are Protestants, and many of the Catholics also are in favor of schools. Some years ago they had a schoolmaster, a Protestant, whom they liked very well. The priest came and said that they must send him away, and finally he had such influence, telling them that they would go to the bad place at last if they retained him, that they sent him away. The school party, though numerous, were about giving up. Bishop Fenwick came from Boston and used his influence against them. But our Indian told his side that they must not give up, must hold on, they were the strongest. If they gave up, then they would have no party. But they answered that it was "no use, priest too strong, we 'd better give up." At length he persuaded them to make a stand.

The priest was going for a sign to cut down the liberty-pole. So Polis and his party had a secret meeting about it; he got ready fifteen or twenty stout young men, "stript 'em naked, and painted 'em like old times," and told them that when the priest and his party went to cut down the liberty-pole, they were to rush up, take hold of it, and prevent them, and he assured them that there would be no war, only a noise, "no war where priest is." He kept his

men concealed in a house near by, and when the
priest's party were about to cut down the liberty-pole, the fall of which would have been a
death-blow to the school-party, he gave a signal,
and his young men rushed out and seized the
pole.   There was a great uproar, and they were
about coming to blows, but the priest interfered,
saying, "No war, no war," and so the pole
stands, and the school goes on still.

We thought that it showed a good deal of
tact in him, to seize this occasion and take his
stand on it; proving how well he understood
those with whom he had to deal.

The Olamon River comes in from the east in
Greenbush a few miles below the Passadumkeag.
When we asked the meaning of this name, the
Indian said there was an island opposite its
mouth which was called *Olarmon*.   That in old
times, when visitors were coming to Oldtown,
they used to stop there to dress and fix up or
paint themselves.   "What is that which ladies
used?" he asked.   Rouge?   Red Vermilion?
"Yer," he said, "that is *larmon*, a kind of clay
or red paint, which they used to get here."

We decided that we, too, would stop at this
island, and fix up our inner man, at least, by
dining.

It was a large island, with an abundance of
hemp nettle, but I did not notice any kind

of red paint there. The Olamon River, at its mouth at least, is a dead stream. There was another large island in that neighborhood, which the Indian called "*Soogle*" (*i. e.*, Sugar) Island.

About a dozen miles before reaching Oldtown he inquired, "How you like 'em your pilot?" But we postponed an answer till we had got quite back again.

The *Sunkhaze*, another short dead stream, comes in from the east two miles above Oldtown. There is said to be some of the best deer ground in Maine on this stream. Asking the meaning of this name, the Indian said, "Suppose you are going down Penobscot, just like we, and you see a canoe come out of bank and go along before you, but you no see 'em stream. That is *Sunkhaze*."

He had previously complimented me on my paddling, saying that I paddled "just like anybody," giving me an Indian name which meant "great paddler." When off this stream he said to me, who sat in the bows, "Me teach you paddle." So turning toward the shore he got out, came forward and placed my hands as he wished. He placed one of them quite outside the boat, and the other parallel with the first, grasping the paddle near the end, not over the flat extremity, and told me to slide it back and forth on the side of the canoe. This, I found, was a great improvement which I had not thought of, saving me the labor of lifting the paddle each time, and I wondered that he had not suggested it before. It is true, before our baggage was reduced we had been obliged to sit with our legs drawn up, and our knees above the side of the canoe, which would have prevented our paddling thus, or perhaps he was afraid of wearing out his canoe, by constant friction on the side.

I told him that I had been accustomed to sit in the stern, and lifting my paddle at each stroke, getting a pry on the side each time, and I still paddled partly as if in the stern. He then wanted to see me paddle in the stern. So, changing paddles, for he had the longer and better one, and turning end for end, he sitting flat on the bottom and I on the crossbar, he began to paddle very hard, trying to turn the canoe, looking over his shoulder and laughing, but finding it in vain he relaxed his efforts, though we still sped along a mile or two very swiftly. He said that he had no fault to find with my paddling in the stern, but I complained that he did not paddle according to his own directions in the bows.

Opposite the Sunkhaze is the main boom of the Penobscot, where the logs from far up the river are collected and assorted.

As we drew near to Oldtown I asked Polis if he was not glad to get home again; but there was no relenting to his wildness, and he said, "It makes no difference to me where I am." Such is the Indian's pretense always.

We approached the Indian Island through the narrow strait called "Cook." He said, "I 'xpect we take in some water there, river so high, — never see it so high at this season. Very rough water there, but short; swamp steamboat once. Don't you paddle till I tell you, then you paddle right along." It was a very short rapid. When we were in the midst of it he shouted "paddle," and we shot through without taking in a drop.

Soon after the Indian houses came in sight, but I could not at first tell my companion which of two or three large white ones was our guide's. He said it was the one with blinds.

We landed opposite his door at about four in the afternoon, having come some forty miles this day. From the Piscataquis we had come remarkably and unaccountably quick, probably as fast as the stage or the boat, though the last dozen miles was dead water.

Polis wanted to sell us his canoe, said it would last seven or eight years, or with care, perhaps ten; but we were not ready to buy it.

We stopped for an hour at his house, where

my companion shaved with his razor, which he pronounced in very good condition. Mrs. P. wore a hat and had a silver brooch on her breast, but she was not introduced to us. The house was roomy and neat. A large new map of Oldtown and the Indian Island hung on the wall, and a clock opposite to it. Wishing to know when the cars left Oldtown, Polis's son brought one of the last Bangor papers, which I saw was directed to "Joseph Polis," from the office.

This was the last that I saw of Joe Polis. We took the last train, and reached Bangor that night.

APPENDIX

I. TREES.

THE prevailing trees (I speak only of what I saw) on the east and west branches of the Penobscot and on the upper part of the Allegash were the fir, spruce (both black and white), and arbor-vitæ, or "cedar." The fir has the darkest foliage, and, together with the spruce, makes a very dense "black growth," especially on the upper parts of the rivers. A dealer in lumber with whom I talked called the former a weed, and it is commonly regarded as fit neither for timber nor fuel. But it is more sought after as an ornamental tree than any other evergreen of these woods except the arbor-vitæ. The black spruce is much more common than the white. Both are tall and slender trees. The arbor-vitæ, which is of a more cheerful hue, with its light-green fans, is also tall and slender, though sometimes two feet in diameter. It often fills the swamps.

Mingled with the former, and also here and there forming extensive and more open woods by themselves, indicating, it is said, a better soil, were canoe and yellow birches (the former was always at hand for kindling a fire, — we saw no small white-birches in that wilderness), and sugar and red maples.

The Aspen (*Populus tremuloides*) was very common on burnt grounds. We saw many straggling white pines, commonly unsound trees, which had therefore been skipped by the choppers; these were the largest trees we saw; and we occasionally passed a small wood in which this was the prevailing tree; but I did not notice nearly so many of these trees as I can see in a single walk in Concord. The speckled or hoary alder (*Alnus incana*) abounds everywhere along the muddy banks of rivers and lakes, and in swamps. Hemlock could commonly be found for tea, but was nowhere abundant. Yet F. A. Michaux states that in Maine, Vermont, and the upper part of New Hampshire, &c., the hemlock forms three fourths of the evergreen woods, the rest being black spruce. It belongs to cold hillsides.

The elm and black ash were very common along the lower and stiller parts of the streams, where the shores were flat and grassy or there were low gravelly islands. They made a pleasing variety in the scenery, and we felt as if nearer home while gliding past them.

The above fourteen trees made the bulk of the woods which we saw.

The larch (Juniper), beech, and Norway pine (*Pinus resinosa*, red pine), were only occasionally seen in particular places. The *Pinus Banksiana* (gray or Northern scrubpine), and a single small red oak (*Quercus rubra*) only, are on islands in Grand Lake, on the East Branch.

The above are almost all peculiarly Northern trees, and found chiefly, if not solely, on mountains southward.

II. FLOWERS AND SHRUBS

It appears that in a forest like this the great majority of flowers, shrubs, and grasses are confined to the banks of the rivers and lakes, and to the meadows, more open swamps, burnt lands, and mountain-tops; comparatively very few indeed penetrate the woods. There is no such dispersion even of wild-flowers as is commonly supposed, or as exists in a cleared and settled country. Most of our wild-flowers, so called, may be considered as naturalized in the localities where they grow. Rivers and lakes are the great protectors of such plants against the aggressions of the forest, by their annual rise and fall keeping open a narrow strip where these more delicate plants have light and space in which to grow. They are the *protégés* of the rivers. These narrow, and straggling bands and isolated groups are, in a sense, the pioneers of civilization. Birds, quadrupeds, insects, and man also, in the main, follow the flowers, and the latter in his turn makes more room for them and for berry-bearing shrubs, birds, and small quadrupeds. One settler told me that not only blackberries and raspberries, but mountain maples came in, in the clearing and burning.

Though plants are often referred to primitive woods as their locality, it cannot be true of very many, unless the woods are supposed to include such localities as I have mentioned. Only those which require but little light, and can bear the drip of the trees, penetrate the woods, and these have commonly more beauty in their leaves than in their pale and almost colorless blossoms.

The prevailing flowers and conspicuous small plants of the *woods*, which I noticed, were: *Clintonia borealis, Linnœa,* checkerberry (*Gaultheria procumbens*), *Aralia nudicaulis* (wild sarsaparilla), great round-leaved orchis, *Dalibarda repens, Chiogenes hispidula* (creeping snowberry), *Oxalis acetosella* (common wood-sorrel), *Aster acuminatus, Pyrola secunda* (one-sided pyrola), *Medeola Virginica* (Indian cucumber-root), small *Circœa* (enchanter's nightshade), and perhaps *Cornus Canadensis* (dwarf-cornel).

Of these, the last of July, 1858, only the *Aster acuminatus* and great round-leaved *orchis* were conspicuously in bloom.

The most common flowers of the *river* and *lake shores*

were: *Thalictrum cornuti* (meadow-rue), *Hypericum ellipti-cum, mutilum,* and *Canadense* (St. John's-wort), horsemint, horehound, *Lycopus Virginicus* and *Europœus,* var. *sinuatus* (bugle-weed), *Scutellaria galericulata* (skull-cap), *Solidago lanceolata* and *squarrosa* East Branch (golden-rod), *Diplo-pappus umbellatus* (double-bristled aster), *Aster radula, Cicuta maculata* and *bulbifera* (water-hemlock), meadow-sweet, *Lysimachia stricta* and *ciliata* (loose-strife), *Galium trifidum* (small bed-straw), *Lilium Canadense* (wild yellow-lily), *Platanthera peramœna* and *psycodes* (great purple orchis and small purple-fringed orchis), *Mimulus ringens* (monkey-flower), dock (water), blue flag, *Hydrocotyle Americana* (marsh pennywort), *Sanicula Canadensis ?* (black snake-root), *Clematis Virginiana ?* (common vir-gin's-bower), *Nasturtium palustre* (marsh cress), *Ranun-culus recurvatus* (hooked crowfoot), *Asclepias incarnata* (swamp milkweed), *Aster Tradescanti* (Tradescant's as-ter), *Aster miser,* also *longifolius, Eupatorium purpureum* apparently, lake shores (Joe-Pye-weed), *Apocynum Can-nabinum* East Branch (Indian hemp), *Polygonum cilinode* (bindweed), and others. Not to mention among inferior orders wool-grass and the sensitive fern.

In the water, *Nuphar advena* (yellow pond-lily), some *potamogetons* (pond-weed), *Sagittaria variabilis* (arrow-head), *Sium lineare ?* (water-parsnip).

Of these, those conspicuously in flower the last of July, 1857, were: rue, *Solidago lanceolata* and *squarrosa, Diplo-pappus umbellatus, Aster radula Lilium Canadense,* great and small purple orchis, *Mimulus ringens,* blue flag, vir-gin's-bower, &c.

The characteristic flowers in *swamps* were: *Rubus triflorus* (dwarf-raspberry), *Calla palustris* (water-arum), and *Sar-racenia purpurea* (pitcher-plant). On *burnt grounds : Epi-lobium angustifolium,* in full bloom (great willow-herb), and *Erechthites hieracifolia* (fire-weed). On *cliffs : Campanula rotundifolia* (harebell), *Cornus Canadensis* (dwarf cornel), *Arctostaphylos uva-ursi* (bearberry), *Potentilla tridentata* (mountain cinquefoil), *Pteris aquilina* (common brake). At *old camps, carries, and logging-paths: Cirsium arvense* (Canada thistle), *Prunella vulgaris* (common self-heal), clover, herds-grass, *Achillea millefolium* (common yarrow), *Leucanthemum valgare* (white-weed), *Aster macrophyllus, Halenia deflexa* East Branch (spurred gentian), *Antennaria margaritacea* (pearly everlasting), *Actœa rubra* and *alba*, wet carries (red and white cohosh), *Desmodium Canadense* (tick-trefoil), sorrel.

The handsomest and most interesting flowers were the great purple orchises, rising ever and anon, with their great purple spikes perfectly erect, amid the shrubs and grasses of the shore. It seemed strange that they should be made to grow there in such profusion, seen of moose and moose-hunters only, while they are so rare in Concord. I have never seen this species flowering nearly so late with us, or with the small one.

The prevailing underwoods were: *Dirca palustris* (moosewood), *Acer spicatum* (mountain maple), *Viburnum lantanoides* (hobblebush), and frequently *Taxus baccata,* var. *Canadensis* (American yew).

The prevailing shrubs and small trees along the shore were: *osie rouge* and alders (before mentioned); sallows, or small willows, of two or three kinds, as *Salis humilis, rostrata*, and *discolor ?, Sambucus Canadensis* (black elder), rose, *Viburnum opulus* and *nudum* (cranberry-tree and withe-rod), *Pyrus Americana* (American mountain-ash), *Corylus rostrata* (beaked hazel-nut), *Diervilla trifida* (bush-honeysuckle), *Prunus Virginiana* (choke-cherry), *Myrica gale* (sweet-gale), *Nemopanthes Canadensis* (mountain holly), *Cephalanthus occidentalis* (button-bush), *Ribes prostratum*, in some places (fetid currant).

More particularly of shrubs and small trees in *swamps :*

some willows, *Kalmia glauca* (pale laurel), *Ledum latifo-lium* and *palustre* (Labrador tea), *Ribes lacustre* (swamp gooseberry), and in one place *Betula pumila* (low birch). At *camps and carries:* raspberry, *Vaccinium Canadense* (Canada blueberry), *Prunus Pennsylvanica,* also along shore (wild red cherry), *Amelanchier Canadensis* (shad-bush), *Sambucus pubens* (red-berried elder). Among those peculiar to the *mountains* would be the *Vaccinium vitis-idæa* (cow-berry).

Of plants commonly regarded as *introduced* from Europe, I observed at Ansel Smith's clearing, Chesuncook, abundant in 1857: *Ranunculus acris* (buttercups), *Plantago major* (common plantain), *Chenopodium album* (lamb's-quarters), *Capsella bursa-pastoris,* 1853 (shepherd's-purse), *Spergula arvensis,* also, north shore of Moosehead, in 1853, and elsewhere, 1857 (corn-spurry), *Taraxacum dens-leonis* — regarded as indigenous by Gray, but evidently introduced there — (common dandelion), *Polygonum Persicaria* and *hydropiper,* by a logging-path in woods at Smith's (lady's-thumb and smart-weed), *Rumex acetosella,* common at carries (sheep-sorrel), *Trifolium pratense,* 1853, and carries frequent (red clover), *Leucanthemum vulgare,* carries (white weed), *Phleum pratense,* carries, 1853–7 (herd's-grass), *Verbena hastata* (blue vervain), *Cirsium arvense,* abundant at camps 1857 (Canada thistle), *Rumex crispus ?,* West Branch, 1853 ? (curled dock), *Verbascum thapsus,* between Bangor and lake, 1853 (common mullein).

It appears that I saw about a dozen plants which had accompanied man as far into the woods as Chesuncook, and had naturalized themselves there, in 1853. Plants begin thus early to spring by the side of a logging-path, — a mere vista through the woods, which can only be used in the winter, on account of the stumps and fallen trees, — which at length are the roadside plants in old settlements. The pioneers of such are planted in part by the first cattle, which cannot be summered in the woods.

III. LIST OF PLANTS

THE following is a list of the plants which I noticed in the Maine woods, in the years 1853 and 1857. (Those marked * not in woods.)

1. THOSE WHICH ATTAINED THE HEIGHT OF TREES

Alnus incana (speckled or hoary alder), abundant along streams, &c.

Thuja occidentalis (American arbor-vitæ), one of the prevailing.

Fraxinus sambucifolia (black ash), very common, especially near dead water. The Indian spoke of " yellow ash " as also found there.

Populus tremuloides (American aspen), very common, especially on burnt lands, almost as white as birches.

Populus grandidentata (large-toothed aspen), perhaps two or three.

Fagus ferruginea (American beech), not uncommon, at least on the West Branch (saw more in 1846).

Betula papyracea (canoe-birch), prevailing everywhere and about Bangor.

Betula excelsa (yellow birch), very common.

Betula lenta (black birch), on the West Branch, in 1853.

Betula alba (American white birch), about Bangor only.

Ulmus Americana (American or white elm), West Branch and low down the East Branch, i. e., on the lower and alluvial part of the river, very common.

Larix Americana (American or black larch), very common on the Umbazookskus, some elsewhere.

Abies Canadensis (hemlock-spruce), not abundant, some on the West Branch, and a little everywhere.

Acer saccharinum (sugar maple), very common.

Acer rubrum (red or swamp maple), very common.

Acer dasycarpum (white or silver maple), a little low on East Branch and in Chesuncook woods.

Quercus rubra (red oak), one on an island in Grand Lake, East Branch, and, according to a settler, a few on the east side of Chesuncook Lake; a few also about Bangor in 1853.

Pinus strobus (white pine), scattered along, most abundant at Heron Lake.

Pinus resinosa (red pine), Telos and Grand Lake, a little afterwards here and there.

Abies balsamea (balsam fir), perhaps the most common tree, especially in the upper parts of rivers.

Abies nigra (black or double spruce), next to the last the most common, if not equally common, and on mountains.

Abies alba (white or single spruce), common with the last along the rivers.

Pinus Banksiana (gray or Northern scrub-pine), a few on an island in Grand Lake.

Twenty-three in all (23).

2. SMALL TREES AND SHRUBS

Prunus depressa (dwarf-cherry), on gravel bars, East Branch, near Hunt's, with green fruit, obviously distinct from the *pumila* of river and meadows.

Vaccinium corymbosum (common swamp blueberry), Bucksport.

Vaccinium Canadense (Canada blueberry), carries and rocky hills everywhere as far south as Bucksport.

Vaccinium Pennsylvanicum (dwarf-blueberry ?), Whetstone Falls.

Betula pumila (low birch), Mud Pond Swamp.

Prinos verticillata (black alder, '57), now placed with *Ilex* by Gray, 2d ed.

Cephalanthus occidentalis (button-bush).

Prunus Pennsylvanica (wild red cherry), very common at camps, carries, &c., along rivers; fruit ripe August 1, 1857.

Prunus Virginiana (choke-cherry), river side, common.

Cornus alternifolia (alternate-leaved cornel), West Branch, 1853.

Ribes prostratum (fetid currant), common along streams, on Webster Stream.

Sambucus Canadensis (common elder), common along river sides.

Sambucus pubens (red-berried elder), not quite so common, roadsides toward Moosehead, and on carries afterward, fruit beautiful.

Ribes lacustre (swamp-gooseberry), swamps, common Mud Pond Swamp and Webster Stream; not ripe July 29 1857.

Corylus rostrata (beaked hazel-nut), common.

Taxus baccata, var. *Canadensis* (American yew), a common under-shrub at an island in West Branch and Chesuncook woods.

Viburnum lantanoides (hobble-bush), common, especially in Chesuncook woods; fruit ripe in September, 1853, not in July, 1857.

Viburnum opulus (cranberry-tree), on West Branch; one in flower still, July 25, 1857.

Viburnum nudum (withe-rod), common along rivers.

Kalmia glauca (pale laurel), swamps, common, as at Moosehead carry and Chamberlain swamp.

Kalmia angustifolia (lamb-kill), with *Kalmia glauca*.

Acer spicatum (mountain maple), a prevailing underwood.

Acer striatum (striped maple), in fruit July 30, 1857;

green the first year; green, striped with white, the second; darker, the third, with dark blotches.

Cornus stolonifera (red-osier dogwood), prevailing shrub on shore of West Branch; fruit still white in August, 1857.

Pyrus Americana (American mountain ash), common along shores.

Amelanchier Canadensis (shad-bush), rocky carries, &c., considerable fruit in 1857.

Rubus strigosus (wild red raspberry), very abundant, burnt grounds, camps, and carries, but not ripe till we got to Chamberlain dam and on East Branch.

Rosa Carolina (swamp-rose), common on the shores of lakes, &c.

Rhus typhina * (stag-horn sumac).

Myrica gale (sweet-gale), common.

Nemopanthes Canadensis (mountain holly), common in low ground, Moosehead carry, and on Mount Kineo.

Cratægus (*coccinea?* scarlet-fruited thorn), not uncommon; with hard fruit in September, 1853.

Salix (near to *petiolaris*, petioled willow), very common in Umbazookskus meadows.

Salix rostrata (long-beaked willow), common.

Salix humilis (low bush-willow), common.

Salix discolor (glaucous willow ?).

Salix lucida (shining willow), at island in Heron Lake.

Dirca palustris (moose-wood), common.

In all, 38.

3. SMALL SHRUBS AND HERBACEOUS PLANTS

Agrimonia Eupatoria (common agrimony), not uncommon.

Circœa Alpina (enchanter's nightshade), very common in woods.

Nasturtium palustre (marsh cress), var. *hispidum*, common as at A. Smith's.

Aralia hispida (bristly sarsaparilla), on West Branch, both years.

Aralia nudicaulis (wild sarsaparilla), Chesuncook woods.

Sagittaria variabilis (arrow-head), common at Moosehead and afterward.

Arum triphyllum (Indian turnip), now *arisœma,* Moosehead carry in 1853.

Asclepias incarnata (swamp milk-weed), Umbazookskus River and after, redder than ours, and a different variety from our var. *pulchra.*

Aster acuminatus (pointed-leaved aster), the prevailing aster in woods, not long open on South Branch July 31st; two or more feet high.

Aster macrophyllus (large-leaved aster), common, and the whole plant surprisingly fragant, like a medicinal herb, just out at Telos Dam July 29, 1857, and after to Bangor and Bucksport; bluish flower (in woods on Pine Stream and at Chesuncook in 1853).

Aster radula (rough-leaved aster), common, Moosehead carry and after.

Aster miser (petty aster), in 1853 on West Branch, and common on Chesuncook shore.

Aster longifolius (willow-leaved blue aster), 1853, Moosehead and Chesuncook shores.

Aster cordifolius (heart-leaved aster), 1853, West Branch.

Aster Tradescanti (Tradescant's aster), 1857. A narrow-leaved one, Chesuncook shore, 1853.

Aster, longifolius like, with small flowers, West Branch, 1853.

Aster puniceus (rough-stemmed aster), Pine Stream.

Diplopappus umbellatus (large *diplopappus* aster), common along river.

Arctostaphylos uva-ursi (bear-berry), Kineo, &c., 1857.

Polygonum cilinode (fringe-jointed false buckwheat), common.

Bidens cernua (bur-marigold), 1853, West Branch.

Ranunculus acris (buttercups), abundant at Smith's dam, Chesuncook, 1853.

Rubus triflorus (dwarf-raspberry), low grounds and swamps, common.

Utricularia vulgaris * (greater bladder-wort), Pushaw.

Iris versicolor (larger blue-flag), common Moosehead, West Branch, Umbazookskus, &c.

Sparganium (bur-reed).

Calla palustris (water-arum), in bloom July 27, 1857, Mud Pond Swamp.

Lobelia cardinalis (cardinal-flower), apparently common, but out of bloom August, 1857.

Cerastium nutans (clammy wild chickweed ?).

Gaultheria procumbens (checkerberry), prevailing everywhere in woods along banks of rivers.

Stellaria media * (common chickweed), Bangor.

Chiogenes hispidula (creeping snowberry), very common in woods.

Cicuta maculata (water-hemlock).

Cicuta bulbifera (bulb-bearing water-hemlock), Penobscot and Chesuncook shore, 1853.

Galium trifidum (small bed-straw), common.

Galium Apparine (cleavers ?), Chesuncook, 1853.

Galium, one kind on Pine Stream, 1853.

Trifolium pratense (red-clover), on carries, &c.

Actœa spicata, var. *alba* (white cohosh), Chesuncook woods 1853, and East Branch 1857.

Actœa, var. *rubra* (red cohosh), East Branch 1857.

Vaccinium vitis idœa (cow-berry), Ktaadn, very abundant.

Cornus Canadensis (dwarf-cornel), in woods Chesuncook

1853; just ripe at Kineo July 24, 1857, common; still in bloom, Moosehead carry September 16, 1853.

Medeola Virginica (Indian cucumber-root), West Branch and Chesuncook woods.

Dalibarda repens (Dalibarda), Moosehead carry and after, common. In flower still, August 1, 1857.

Taraxacum dens-leonis (common dandelion), Smith's 1853, only there. Is it not foreign ?

Diervilla trifida (bush honeysuckle), very common.

Rumex hydrolapathum ? (great water-dock), in 1857; noticed it was large seeded in 1853, common.

Rumex crispus ? (curled-dock), West Branch 1853.

Apocynum cannabinum (Indian hemp), Kineo, *Bradford*, and East Branch 1857, at Whetstone Falls.

Apocynum androsæmifolium (spreading dogbane), Kineo, *Bradford*.

Clintonia borealis (Clintonia), all over woods; fruit just ripening July 25, 1857.

A lemna (duckweed), Pushaw 1857.

Elodea Virginica (marsh St. John's-wort), Moosehead 1853.

Epilobium angustifolium (great willow-herb), great fields on burnt lands; some white at Webster Stream.

Epilobium coloratum (purple-veined willow-herb), once in 1857.

Eupatorium purpureum (Joe-Pye-weed), Heron, Moosehead, and Chesuncook lake shores, common.

Allium (onion), a new kind to me in bloom, without bulbs above, on rocks near Whetstone Falls ? East Branch.

Halenia deflexa (spurred gentian), carries on East Branch, common.

Geranium Robertianum (Herb Robert).

Solidago lanceolata (bushy golden-rod), very common.

Solidago, one of the three-ribbed, in both years.

Solidago thyrsoidea (large mountain golden-rod), one on Webster Stream.

Solidago squarrosa (large-spiked golden-rod), the most common on East Branch.

Solidago altissima (rough hairy golden-rod), not uncommon both years.

Coptis trifolia (three-leaved gold-thread).

Smilax herbacea (carrion-flower), not uncommon both years.

Spiræa tomentosa * (hardhack), Bangor.

Campanula rotundifolia (harebell), cliffs Kineo, Grand Lake, &c.

Hieracium (hawk-weed), not uncommon.

Veratrum viride (American white hellebore).

Lycopus Virginicus (bugle-weed), 1857.

Lycopus Europœus (water-horehound), var. *sinuatus,* Heron Lake shore.

Chenopodium album (lamb's-quarters), Smith's.

Mentha Canadensis (wild mint), very common.

Galeopsis tetrahit (common hemp-nettle), Olarmon Isle, abundant, and below, in prime August 3, 1857.

Houstonia cœrulea (bluets), now *Oldenlandia* (Gray, 2d ed.), 1857.

Hydrocotyle Americana (marsh pennywort), common.

Hypericum ellipticum (elliptical-leaved St. John's-wort), common.

Hypericum mutilum (small St. John's-wort), both years, common.

Hypericum Canadense (Canadian St. John's-wort), Moosehead Lake and Chesuncook shores, 1853.

Trientalis Americana (star-flower), Pine Stream, 1853.

Lobelia inflata (Indian tobacco).

Spiranthes cernuus (ladies' tresses), Kineo and after.

Nabalus (rattlesnake root), 1857; *altissimus* (tall white lettuce), Chesuncook woods, 1853.

Antennaria margaritacea (pearly everlasting), common, Moosehead, Smith's, &c.

Lulium Canadense (wild yellow lily), very common and large, West and East Branch; one on East Branch, 1857, with strongly revolute petals, and leaves perfectly smooth beneath, but not larger than the last, and apparently only a variety.

Linnæa borealis (Linnæa), almost everywhere in woods.

Lobelia Dortmanna (water-lobelia), pond in Bucksport.

Lysimachia ciliata (hairy-stalked loosestrife), very common, Chesuncook shore and East Branch.

Lysimachia stricta (upright loosestrife), very common.

Microstylis ophioglossoides (adder's-mouth), Kineo.

Spiræa salicifolia (common meadow-sweet), common.

Mimulus ringens (monkey-flower), common, lake-shores, &c.

Scutellaria galericulata (skullcap), very common.

Scutellaria lateriflora (mad-dog skullcap), Heron Lake, 1857, Chesuncook, 1853.

Platanthera psycodes (small purple-fringed orchis), very common, East Branch and Chesuncook, 1853.

Platanthera fimbriata (large purple-fringed orchis), very common, West Branch and Umbazookskus, 1857.

Platanthera orbiculata (large round-leaved orchis), very common in woods, Moosehead and Chamberlain carries, Caucomgomoc, &c.

Amphicarpæa monocea (hog peanut).

Aralia racemosa (spikenard), common, Moosehead carry, Telos Lake, &c., and after; out about August 1, 1857.

Plantago major (common plantain), common in open land at Smith's in 1853.

Pontederia cordata * (pickerel-weed), only near Oldtown, 1857.

Potamogeton (pond-weed), not common.

Potentilla tridentata (mountain cinquefoil), Kineo.

Potentilla Norvegica (cinquefoil), Heron Lake shore and Smith's.

Polygonum amphibium (water-persicaria), var. *aquaticum* Second Lake.

Polygonum Persicaria (lady's-thumb), log-path Chesuncook, 1853.

Nuphar advena (yellow pond-lily), not abundant.

Nymphœa odorata (sweet water-lily), a few in West Branch, 1853.

Polygonum hydropiper (smart-weed), log-path, Chesuncook.

Pyrola secunda (one-sided pyrola), very common, Caucomgomoc.

Pyrola elliptica (shin-leaf), Caucomgomoc River.

Ranunculus Flammula (spearwort, var. *reptans*).

Ranunculus recurvatus (hooked crowfoot), Umbazookskus landing, &c.

Typha latifolia * (common cat-tail or reed-mace), extremely abundant between Bangor and Portland.

Sanicula Marylandica (black snake-root), Moosehead carry and after.

Aralia nudicaulis (wild sarsaparilla).

Capsella bursa-pastoris (shepherd's-purse), Smith's, 1853.

Prunella vulgaris (self-heal), very common everywhere.

Erechthites hieracifolia (fireweed), 1857, and Smith's open land, 1853.

Sarracenia purpurea (pitcher-plant), Mud Pond swamp.

Smilacina bifolia (false Solomon's-seal), 1857, and Chesuncook woods, 1853.

Smilacina racemosa (false spikenard ?), Umbazookskus carry (July 27, 1853).

Veronica scutellata (marsh speedwell).

Spergula arvensis (corn spurrey), 1857, not uncommon, 1853, Moosehead and Smith's.

Fragaria (strawberry), 1853 Smith's, 1857 Bucksport.

Thalictrum Cornuti (meadow-rue), very common, especially along rivers, tall, and conspicuously in bloom in July, 1857.

Cirsium arvense (Canada thistle), abundant at camps and highway sides in the north of Maine.

Cirsium muticum (swamp-thistle), well in bloom Webster Stream, August 31.

Rumex acetosella (sheep-sorrel), common by river and log paths, as Chesuncook log-path.

Impatiens fulva (spotted touch-me-not).

Trillium erythrocarpum (painted trillium), common West Branch and Moosehead carry.

Verbena hastata (blue vervain).

Clematis Virginiana (common virgin's-bower), common on river banks, feathered in September, 1853, in bloom July, 1857.

Leucanthemum vulgare (white-weed).

Sium lineare (water-parsnip), 1857, and Chesuncook shore, 1853.

Achillea millefolium (common yarrow), by river and log-paths, and Smith's.

Desmodium Canadense (Canadian tick-trefoil), not uncommon.

Oxalis acetosella (common wood-sorrel), still out July 25, 1853, at Moosehead carry and after.

Oxalis stricta (yellow wood-sorrel), 1853, at Smith's and his woodpath.

Liparis liliifolia (tway-blade), Kineo, *Bradford.*

Uvularia grandiflora (large-flowered bellwort), woods, common.

Uvularia sessilifolia (sessile-leaved bellwort), Chesuncook woods, 1853.

In all, 145.

4. OF LOWER ORDER.

Scirpus Eriophorum (wool-grass), very common, especially on low islands. A coarse grass, four or five feet high, along the river.

Phleum pratense (herd's-grass), on carries, at camps and clearings.

Equisetum sylvaticum (sylvatic horse-tail).

Pteris aquilina (brake), Kineo and after.

Onoclea sensibilis (sensitive-fern), very common along the riversides; some on the gravelly shore of Heron Lake Island.

Polypodium Dryopteris (brittle polypody).

Woodsia Ilvensis (rusty Woodsia), Kineo.

Lycopodium lucidulum (toothed club-moss).

Usnea (a parmeliaceous lichen), common on various trees.

IV. LIST OF BIRDS

WHICH I SAW IN MAINE BETWEEN JULY 24 AND AUGUST 3, 1857.

A very small hawk at Great Falls, on Webster Stream.

Haliœtus leucocephalus (white-headed or bald-eagle), at Ragmuff, and above and below Hunt's, and on pond below Mattawamkeag.

Pandion haliœtus (fish-hawk or osprey), heard, also seen on East Branch.

Bubo Virginianus (cat-owl), near Camp Island, also above mouth of Schoonis, from a stump back and forth, also near Hunt's on a tree.

Icterus phœniceus (red-winged blackbird), Umbazook-skus River.

Corvus Americanus (American crow), a few, as at outlet of Grand Lake; a pecular cawing.

Fringilla Canadensis (tree-sparrow), think I saw one on Mount Kineo July 24, which behaved as if it had a nest there.

Garrulus cristatus (blue-jay).

Parus atricapillus (chicadee), a few.

Muscicapa tyrannus (king-bird).

Muscicapa Cooperii (olive-sided fly-catcher), everywhere a prevailing bird.

Muscicapa virens (wood-pewee), Moosehead, and I think beyond.

Muscicapa ruticilla (American redstart), Moosehead.

Vireo olivaceus (red-eyed vireo), everywhere common.

Turdus migratorius (red-breasted robin), some everywhere.

Turdus melodus (wood-thrush), common in all the woods.

Turdus Wilsonii (Wilson's thrush), Moosehead and beyond.

Turdus aurocapillus (golden-crowned thrush or ovenbird), Moosehead.

Fringilla albicollis (white-throated sparrow), Kineo and after, apparently nesting; the prevailing bird early and late.

Fringilla melodia (song-sparrow), at Moosehead or beyond.

Sylvia pinus (pine warbler), one part of voyage.

Muscicapa acadica (small pewee), common.

Trichas Marylandica (Maryland yellow-throat), everywhere.

Coccyzus Americanus? (yellow-billed cuckoo), common.

Picus erythrocephalus (red-headed woodpecker), heard and saw, and good to eat.

Sitta Carolinensis? (white-breasted American nuthatch), heard.

Alcedo alcyon (belted kingfisher), very common.

Caprimulgus Americanus (night-hawk).

Tetrao umbellus (partridge), Moosehead carry, &c.

Tetrao cupido? (pinnated grouse), Webster Stream.

Ardea cærulea (blue heron), lower part of Penobscot.

Totanus macularius (spotted sandpiper or peetweet), everywhere.

Larus argentatus? (herring-gull), Heron Lake on rocks, and Chamberlain. Smaller gull on Second Lake.

Anas obscura (dusky or black duck), once in East Branch.

Anas sponsa (summer or wood duck), everywhere.

Fuligula albicola (spirit duck or dipper), common.

Colymbus glacialis (great Northern diver or loon), in all the lakes. A swallow; the night-warbler? once or twice.

Mergus Merganser (buff-breasted merganser or sheldrake), common on lakes and rivers.

V. QUADRUPEDS.

A bat on West Branch; beaver skull at Grand Lake; Mr. Thatcher ate beaver with moose on the Caucomgomoc. A muskrat on the last stream; the red squirrel is common in the depths of the woods; a dead porcupine on Chamberlain road; a cow moose and tracks of calf; skin of a bear, just killed.

VI. OUTFIT FOR AN EXCURSION.

The following will be a good outfit for one who wishes to make an excursion of *twelve* days into the Maine woods in July, with a companion and one Indian, for the same purposes that I did.

Wear, — a check shirt, stout old shoes, thick socks, a neck ribbon, thick waistcoat, thick pants, old Kossuth hat, a linen sack.

Carry, — in an India-rubber knapsack, with a large flap, two shirts (check), one pair thick socks, one pair drawers, one flannel shirt, two pocket-handkerchiefs, a light India-rubber coat or a thick woolen one, two bosoms and collars to go and come with, one napkin, pins, needles, thread, one blanket, best gray, seven feet long.

Tent, — six by seven feet, and four feet high in middle, will do; veil and gloves and insect-wash, or, better, mosquito-bars to cover all at night; best pocket-map, and perhaps description of the route; compass; plant-book and red blotting-paper; paper and stamps, botany, small pocket spy-glass for birds, pocket-microscope, tape-measure, insect-boxes.

Axe, full size if possible, jackknife, fish-lines, two only apiece, with a few hooks and corks ready, and with pork for bait in a packet, rigged; matches (some also in a small vial in the waistcoat pocket); soap, two pieces; large knife and iron spoon (for all); three or four old newspapers, much twine, and several rags for dishcloths; twenty feet of strong cord, four-quart tin pail for kettle, two tin dippers, three tin plates, a fry-pan.

Provisions. — Soft hardbread, twenty-eight pounds; pork, sixteen pounds; sugar, twelve pounds; one pound black tea or three pounds coffee; one box or a pint of salt; one quart Indian meal, to fry fish in; six lemons, good to correct the pork and warm water; perhaps two or three pounds of rice, for variety. You will probably get some berries, fish, &c., beside.

A gun is not worth the carriage, unless you go as hunters. The pork should be in an open keg, sawed to fit; the sugar, tea or coffee, meal, salt, &c., should be put in separate water-tight India-rubber bags, tied with a leather string; and all the provisions, and part of the rest of the baggage, put into two large India-rubber bags, which have been proved to be water-tight and durable.   Expense of preceding outfit is twenty-four dollars.

An Indian may be hired for about one dollar and fifty cents per day, and perhaps fifty cents a week for his canoe (this depends on the demand).   The canoe should be a strong and tight one.   This expense will be nineteen dollars.

Such an excursion need not cost more than twenty-five dollars apiece, starting at the foot of Moosehead, if you already possess or can borrow a reasonable part of the outfit.   If you take an Indian and canoe at Oldtown, it will cost seven or eight dollars more to transport them to the lake.

VII.   A LIST OF INDIAN WORDS.

1. *Ktaadn,* said to mean *Highest Land,* Rale puts for *Mt. Pemadene;* for *Grai, pierre à aiguiser, Kitadaügan.* (v. Potter.)

Mattawamkeag, place where two rivers meet.   (Indian of carry.)   (v. Williamson's History of Maine, and Willis.)

Molunkus.

Ebeeme, rock.

Noliseemack ; other name, Shad Pond.

Kecunnilessu, chicadee.

Nipsquecohossus, woodcock.

Skuscumonsuk, kingfisher.   Has it not the pl. termination *uk* here, or *suk?*

Wassus, bear, *aouessous.*   Rale.

Lunxus, Indian-devil.

Upahsis, mountain-ash.

} Joe.

Moose (is it called, or does it mean, wood-eater ?), *mous,* Rale.

Katahdinauguoh, said to mean mountains about Ktaadn.

Ebemena, tree-cranberry. *Ibibimin, nar,* red, bad fruit. Rale. } Joe.

Wighiggin, a bill or writing, *aouixigan,* " *Livre, lettre, peinture, ceinture.*" Rale. } Ind'n of carry.

Sebamook, Large-bay Lake, *Peqouasebem;* add *ar* for plural, *lac* or *étang.* Rale. *Ouaürinaügamek, anse dans un lac.* Rale. *Mspame,* large water. Polis. } Nicholai.

Sebago and *Sebec,* large open water.

Chesuncook, place where many streams empty in. (v. Willis and Potter.)

Caucomgomoc, Gull Lake. (*Caucomgomoc,* the lake; *caucomgomoc-took,* the river, Polis.) } Tahmunt, &c.

Pammadumcook.

Kenduskieg, Little Eel River. (v. Willis.) Nicholai.

Penobscot, Rocky River. *Puapeskou,* stone. (Rale v. Springer.) } Ind'n of carry.

Umbazookskus, meadow stream. (Much-meadow river, Polis.)

Millinocket, place of Islands.

Souneunk, that runs between Mountains.

Aboljacarmegus, Smooth-ledge Falls and Dead-water. } Nicholai.

Aboljacarmeguscook, the river there.

Muskiticook, Dead Stream. (Indian of carry.) *Meskikou,* or *Meskikouikou,* a place where there is grass. (Rale.) *Muskéeticook,* Dead-water. (Polis.)

Mattahumkeag, Sand-creek Pond.

Piscataquis, branch of a river. } Nicholai.

Shecorways, sheldrakes.

Naramekechus, peetweet. } Polis.

Medawisla, loon.

Orignal, Moosehead Lake. (Montresor.)

Chor-chor-que, usnea.

Adelungquamooktum, wood-thrush.

Bematruichtik, high land generally. (*Mt. Pema-dené.* Rale.)

Maquoxigil, bark of red osier, Indian tobacco. } Polis.

Kineo, flint (Williamson; old Indian hunter). (Hodge.)

Artoosoqu', phosphorescence.

Subekoondark, white spruce.

Skusk, black spruce.

Beskabekuk, the " Lobster Lake " of maps.

Beskabekuk shishtook, the dead-water below the island.

Paytaytequick, Burnt-Ground Stream, what Joe called *Ragmuff.*

Nonlangyis, the name of a dead-water between the last and Pine Stream.

Karsaootuk, Black River (or Pine Stream). *Mka-zéouighen,* black. Rale. } Polis.

Michigan, fimus. Polis applied it to a sucker, or a poor, good-for-nothing fish. *Fiante* (?) *mitsegan,* Rale. (Pickering puts the ? after the first word.)

Cowosnebagosar, Chiogenes hispidula, means, grows where trees have rotted.

Pockadunkquaywayle, echo. *Pagadaükoueouérré.* Rale. *Bororquasis,* moose-fly.

Nerlumskeechtcook (or *quoik?*), (or *skeetcook*), Dead-water, and applied to the mountains near.

Apmoojeuegamook, lake that is crossed.

Allegash, hemlock-bark. (v. Willis.)

Paytaywecongomec, Burnt-Ground Lake, *Telos.* } Polis.

Madunkehunk, Height-of-land Stream (Webster Stream).

Madunkehunk-gamooc, Height-of-land Lake.

Matungamooc, Grand Lake.

Uncardnerheese, Trout Stream.

Wassataquoik (or *-cook*), Salmon River, East Branch. (v. Willis.)

Pemoymenuk, Amelanchier berries, " *Pemouaimin, nak*, a black fruit. Rale." Has it not here the plural ending ?

Sheepnoc, Lilium Canadense bulbs. " *Sipen, nak*, white, larger than *penak*." Rale.

Paytgumkiss, Petticoat (where a small river comes into the Penobscot below Nickatow).

Burntibus, a lake-like reach in the Penobscot.

} Polis.

Passadumkeag, " where the water falls into the Penobscot above the falls." (Williamson.) *Paüsidaükioui* is, *au dessus de la montagne.* Rale.

Olarmon, or *larmon*, (Polis) red paint. " Vermilion, paint, *Ouramaü*." Rale.

Sunkhaze, " See canoe come out; ho, see 'em stream." (Polis.) The mouth of a river, according to Rale, is *Saüghedétegoue.* The place where one stream empties into another, thus ȣ is *saüktaüoui.* (v. Willis.)

Tomhegan Br. (at Moosehead). " *Hatchet, temahigan*." Rale.

Nickatow, " *Nicketaoutegué*, or *Niketoutegoue, rivière qui fourche.*" Rale.

2. From WILLIAM WILLIS, on the Language of the Abnaquies, Maine Hist. Coll., Vol. IV.

Abalajako-megus (river near Ktaadn).

Aitteon (name of a pond and sachem).

Apmogenegamook (name of a lake).

Allagash (a bark camp). Sockbasin, a Penobscot, told him, " The Indians gave this name to the lake from the fact of their keeping a hunting-camp there."

Bamonewengamock, head of Allagash, Cross Lake. (Sockbasin.)

Chesuncook, Big Lake. (Sockbasin.)

Caucongamock (a lake).

Ebeeme, mountains that have plums on them. (Sockbasin.)

Ktaadn. Sockbasin pronounces this Ka-tah-din, and said it meant "large mountain or large thing."

Kenduskeag (the place of Eels).

Kineo (flint), mountain on the border, &c.

Metawamkeag, a river with a smooth, gravelly bottom. (Sockbasin.)

Metanawcook.

Millinoket, a lake with many islands in it. (Sockbasin.)

Matakeunk (river).

Molunkus (river).

Nicketow, Neccotoh, where two streams meet ("Forks of the Penobscot").

Negas (Indian village on the Kenduskeag).

Orignal (Montresor's name for Moosehead Lake).

Ponguongamook, Allagash, name of a Mohawk Indian killed there. (Sockbasin.)

Penobscot, Penobskeag, French *Pentagoet*, &c.

Pougohwaken (Heron Lake).

Pemadumcook (lake).

Passadumkeag, where water goes into the river above falls. (Williamson.)

Ripogenus (river).

Sunkhaze (river), Dead-water.

Souneunk.

Seboomook. Sockbasin says this word means "the shape of a Moose's head, and was given to the lake," &c. *Howard* says differently.

Seboois, a brook, a small river. (Sockbasin.)

Sebec (river).

Sebago (great water).

Telos (lake).

Telasiuis (lake).

Umbagog (lake), doubled up; so called from its form. (Sockbasin.)

Umbazookskus (lake).

Wassatiquoik, a mountain river. (Sockbasin.)

Judge C. E. Potter of Manchester, New Hampshire, adds in November, 1855: —

" *Chesuncook.* This is formed from *Chesunk,* or *Schunk* (a goose), and *Auke* (a place), and means 'The Goose Place.' Chesunk, or Schunk, is the sound made by the wild geese when flying."

Ktaadn. This is doubtless a corruption of *Kees* (high), and *Auke* (a place).

Penobscot, Penapse (stone, rock-place), and *Auke* (place).

Suncook, Goose-place, *Schunk-auke.*

The Judge says that *schoot* means to rush, and hence *schoodic* from this and *auke* (a place where water rushes), and that *schoon* means the same; and that the Marblehead people and others have derived the words *scoon* and *scoot* from the Indians, and hence schooner ; refers to a Mr. Chute.

INDEX

Abbot (Me.), 118.
Aboljacarmegus Falls, 69, 99; Indian meaning of, 192.
Aboljacarmegus, Lake, 60.
Aboljacknagesic stream, 61, 70, 71, 74.
Aitteon, Joe, 114, 120, 259, 288, 389.
Allegash and East Branch, the, 214–407.
Allegash Lakes, the, 97, 215, 310, 319.
Allegash River, the, 48, 97, 197, 219, 288, 310, 315, 316, 318, 319, 322, 335.
Ambejijis Falls, 60; portage round, 62; 102.
Ambejijis Lake, 54, 55, 56, 58, 60, 102, 362.
Ambejijis stream, 60.
America, the newness of, 109.
Androscoggin River, the, 4.
Apmoojenegamook Lake, 302, 303; meaning of, 310; 322; a storm on, 326, 327; hard paddling on, 331.
Aroostook (Me.) road, 2, 14; river, 2; wagon, an, 15; valley, 26; sleds of the, 323.
Assabet River, the, 142.
Asters, 117.
Atlas, the General, 115.

Bailey, Prof. J. W., 2.
Bald Mountain, 238.
Bangor (Me.), 1, 3, 9, 12, 13; passage to, 17; 26, 42, 45, 89, 104, 111, 113, 114, 115, 116, 118; the deer that went a-shopping in, 188; 196, 197, 203, 204, 205, 214, 216; House, the, 218, 219; 310, 312, 318, 319, 360, 382, 407.
Batteaux, 4, 41.
Beards, growing, for sylvan appearance, 209.
Bears, abundance of, 290.
Bed, a cedar-twig, 72; of arbor-vitæ twigs, 329; the primitive, by all rivers, 394.

Birds, in the wilderness, 143; about Moosehead Lake, 229; about Mud Pond carry, 293; near Chamberlain Lake, 298; on Heron Lake, 316; on East Branch, 384.
Black flies, protection against, 292; 304.
Blueberries, 79, 370.
Boston (Mass.), countrified minds in towns about, 28.
Bowlin Stream, 383.
Burnt Ground, the, 370.
Burnt Land, the, 34, 93.
"Burntibus," 397.

Camden Hills, 114.
Camp, loggers', 22; reading matter in a, 44; on side of Ktaadn, ?, 82; the routine for making, 259–261; darkness about a, 376–379.
Canadian, boat-song, 49; a blind, 289; avoiding the, 320.
Canoe, a birch, 128; used in third excursion to Maine Woods, 223; shipping water in a, 233; crossing lakes in a, 254; carrying a, 255, 256; running rapids in a, 341, 343, 347.
Carbuncle Mountain, 361.
Caribou Lake, 267.
Carry, Indian's method with canoe at a, 255, 256; a wet, 291–303; berries at each, 379, 380; race at a, 390–392.
Caucomgomoc Lake, 275.
Caucomgomoc Mountain, 288.
Caucomgomoc stream, 173, 180; Indian meaning of, 191; river, 271, 307; 283, 316, 369.
Cedar-tea, arbor-vitæ, or, 73.
Chaleur, Bay of, 220.
Chamberlain Farm, the, 303, 327, 328.
Chamberlain Lake, 122, 177, 197, 289, 294, 296, 297; Apmoojenega-mook or, 303; dams about, 312; 325, 332.